THE TORON

Here are the restaura
neighbourhoods and a
about—whether you'r   onian
who wants to get the m   ity.

Allan Gould tips you   the inside information that
will help you find the places to go and things to do that
make Toronto one of the most vibrant cities in the world.

THE TORONTO BOOK

Allan Gould

KEY PORTER BOOKS

Key Porter Books
59 Front Street East
Toronto M5E 1B3

CANADIAN CATALOGUING IN PUBLICATION DATA

Gould, Allan 1944-
The Toronto book

Includes index.
ISBN 0-919493-06-8

1. Toronto (Ont.)—Description—Guide-books.
I. Title.

FC3097.18.G68   917-13'541   C83-098379-1
F1059.5.T68G68

Illustrations by Graham Pilsworth
Designed by Ken Rodmell and Gerry Takeuchi

Printed and bound in Canada

DEDICATION
GIVING CREDIT WHERE CREDIT IS DUE

A heartfelt thank-you to Bayla Gross and Queenie Teichmann of Insight Planners, who provided invaluable suggestions on galleries and antique shops; to Annette Poizner and Anne Gorman, who did most of the leg work and smoke breathing, dragging themselves from pub to nightclub to disco to help me with the night-life section; to Larry LeBlanc, radio genius, who assisted on what-to-listen-to-in-Toronto in the media section; to Sandra Folk, for her excellent suggestions on a number of sections; to Miss Suzette of AHA (After Hours Assistance) for her generous assistance on after-hours establishments in Toronto; to Lang Prue at Metro Parks for non-stop tips; to Judah and Elisheva Gould, who kindly informed me of what they loved and, rarely, didn't love about Toronto sites and sights; to Merle Gould, to whom I am only related through marriage, but with this book we can claim blood as well (in fact, she is the reason I use the Royal We throughout this book). Together we went on many of the walks and shopping tours described in the following pages, and it would not have been proper, honest, or feminist to leave her out. I truly could *not* have done it without her.

And, perhaps most of all, to Toronto, for making it easy, by being such a very good place to live, work, and visit.

CONTENTS

Points of Interest

1 North Yonge Street
2 Forest Hill
3 Casa Loma
4 Rosedale
5 Metropolitan Toronto Library
6 Yorkville
7 The Annex
8 Mirvish Village
9 Kensington Market
10 Ecology House
11 Varsity Stadium
12 Royal Ontario Museum
13 McLaughlin Planetarium
14 Queen's Park
15 University of Toronto
16 Canadiana Building
17 Baldwin Street
18 Spadina Avenue
19 Chinatown
20 Bus Terminal
21 Maple Leaf Gardens
22 Massey Hall
23 Allen Gardens
24 Art Gallery of Ontario
25 The Grange
26 Eaton Centre
27 Queen Street West
28 Village By the Grange
29 Campbell House
30 Toronto City Hall
31 Old City Hall
32 Mackenzie House
33 Royal Alexandra Theatre
34 Toronto Stock Exchange
35 Royal York Hotel
36 Roy Thomson Hall
37 Union Station
38 O'Keefe Centre
39 St Lawrence Centre
40 The Esplanade
41 St Lawrence Market
42 Enoch Turner Schoolhouse
43 CN Tower
44 Harbourfront Park
45 Harbour Castle Hotel
   (Convention Centre)
46 Old Fort York
47 Toronto Islands
48 Ontario Place
49 Marine Museum
50 Canadian National Exhibition
51 CNE Stadium
52 Sports/Hockey Hall of Fame
53 Leslie Street Spit
54 The Beaches
55 Cabbagetown
56 Riverdale Farm
57 The Danforth
58 Todmorden Mills
59 Ontario Science Centre
60 Edwards Gardens

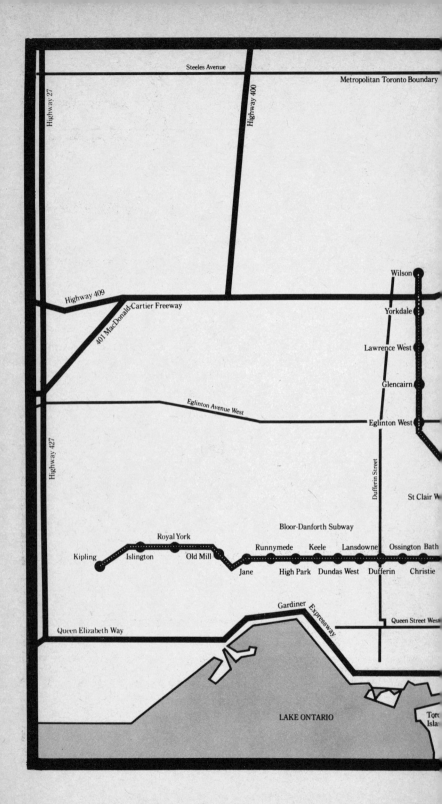

Steeles Avenue

Metropolitan Toronto Boundary

Highway 27

Highway 400

Wilson

Highway 409

Yorkdale

401 MacDonald-Cartier Freeway

Lawrence West

Glencairn

Eglinton Avenue West

Eglinton West

Highway 427

Dufferin Street

St Clair W

Bloor-Danforth Subway

Royal York

Runnymede   Keele   Lansdowne   Ossington   Bath

Kipling   Islington   Old Mill

Jane   High Park   Dundas West   Dufferin   Christie

Gardiner Expressway

Queen Street West

Queen Elizabeth Way

LAKE ONTARIO

Toro
Isla

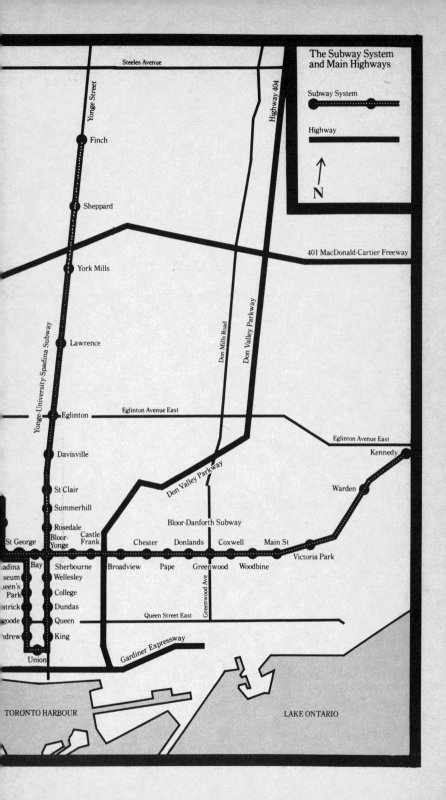

The Subway System
and Main Highways

Subway System

Highway

N

11

NOTES OF A NON-NATIVE SON

WHY WE LOVE TORONTO

Can a dreary city become a dream city in a quarter-century? Can a city whose citizens escaped to Detroit or Buffalo for a good time less than two decades ago suddenly attract twenty-five million visitors each year? When the folks down south at *Fortune* magazine label Toronto "the World's Newest Great City," should we believe them?

It was not always thus. Canada's popular historian, Pierre Berton, recently described a Toronto Sunday during the Second World War: "It wasn't much of a city if you ask me; it was terrible. There were no movies, you couldn't get a drink, there were no sports in the city, you'd just wander around or go to church. And the food was terrible." Not exactly public relations, is it?

Another Canadian writer in the 1940s penned a radio play entitled *We All Hate Toronto*. And they did, too. They called Toronto Hogtown. And they meant it.

And now, a great leap forward to the autumn of 1982, when the International Conference on Urban Design was held in Toronto. Reporters interviewed the participants:

"I hear nothing but good things about Toronto; that it is the most livable city in North America."

"It is an example of how a city could grow."

"Toronto reminds me of the services and cleanliness of a European city. It has the diversity of ethnic groups and culturally it has become international."

And that's from the world's urban designers, not our mayor.

The new Michelin guidebook to Canada has proclaimed Toronto "innovative, energetic, stimulating" and worth three stars. We're thinking of wearing them on our foreheads, as we did in grade school.

Whatever it is, *something* has happened to Toronto or a book like this would be as superfluous as a charity for Steven Spielberg.

For a start, much of Toronto's excitement, dynamism, and all-round worthiness as a place to live and visit is explained by our ethnic diversity. More than 60 per cent of the close to three million people in the metropolitan Toronto area were born and raised somewhere else. And that somewhere was often very far away.

Nearly 500,000 Italians make this city the largest community of its kind outside Italy. Toronto has the largest Portuguese community in North America. More than 120,000 Jews. Nearly 90,000 Greeks. Tens of thousands of Germans. Chinese. Hungarians. East Indians. West Indians. Chileans. Maltese. Nigerians. And enough others to make the United Nations move here from Manhattan.

What all that has meant to Toronto is a vibrant mixture of cultures that has echoes of New York City at the turn of the century – but without the slums, crowding, disease, and tensions (which we probably would have had too, had Canada opened her gates back then).

There are still critics, of course. They say that Toronto is still too smug (well, yes); too regulated (they'd prefer chaos?); too provincial (actually it's municipal; Ontario is provincial); too prim and proper (they miss being mugged?); too young (we weren't born yesterday, ya know).

And we weren't. Toronto formally became "Toronto" on March 6, 1834, only a century and a half ago, but its roots go back to 1615.

A Frenchman named Etienne Brûlé was sent into the not-yet-Canadian wilderness in 1610 by explorer Samuel de Champlain to see what he could discover. And he discovered plenty: the river and portage routes from the St. Lawrence to Lake Huron, possibly lakes Superior and Michigan and, eventually, Lake Ontario.

His discoveries surprised the local Indians, who had known about these places for hundreds of years; and they had long since named the area Brûlé "discovered" between the Humber and Don rivers Toronto, which is believed to mean "a place of meetings." It was later a busy Indian village named Teiaiagon, a French trading post, a British town named York (the British won the Seven Years' War in the late 1700s; if they hadn't, you'd probably be reading this in French) and finally, back to the original Indian name of Toronto.

Toronto was invaded by the Americans in 1812; there were many Great Fires, a rebellion in 1837, and a slow but steady growth of White Anglo-Saxon Protestants, from about nine thousand in the 1830s to almost half a million before the Second World War, when they outnumbered the non-WASPs five to two.

And today, behold what is becoming a Great World City. There are dozens of reasons why Toronto has become the centre of Canadian culture, commerce, and communications. They range from chance – in 1974 Mikhail Baryshnikov chose to defect from the Bolshoi here – to sensitive and thoughtful government action: during the 1970s the city council set limits on the number and size of new buildings, and the Ontario Government put a stop to the Spadina Expressway before it could cut through the city. Many building projects mix low-rental housing with luxury condos, restaurants, offices, and businesses. Toronto encourages urban renewal without having gone through the urban removal that has plagued many other cities. And the city boasts such ethnic inspirations as Caravan, the International Picnic, Caribana, Kensington Market, and some of the best restaurants anywhere. Really.

That Toronto is such a good place to visit and live, is all the more impressive because we have so much working against us. First, our weather is not very good: our winters are often damp and cold, our summers often hot and sticky. Second, our God-given geographical attractions do not rival those of Vancouver, San Francisco, Montreal, or Paris; our topography is more Woody Allen than Orson Welles.

Torontonians are people who, to quote our former mayor, David Crombie, "stuff little bunches of paper into their pockets" until they can find a garbage can, because they are so compulsively neat and civic-minded. They are people who rarely resort to violence, so other people walk kilometres (and even miles) at night without fear. People who, in 1953, had the foresight and brains to create the first metropolitan system of government in North America, improving efficiency by consolidating public transit, courts, tax assessment, and police within a 240-square-mile area. People who, when they undertake a major building project, often will be creative and even daring in their architecture, as you can see in our New City Hall, Ontario Science Centre, Metro Toronto Library, Scarborough College, Roy Thomson Hall, Ontario Place, Scarborough Civic Centre, Royal Bank Tower, and Metro Toronto Zoo.

I have a personal confession here. I was born and raised in Detroit. I came here in 1968 to marry a Torontonian and have been a Canadian citizen since 1974. I think this is a relevant confession, because it underlines a fact about this book that you should know. I am not a civic booster or a PR man for the city. I am a new Torontonian like most of the people in this city, from another town, another country, another world. I have grown to know and love Toronto, and I am more impressed with each passing day at how decent, vibrant, alive, attractive, and interesting a place it is. And being forced at gunpoint (unloaded of course – this *is* Toronto) by an adamant editor to keep visiting and writing about more and more of the city provided remarkable incentive.

However, I will be the first to admit that Toronto has flaws. Most of its professional sports teams give new meaning to the word amateur. It lacks the physical beauty and sophisticated charm of Montreal. Its housing and food seem to cost too much. (To be fair, a recent international survey found Toronto's living costs way down on the list of the world's major cities – far cheaper than Tokyo, Buenos Aires, London, Vienna, Zurich, Amsterdam, New York, Hong Kong, Johannesburg, Madrid, Los Angeles, Paris, Rome, Tel Aviv, and Washington, D.C.).

But any city that has the Ontario Science Centre, Harbourfront, the CN Tower, Eaton Centre, Casa Loma, High Park, Toronto Islands, and Black Creek Pioneer Village can't be all bad, can it?

So, welcome to Toronto. I hope this city will welcome you as it welcomed me. Why, I even got to write a book about it.

Allan Gould
Winter 1983

HOW TO MAKE LIVING/VISITING EASIER

WORDS TO THE VERY WISE

The soul of man is a far country, wrote Sigmund Freud. The soul of Toronto must seem just as complex, confusing, and consternating at times. Hence the following, one hopes helpful, list of information.

GETTING AROUND
We have often wished that Toronto had the lovely simplicity of Manhattan, with its numbered streets going east-west and its numbered avenues running north-south.

No such luck. But Toronto is not a terribly difficult city to get around in. It's laid out pretty much on a grid. Yonge Street (pronounced "young") is the main north-south artery, much like New York's Fifth Avenue or Detroit's Woodward. The cross-streets are numbered east and west from Yonge. So, if you are looking for 300 Eglinton Avenue West, you want a building a few blocks *west* of Yonge, while 80 King Street East would be just a block or two *east* of Yonge. Right? Right.

If you study the subway map on pages 10-11, you'll get a good sense of Toronto. And if you take the subway, which goes near most of the places mentioned in this book, you'll be showing good sense as well: it's clean, fast, easy to use, fairly reasonable, and very safe. And there is excellent bus and streetcar service from most subway stops. If you get a transfer when you get on the subway or surface transit, you can use it to board any connecting service free.

A Sunday/Holiday Transit Pass costs $2.50. It's valid for one full day, and will get up to two adults and three children (anyone under eighteen) on to TTC buses, streetcars, and subways any number of times during the day.

If you are driving, just remember: Lake Ontario is the southern boundary of Toronto; Highway 401, running east-west, cuts through the northern portion of the city; and there are two highways that run through the city north-south from Highway 401 down to the waterfront: Highway 427 in the west, and the Don Valley Parkway in the east.

We recommend that you study the maps on pages 8-11, to get a sense of the driving/walking layout of Toronto. As you will see, we've identified some Toronto highlights. For places a bit out of town, such as the new Metro Zoo, or a bit hard to find, such as Fort York, we have provided a "How To Get There" at the end of the description in the text.

In a word, Don't Panic. If you remember that Highway 401 is north, the lake is south, Highway 427 is west (near the airport), and the Don Valley Parkway is east, you know as much as you really need to. Anything south of Bloor is considered "downtown." And every subway car has a map of the entire underground system, so you can feel at home even down there. Welcome home.

If you are driving in the city, here are a few things to remember:

By law, everyone in a car must wear a seat-belt.

Don't forget that we have reluctantly gone metric, so gas is sold by the litre (about 4.5 to the Imperial gallon), and the 100 km signs on the highway are not an invitation to floor it; it's about 60 miles per hour.

Pedestrian Crossings are marked by large Xs and found all about the city: they give pedestrians the right of way, so be prepared to stop when you see one. If you're a pedestrian, wait until the traffic stops before venturing into a crosswalk. We don't want to lose you to a driver who didn't read this book.

Winter road reports are given from November to April. Phone 248-3561.

Cheapo car rentals. All the big ones are here, but so are such places as Rent-a-Wreck at 390 Dupont near Spadina (961-7500), which will rent you cars around five years old for $100 a week and less.

If you don't want to drive or go exploring on the subway, here are some alternatives:

Taxis include Co-op (364-8161), Diamond (366-6868), Metro Cab (364-1111). In the north, ABC Taxi (534-1111); in the west, Yellow Cab (363-4141); in the east, East End Taxi (461-1111). All cabs can pick up and deliver anywhere in the city and can simply be hailed on busy streets. Tipping is welcome and even encouraged.

City tours include **Gray Coach Line** (979-3511), which provides tours ranging from 90 minutes (in the summer) to 2½ hours and more. **Toronto by Trolley Car** (869-1372) tours downtown Toronto in a lovely, sixty-year-old streetcar. **Insight Tours** (482-2626) puts together highly creative tours of art galleries, antique shops, and more. **Boat Tours International** (364-2412) gives you a fish-eye view of Toronto by water. And for the very lazy, the **Great Toronto Adventure** (922-1212) at 131 Bloor Street West, at University, gives you an hour of Toronto, via eight screens, sixty projectors, and loud, loud sound.

Four intercity bus lines (Gray Coach, Greyhound, Voyageur, and Travelways) come and go from the bus terminal (979-3511) at Bay and Dundas.

However you travel, you should know the following:

The **emergency number** is 911. Just dial it and state your problem. Police, fire, or ambulance services will come running on the triple.

For the handicapped, a booklet is available listing buildings with special facilities and those to avoid. Phone 863-0505.

Hotel information is available from **Accommodation Toronto** (596-7117), Mon.-Fri., 9:00 a.m.-5:00 p.m. in winter and 9:00 a.m.-9:00 p.m. during May to November; Sat., 9:00 a.m.-6:00 p.m., and Sun., 9:00 a.m.-5:00 p.m. year-round.

Visitors' information is magnificent in Toronto. The **Convention and Tourist Bureau of Metro Toronto** (979-3133), located in Suite 110, the Eaton Centre has wisely placed booths bursting with maps, brochures, and other goodies all over the city, including Bloor and University and next to the Eaton Centre. Don't start to explore Toronto without diving into their material. **Travellers Aid** also helps out: at Union Station (366-7788) and at the airport (676-2868), both open daily 9:00 a.m.-9:00 p.m. On weekends, the offices at both airport terminals keep approximately the same hours as Union Station: 10:00 a.m.-5:00 p.m.

Holidays in Toronto tend to be the same as elsewhere, with such basics as Christmas, Labour Day, and so on. But there are some differences: Victoria Day is the fourth Monday in May, and most things are closed. Dominion Day, alias Canada Day, is July 1st. Civic Holiday is the first Monday in August and provides overworked Torontonians with an extra long weekend in the summer. Canadian Thanksgiving is the second Monday in October. Boxing Day is the day after Christmas, December 26. It is a day of fantastic sales at many stores and is anticipated almost as much as Christmas, if for less spiritual reasons.

Booze is not sold in your neighbourhood pharmacy, grocery store, or pinball arcade in Toronto. Look up Beer & Ale in the yellow pages for locations of **Brewers' Retail Stores**, usually open weekdays 10:00 a.m.-10:00 p.m., and Sat., 10:00 a.m.-8:00 p.m. Liquor and wine can be bought only at the **Liquor Control Board of Ontario** locations (LCBO), which are usually open Mon. to Sat., 10:00 a.m.-6:00 p.m. Some locations, usually in shopping plazas or malls, are open until 10:00 p.m.

Postal information: Beer and wine may not be offered on every corner of Toronto, but stamps are. Many variety, milk, and drugstores have a little post office where you may purchase Canadian stamps to mail letters in Canada, the United States, and elsewhere. The phone number of the main post office is 366-7492.

There are three places where you can get terrific views of Toronto. And they are free, which is almost as remarkable as the view: the **Toronto-Dominion Tower** has an observation deck on the fifty-fourth floor; you can reach it from King Street just west of Bay. The **Westin Hotel**, at the southeast corner of Richmond and University, has two glass-enclosed elevators that are almost as thrilling as the CN Tower elevator. Our kids love it, and if you don't bug the legitimate guests of the hotel, they probably won't throw you off it. If they do, there's still the see-through elevator at the **Hilton Harbour Castle** at the foot of Bay Street by the lake.

Stinky Weather and the Underground City is not the name of a rock group; it's our way of telling you that there is a thermostat-controlled Toronto that flows under large buildings, all the way from Union Station at Bay and Front up to the Eaton Centre, which ends at Dundas and Yonge. You can start underground at the train station; continue north under the Royal Bank Plaza; then on to the Toronto-Dominion Centre, with a jog east to Commerce Court (east of Bay); then back west and north to First Canadian Place north of King Street; then a quick dash across snow-and-salt-filled Adelaide Street to the Richmond-Adelaide Centre near York Street; then north under Richmond Street to the Four Seasons Sheraton; then either north to the City Hall or east to Simpsons at Queen east of Bay. From Simpsons there's an enclosed bridge to the Eaton Centre.

A phone number that should be engraved on every wall in Toronto is 484-4544, the **Toronto Transit Commission**'s magic number. They will tell you what subway, bus, or streetcar to take from anywhere to anywhere. Use it often. But remember, unless you have a transfer, exact fares – coins, tokens, or tickets – are necessary on all surface routes. You can buy tickets, etc. in any subway station.

THE MEDIA HAVE THE MESSAGE

In communications, Toronto is to Canada what New York is to the United States. The big magazines are here; the big newspapers are here; the major TV and radio stations are here. (And don't think that makes the rest of the country too happy, either.) As the best way to learn about a city is to follow its media, here is a quick guide to what to watch, listen to, and read.

TELEVISION

Toronto was one of the best-served areas for TV choice, even before cable came down the telephone wires. In addition to Toronto stations, networks come in from Buffalo; other stations can be drawn in from Barrie, Peterborough, and Kitchener on cable.

All three Toronto newspapers have excellent TV guides in their weekend editions. The daily papers also carry listings. But be warned: stations appear on different channels depending on which cable system your home or hotel is using. But then, searching for the show is usually better entertainment than the show itself.

CBLT, channel 5, is the local English-language station of the Canadian Broadcasting Corporation. It's a government-owned network, and its programming runs from so-so to inspired. Many programs are bought from the usual American factories, but occasionally some fine British series are broadcast. It shines in public affairs and information. Try to catch *The National* at 10:00 p.m. each weeknight, followed by *The Journal* at 10:22 p.m. (yup, 10:22). It gives you more than the usual ninety-second news reports; its documentaries and interviews are interesting and occasionally excellent.

CFTO, channel 9, is the local outlet of CTV, Canada's major private network. With the exception of some fine news shows such as *W5*, *Canada AM* from (7:00-9:00), and the evening news at 11:00 p.m., the station is hard to differentiate from any American network.

Global TV, channel 22, is a primarily Ontario-based network, although it has been picking up syndicated stations in the West. Its 11:00 p.m. news is quite good, American style.

City-TV, channel 79, is a highly innovative attempt at local programming for Toronto. Although most of its schedule is American, it often does fascinating work on its 10:00 p.m. newscasts, which were probably taped outside your hotel or home fifteen minutes ago.

TVOntario, channel 19, is the educational network of the Ontario government. It does some fine work, especially *Speaking Out*, a phone-in show, and *Saturday Night at the Movies*, where you can catch double bills such as *Citizen Kane* and *The Magnificent Ambersons* – without commercials. And between the two films are interviews with the actors, writers, directors, and producers who worked on the films. It's a good reason to stay home on Saturday evening.

CBLFT, channel 25, is the CBC French-language station. You haven't lived until you've seen *Goldfinger en français*.

WNED, channel 17, is the Buffalo branch of PBS (Public Broadcasting System), beaming all the major public broadcasting shows from *Cosmos* to *Nova* to *Sneak Previews*. Some Torontonians feel that channel 17 is the only reason for having a TV.

CHCH, channel 11, is an independent channel out of Hamilton, Ontario. It's mainly American sit-coms and dramas.

WUTV, channel 29 out of Buffalo, is a mishmash of old MASHes.

Since February, 1983, Torontonians have also had the joy of choosing between three Pay-TV stations: First Choice and Superchannel show movies, movies, concerts, sports, and movies. C-Channel is Culture.

RADIO

Ever since 1919, when broadcasting began in Canada, radio has been a favourite with Canadians. Part of this is due to our incredible size – there are about 8,500 kilometres (6,000 miles) from the tip of Newfoundland to the islands of British Columbia. Until recently, large areas of Canada received radio signals, but not television. But radio's popularity is also due to the Canadian Broadcasting Corporation (known as the CBC), which has kept this country hanging together in spite of its politicians.

AM Stations

CBL (740) is it. No advertisements; nothing but intelligent talk and music. This is the CBC outlet in Toronto, and much of the country listens to what is spoken, played, and performed right here in Toronto, down at Jarvis and Carlton streets. From the local drive-to-work show, *Metro Morning*, to *Morningside*; *RSVP*, a classical music show out of Edmonton; *The World at Six*, the thirty-minute news broadcast; and the award-winning phone-out show *As It Happens* (which has interviewed everyone the world over) as well as the inspired lunacy of *Eclectic Circus*, this is the station for news (on the hour), lively talk, and fine music. And best of all is *Sunday Morning*, a *New York Times* of the air. You won't regret listening to this station. And no commercials. Ever.

CKEY (590) is almost completely news and talk. And according to the best predictions, that is what will happen to more and more AM stations over the next decade.

CFTR (680) is pop rock, with strongest appeal to 15-to-35-year-olds. Don't knock it.

CFRB (1010) is the number one station in numbers of listeners, advertising bucks, everything. It's called Easy Listening in the business. Between the commentaries and the talk spots, nothing but MOR (middle-of-the-road) music. Barry Manilow, Kenny Rogers, Willie Nelson, the Beatles. Hundreds of thousands of Torontonians swear by it; few swear at it as it's an institution like Casa Loma or Rosedale.

CHUM (1050) is the number one rock station. Big with the teens and the top fifty singles, but they're playing more album cuts now.

CFGM (1320) is "Well, she loved me but she was hit by a truck." You guessed it: pop country. Just count how many times Hank Williams, Jr. is heard on any day, and you'll get the idea.

CJCL (1430) is the station that brings you the Toronto Blue Jays and the Toronto Maple Leafs, but it also has very winning, very soft rock. It's adult contemporary all the way.

CHIN (1640) is the ethnic station: the Greek hour, the Jewish hour, the Italian hour. If you happen to be Greek, Jewish, Italian, or any of a dozen different nationalities and religions, you can hear your music, your language, your news for an hour or two.

FM Stations

CJRT (91.1) is a wonder. A private, non-profit station that somehow struggles along from day to week to year on government grants and donations from its listeners. About seventy hours of classical music a week, thirty hours of jazz. If you wish to hear a complete symphony or concert, this is the place. You may be so impressed you'll mail in some money, so you won't feel guilty about listening and hearing no commercials to pay for it.

CBL-FM (94.1) is the other dream station for serious music and talk lovers in Toronto; it is the FM station of the CBC, and its highlights include *Off the Record*, two hours of music and commentary daily from Vancouver, and *Ideas*, a series of one-hour studies each weekday evening. Next to CJRT, this is *the* classical music station in Toronto.

CHFI (98.1) is adult contemporary on FM – Ray Coniff, Chuck Mangione – you get the idea.

CKO (99.1) is the all-news station, heard across Canada. It should certainly be on AM, and it's hard to listen for more than four minutes at a time. But if there has been a political assassination or an earthquake in your home town, this is the station to turn to.

CKFM (99.9) is the FM sister of CFRB. It's AC but getting rockier, musically speaking. If you are about thirty-five and grew up with pop music, you'll probably enjoy this station a lot.

CHIN-FM (101.1) is ethnicity on FM. Its programming is a lot like that of its non-stereo affiliate CHIN-AM, listed on p. 23.

CFNY (102.1) is the sound of progressive rock. You'll hear the newest British wave, underground music, imported records, oldies. For listeners eighteen to thirty-five, this one is popular, indeed.

CHUM-FM (104.5) is the hit-parade station of FM. You'll hear the top fifty albums played over and over and over. It's very popular and often neck-in-neck for listeners with the following stations:

CILQ (107) is known by all as Q107 and is a lot harder than CHUM—FM. Here is where to find or avoid the Stones, heavy metal, punk. Its audience is much younger than CHUM-FM's and it's right there in the streets.

There are other, smaller stations, of course, including all-Italian ones, all-Greek ones, and so on. If you want to find out more, check your yellow pages under Radio Stations. And give your eyes a rest from TV.

NEWSPAPERS

The Toronto Star is the biggest newspaper in Canada. It had left-wing, even socialist, beginnings, and by supporting the occasional Communist candidate between the wars, it earned the epithet of "The Red Star." But like most old lefties, the paper has become conservative in its old age. The entertainment section is often good, as are its foreign news and local coverage. Picking up the Saturday edition is a must, if only for its TV guide. The award-winning food editor, Jim

White, is very clever; Michele Landsberg's heart bleeds in the right place; and Richard Gwyn is tops for political analysis. And the *Star* has the best comics anywhere.

The Globe and Mail, Canada's answer to a national newspaper, is zapped from Toronto across the country by satellite every night and printed in other provinces. One of the best things about its news coverage is its subscription to *The New York Times* service: you'll often find *Globe* stories were in the *Times* a few hours earlier – verbatim.

Its movie critic, Jay Scott, is magnificent and rarely wrong. Some of its columnists are excellent, especially George Bain and John Fraser on political issues and Rick Groen on TV. And its business section is the one to read carefully. Overall, this is the paper bought by the bankers, university professors, and anyone who wants to know as much as you might be expected to know without buying *The New York Times*. Whew.

The Toronto Sun: Hoi polloi live. Populist, snappy, and slightly to the political right of Attila the Hun. Big pictures of scantily clothed women and men. This is Toronto's *New York Daily News*: shrill, vulgar, reactionary, and fun. If you want to know what the people feel or are talking about, this is, alas, the place to find out. The columns by Barbara Amiel and Allan Fotheringham are a must. And when you've finished reading the editorials and most of the columns, you'll think that Ottawa is run by Commies.

SITES AND SIGHTS

For a city of its size (close to three million, if you include the suburbs, which are rapidly expanding everywhere except in Lake Ontario), Toronto is rich with countless sites and sights. From the obvious – Casa Loma, Ontario Place, the Ontario Science Centre – to the obscure living museums found all over town, Toronto is a guidebook-writer's paradise.

Still, there are problems: the Royal Ontario Museum is one of the world's major collections, but should it go in this chapter or under The Arts? Or what of The Grange, that delightful building which stands smack behind the Art Gallery of Ontario? It *should* be listed with the AGO, but then, it *is* an Historic House....

But that's *your* problem, as the psychiatrist says. With the help of our fine index on pp. 254-256, you'll be able to track down everything you wanted to know about what to see and do in Toronto.

Nearly all the major sites/sights in this chapter and those that follow are for kids as well as adults (something that cannot be said for the Must See Places in most cities around the world). From the obvious – the Zoo and Canada's Wonderland – to the less obvious – Fort York and the Eaton Centre (where the architecture, fabulous fountain, and glass-enclosed elevator can keep almost any child happy, while mom and dad do a bit of shopping), Toronto really *is* a kid-oriented city.

THE CN TOWER
PHALLACY OR DELIGHT?

The trivia abounds: it weighs 130,000 tons, which is twice as heavy as the world's biggest luxury liner and about the weight of 23,214 large elephants. Its height, 553.33 metres (1,815 feet 5 inches), is the equivalent of about 5½ Canadian football fields tilted up end to end, which might be the best excuse for the Toronto Argonauts' record over most of the past decade. It contains enough concrete to build a curb along Highway 401 from Toronto to Kingston, some 259 km (163) miles away.

Don Harron insists that the **CN Tower** was built to teach Canadian men humility. Perhaps. But the official reason is that so many tall buildings had been built in Toronto that radio and TV transmission towers could not broadcast over them. Signal bounce or "ghosting" was becoming endemic. The answer: build something taller.

Love it or hate it, the CN Tower is hard to ignore. Like the Eiffel Tower, it is wonderful to visit because it is the only place in the city where you don't have to look at the damn thing. It is also in the *Guinness Book of World Records* as the world's tallest free-standing structure. (Yes, there is a taller structure, but it is supported by guy wires.)

It was built over a forty-month period by Canadian National, the government-owned railroad and telecommunications firm, at the cost of $57 million. At the time it was to be the centrepiece of a giant downtown office and residential development that did not work out. But the **CN Tower** rose, regardless.

The builders have wisely made the tower interesting as well as safe. In the main lobby a bank of twenty-four colour monitors show the television signals being broadcast from the tower. There is a restaurant (irresistibly called "The Lunching Pad"), and the chance to have a computer portrait made of you and the gang.

Four elevators zoom up the outside of the tower at 6 metres (20 feet) per second or 360 metres (1,200 feet) in the one-minute ride – a rate of ascent similar to a jet-plane take-off. No, you probably will not get sick, as environmental psychologists were hired to protect you. To prevent vertigo, for example, each elevator has only one floor-to-ceiling glass wall. Indeed, there is such a sense of cocoon-like security that when you step out onto the observation area, you feel more like a butterfly than an advertisement for Gravol.

The Skypod, about two-thirds up the tower, is seven storeys (30.48 metres) high. It is the main activity area: two observation decks, a night-club, a revolving restaurant, and various technical levels (not open to the public) that are filled with microwave equipment.

At Level 2 of the Skypod, the outdoor observation deck at 342 metres (1,122 feet) has an enclosed promenade, and an outdoor balcony for looking straight down at the ground (and your lunch if you can't cope with heights).

Level 3 of the Skypod, the indoor observation deck, has not only conventional telescopes but high-powered peritelescopes, sophisticated 200-power zoom scopes that can simulate flight without a trip to the airport.

The Space Deck is thirty-three storeys higher, forty seconds on the elevator, another dollar, and, at an elevation of 446.53 metres (1,465 feet), the world's highest public observation gallery. They claim that you can see almost 160 km (100 miles) from here. But even from Skypod, on a clear day you can see, if not forever, at least Lake Simcoe to the north and the eternal mist rising from Niagara Falls to the south.

Peak visiting hours tend to be between 11:00 a.m. and 4:00 p.m., so if you get there just after the 10:00 a.m. opening, and on a weekday rather than weekend, you'll have less of a wait. And there *can* be quite a wait, with 1.8 million visitors a year (and more than half of them coming on the very day you do).

How to Get There:

The CN Tower is located at 301 Front Street West. Enter via Lakeshore Boulevard West, between York and Spadina, or drive down University to Front, and then west a few short blocks. There is good on-site parking. It is probably easier, however, to take the north-south subway to Union Station, and then walk a few short blocks west. You can't miss it.

Phone 360-8500 for information about the tower.

CASA LOMA:
IS THIS TORONTO OR DISNEYLAND?

There it is, smack in the middle of the city. **Casa Loma**, Spanish for "house on the hill," with ninety-eight rooms, two towers, secret panels, and passageways.

Not a cheap, plastic imitation, **Casa Loma** is as real as the greed, fantasies, and erstwhile wealth of its creator, **Sir Henry Pellatt** – known as "Pellatt the Plunger" from his entrepreneurial days at the turn of the century, running electric-light companies, Brazilian power and transportation developments, lumber and silver mining, and the Grand Trunk Pacific Railroad. And when he died aged eighty, living in the tiny house of his former chauffeur, his cash assets were $185.08. There's a moral here somewhere.

Casa Loma will remain Sir Henry's greatest monument. And what a monument! It has a pipe organ larger than those in many cathedrals, and a reproduction of Windsor Castle's Peacock Alley. The stable, which can be reached by underground passage, is furnished in mahogany and marble, with porcelain troughs that would put modern bathrooms to shame.

The castle was built between 1909 and 1913, at a cost of about $1,700,000. The stone fence surrounding it cost $250,000. Master stonemasons (and their stones) were imported from Scotland to build the massive walls. Sir Henry paid a dollar per stone, which was a better deal than the masons got. They finally went on strike for 47¢ an hour.

The castle has no single style of architecture; Pellatt visited dozens of castles across Europe, picking up glimmerings as he went: English turrets, hints of Spain, motifs of Scotland, smatterings of Austria. The architect, **E.J. Lennox**, who also built Toronto's Old City Hall, apparently believed that Casa Loma was French baronial style. Who cares? Any five-year-old can tell you that it looks like a castle.

And it has the required romance and intrigue. There is a hidden button in Sir Henry's den. Press it, and the panel swings out, revealing a staircase that leads to his bedroom, through another door concealed in a panel. And in the bedroom is a hidden locker.

Alas, he should have kept more money in it. In a few short years, soon-to-be-poor Sir Henry saw his taxes skyrocket from $600 to $12,000. And so, in 1924, barely a decade after he moved in, Sir Henry retreated to his 1,000-acre farm near King City, north of the city, where, he muttered, he should have built his dream castle in the first place.

For most of the 1920s and 1930s, Pellatt's Folly was home to bats, owls, and pigeons, who obviously found the city taxes manageable. In 1937, the Kiwanis Club took **Casa Loma** over as a tourist attraction, charging 25¢ per person for a tour, "the cost of a shave and a haircut." Your visit will cost somewhat more, but the money goes for the same good cause: over the years a million dollars has been donated to charity by the Kiwanis.

There are no guided tours of the castle, which is probably for the best: you can come and go as you please, and the kids will probably want to race off to the stables or towers. You'll probably walk at least a mile by the time you leave, so wear comfortable shoes. And don't forget your camera.

A visit to the towers makes it all worthwhile, especially for kids, since the little ones may well be bored with much of the opulence and grandeur of the lower floors. You climb up spiral staircases until you get to the top – and it really *is* the top. The Scotch Tower at the east end is enclosed, but the open-air Norman Tower is great for taking pictures of downtown Toronto and each other, and for peering over the carved unicorns and lions, red-tiled roofs, and turrets and battlements of this fairy-tale castle.

How to Get There:

Casa Loma is at 1 Austin Terrace, which is just a few blocks south of St. Clair, going along Spadina. There is a considerable amount of free parking, right at the entrance of the castle.

Phone 923-1171 for information on group tours. (For ten and more, prices are chopped considerably for adults and children under twelve.) Casa Loma is open daily all year except for Christmas and New Year's day.

THE ONTARIO SCIENCE CENTRE: WE HAVE SEEN THE FUTURE AND IT BEEPS

When we were in our teens, we visited the Museum of Science and Industry in Chicago, and our minds were boggled. You poked, jabbed, and pressed buttons to make machines do all kinds of things. We thought we would never see its like again.

Think again. Right here in muddy York, just fifteen minutes from City Hall, just twenty-five minutes from the airport, there it is: the **Ontario Science Centre**, in one of the most extraordinary buildings and with some of the most astonishing exhibits you've ever seen. **Raymond Moriyama**, the genius who designed the Metropolitan Toronto Library and Scarborough Civic Centre, made brilliant use of the landscape. Three linked pavilions float gracefully down the side of a ravine in a 180-acre conservation area on the southwest corner of Don Mills Road and Eglinton Avenue East. The **Ontario Science Centre** cost $25 million, and never has money been better spent.

But before you begin, pick up some free maps and flyers from a booth just inside the main entrance, to help you plan your time. There are more than five hundred exhibits and they are always changing, so you will have to make some choices.

At **Exploring the Molecule**, you can watch a laser slice through wood, bricks, and junior's hand if he's not careful. Crawl inside a simulated space capsule in **Exploring Space** and dock your ship by watching a closed-circuit TV screen.

In the **Hall of Communication** (our favourite, we confess), "logic gates" teach you how computers "think." You can take on a computer at tic-tac-toe, whisper into a "sound focus dish" and be heard across a crowded room or stagger through a disorientation room that plays sneaky but harmless tricks on your inner ear.

The **Hall of Life** has a reproduction of Banting and Best's lab where they discovered insulin, and the reproduction and birth exhibit will tell your kids how it all happens without your stammering and stuttering.

In the **Science Arcade** you can play musical instruments

in soundproof glass rooms, operate water pumps, and generate electricity by pedalling a bike. You can take a driver reaction test in the **Hall of Transportation**. The **Hall of Engineering** has one of the most popular exhibits of all: someone puts their hand on a funny round thing, and the electricity makes their hair stand on end, right?

The **Ontario Science Centre** does what your grade-nine teacher didn't: make science fascinating, exciting, and irresistible. But it would take a person about forty hours to see, hear, touch, and experience all the exhibits, so try to cover one or two halls, but not many more, during each visit. Like a museum, it can be quite overwhelming unless you just go with the flow and drift from room to room, jabbing, reading, pedalling, staring, pressing, pushing, and enjoying whatever strikes your fancy.

How to Get There:
By car, take the Don Valley Parkway north and exit at Don Mills Road North or take it south and exit at Eglinton Avenue westbound; turn left (south) off Eglinton to Don Mills Road. The Eglinton East bus serves the centre from the Eglinton subway station, and the Don Mills bus will take you there from the Pape station. The address is 770 Don Mills Road. Try to go weekday mornings or afternoons. Phone 429-4423 for a recorded message on prices and times, or 429-4100 for further information.

EATON CENTRE:
THE MEETIN', TREATIN', AND EATIN' CENTRE

"Death of a Main Drag," headlined an anti-Eaton Centre newspaper article in 1979. It will kill Yonge Street, the journalist warned. "Closed at both ends by doors, and climate controlled, the Galleria is essentially a sterile and artificial environment masquerading as an organic one."

Not so, argued an impassioned letter to the editor the following week. "People like the environment of the Galleria. Its popularity has lessons for Yonge Street." The letter was signed Jane Jacobs, the world-renowned urbanist and author of *Death and Life of Great American Cities*, who chose to live in Toronto because of its excitement and hope.

Jacobs is correct; people do love the Eaton Centre. It has rapidly become one of Toronto's most popular attractions. Not bad when you consider that most of the stores can be found in suburban shopping centres.

The **Eaton Centre** is North America's largest indoor shopping complex if you throw in **Simpsons** just to the south, on the other side of Queen Street. More than a million shoppers a week visit the $300-million, 300,000-square-metre (3,000,000-square-foot) building. It employs 15,000 people, and grosses some $500 million a year in sales.

Why is the centre so popular? Is it the graceful glass roof, arching 38.7 metres (127 feet) above the lowest mall level? Is it **Michael Snow**'s gorgeous flock of fibreglass Canada geese, floating poetically in the open space of the gallery? Is it the glass-enclosed elevators, the porthole windows, the seemingly endless flow of escalators taking thousands of people comfortably from level to level?

It is all those things and more. The sheer size is thrilling rather than exhausting or intimidating. Filling three city blocks, **Eaton Centre** has twenty-one movie theatres, fifty fashion stores, and more than two dozen shoe stores. And it never closes, even when the stores shut their doors at 9:00 p.m. and the last bar closes down at 1:00 a.m. It is really a city under glass. And in a city with weather like Toronto's, being climate-controlled is nothing to sniff at.

There are some clues to finding where you are in the sea of three hundred stores. Level 1, where many of the lower-priced fashion stores are located, has nearly one-third of all the businesses. Level 2, which has higher-priced stores and more fashionable fashions, has sixty stores. Level 3, the highest level, has the highest fashion, the highest prices, and the fewest shops.

Useless information: The **Eaton Centre** has about $300,000 worth of landscaping, plants, and trees. There are nineteen escalators. There are nearly five thousand light fixtures. Sixty people are employed just to keep the centre clean. Below Level 1 are thirty-five huge loading bays to receive the hundreds of thousands of pieces of incoming merchandise. Both Dundas and Queen subway stations, which serve the centre, handle about sixty thousand passengers daily. There are 25,000 square metres (250,000 square feet) of walkways in the centre. There are more than sixty restaurants, fast food outlets, and specialty food shops.

Which brings us to useful information on some of the popular eateries:

Level 1: **Apple Annie's** has rough timber, lots of antiques, and eleven varieties of crepes and pancakes. The giant apple pancake is famous. **Michel's Baguette** is a goldmine, with real silverware, a generous salade Niçoise served in glass bowls, and excellent sandwiches. The buttery croissants, various rolls, and baguettes are made on the premises. The crusty French sticks must be eaten within twelve hours, as they contain no preservatives. **Swenson's Ice Cream Factory**, a branch of the famous original in San Francisco, has expensive and rich, rich ice cream in some two dozen varieties. At **The Sweet Gallery**, Black Forest, German chocolate, and hazelnut and strawberry shortcakes assault both your waistline and your wallet.

Level 2: There are two pubs you might enjoy. **The Nags Head Tavern** has re-created an English pub. There is steak and kidney pie and lots of beer. In **The Elephant & Castle**, dark ceiling beams hold up nothing but your admiration; there are dining booths and massive kegs of draft beer.

Level 3: Try **mmmuffins**, brought to you by the same genius who runs **Michel's Baguette** on Level 1. The trick here is to use no preservatives, additives, or colouring. They sell more than a hundred dozen a day, and are they good! **Chocolate Chocolat** makes its own you-know-what with ingredients sent from Tobler of Switzerland. Watch it being made; then watch yourself shell out about $20 a pound to buy some. You can buy chocolate letters to create yummy messages. **Godiva** chocolates are also about $20 a pound; they are flown in every week from Belgium and the United States. The boxes are exquisite, as are the treats inside.

Level 4: **Mr. Greenjeans**. Its hamburgers cost a lot but are big enough for a family.

The **Marine Room** in Eaton's is the biggest dining area in the Galleria. It's a cafeteria, and the salad bar will prevent you from getting scurvy. Carved roasts, fruit salads, hot meals, and made-to-order sandwiches are also provided.

You'll rarely eat anything that could remotely be called gourmet fare (except perhaps those chocolates), but the wide selection of restaurants and snack-bars – and there are dozens more – make the centre a delightful place to eat, as well as ogle, as well as shop. In its own exciting way it is an ode to capitalism, a CN Tower of stores, uniquely Toronto. No matter what the occasional critic says, the **Eaton Centre** is an enormous success.

ONTARIO PLACE: A PLACE TO PLAY

"A string of hamburger stands down by the waterfront," sniffed one Opposition member when it opened back in May 1971. "A monument to the Conservative Party" snarled another, referring to the government that has been running the province longer than most of its citizens have been alive.

And when **Ontario Place** opened, it all seemed much ado about nothing, except that the nothing cost $19 million of taxpayers' money – our money. But like so many things in this astonishingly successful town, the ninety-six acres of play space soon changed our ideas of entertainment with the impact of the Beatles singing "She Loves You" on *The Ed Sullivan Show*.

The three islands on which **Ontario Place** stands just south of the Canadian National Exhibition grounds were built from the fill taken from the Bloor subway extension and the Toronto-Dominion Centre excavation. The landfill was then sodded, and 1,687 trees and 29,000 shrubs and plants were installed, along with footpaths and waterways.

The original inspiration was Canada's Centennial in 1967, when celebration projects were begun all across this country. There are echoes of Montreal's Expo 67, probably because a number of architects and engineers worked on both.

There is an amazing number of things to do, from visiting the Children's Village, to eating at its many restaurants and bars, to seeing a film on one of the world's largest indoor movie screens, to roller-skating, to . . . Let's put it in a highly personal way: for the past two years, we have had our son's birthday party there, packing about a dozen kids in a car or two and letting them run loose (almost) on the grounds. For six months afterwards all we hear from my son's friends' parents is, "All my kid ever talks about is your son's birthday party at Ontario Place!" But we refuse to be intimidated by their jealousy.

When you enter the grounds, you'll get excellent little brochures describing the joys awaiting you. So we'll just touch on some of the highlights:

HMCS Haida is a Canadian destroyer that was commissioned in England in 1942 and served during the Second World War and the Korean War. It was berthed permanently just east of the entrance to **Ontario Place**. It's really a floating museum, and it's open for touring every day. It costs a bit extra after your general admission, but all the people who tour it agree that it's well worth the price.

Children's Village, located on the east island, is a miraculous two acres of inspired kids' play. It's enough to make even the most self-satisfied adult sympathize with Peter Pan's refusal to grow up. You see, you old codger you, it's only open for kids less than 135 cm (58″) high. Tube slides, roller bins,

hand slides, a moon walk, and lots more make this an imaginative, creative playground, all under an orange, vinyl canopy
so kids can play there even in a rainstorm. And after they
cavort in the water-play area, they can enter a giant
bird-shaped, walk-in "child dryer."

The Forum is an outdoor amphitheatre with three thousand seats and room for three times as many on the grassy
slopes around its sides. For many people, this is the main
reason for flocking to **Ontario Place**; top entertainers play
there – the **Toronto Symphony**, **Peter Allen**, **Rush**, **Kris
Kristofferson**, **Cleo Laine** and **John Dankworth**,
Queen, **Anne Murray**, **Ray Charles**, the **National
Ballet of Canada**, **Chuck Mangione** – and all free once
you're in the grounds. As you might guess, the smart people
get to the **Forum** by mid-afternoon, picnic there, and wait
very patiently for the 8:00 p.m. performance.

The Cinesphere looks a lot like one of Buckminster
Fuller's geodesic domes and helps give **Ontario Place** its
striking visual image from the distance. The six-storey
screen can handle 60′ x 80′ film images, and the theatre itself
holds eight hundred viewers. Whether in 35 mm, 70 mm, or
IMAX (there are only a handful of these projectors and theatres in the world), the films are often all medium and no
message; size is all. But when you sit enveloped in giant
images of humpback whales or space satellites or the Grand
Canyon, the experience transcends the vague story lines.
There are usually a number of different movies shown each
day on the half hour. Each film lasts about twenty minutes.
There is an entry fee of one dollar per person during the CNE.
(See pp. 67-69.) At other times it's free.

Children's Theatre is an entertainment centre with
kids' music, puppet shows, clowns, and magicians. Shows
run for just under an hour from noon to 5:00 p.m. daily. And
as if this isn't enough, there are bumper boats, miniature
golf, jazz bands on the floating showboat, Futurepod, aero-
space, computer games and much, much more. And then
there's the marina for more than three hundred boats and
open-air trains to transport the foot-weary and . . . oh, you get
the idea. **Ontario Place** works. Or rather, plays.

Ontario Place is open from mid-May to mid-September.
In recent years, they have wisely run 70 mm films – usually
family classics such as *Sleeping Beauty* and *Close Encounters
of the Third Kind* – in the **Cinesphere** during the winter
months. Check your daily newspaper for ads regarding times
and prices, or phone **Ontario Place** (965-7711).

How to Get There:
There are two large parking lots just south of Lakeshore Boulevard to the east and west of **Ontario Place**. During the CNE, it will cost a few dollars extra, so you would do well to take public transportation. Dufferin (number 29) buses go south on Dufferin to the Exhibition grounds. The Bathurst streetcar (number 511) goes to the Ex from the Bathurst subway station at Bloor, and the Dundas (number 505) bus heads there from the Dundas West subway station. On weekends and holidays, the TTC has special **Ontario Place** buses that leave the Gray Coach terminal at Bay and Dundas and continue boarding down Bay and Front streets.

HARBOURFRONT:
AN EMBARRASSMENT OF RICHES

Toronto has been exceedingly prodigal with its God-given, man-taken-away waterfront. Over the years we have allowed railway tracks and yards, the multi-lane Lakeshore Boulevard and the Gardiner Expressway cut us off from our watery origins. Successive city governments lacked any sensitivity to the natural beauty of our harbour.

Enter, stage left, hands overflowing with money, the federal government of far-off Ottawa, which knows how to buy votes better than the local politicos. Back in the early 1970s, the feds offered, nay announced, that they were going to buy nearly all the central waterfront of Toronto and present it as a gift to our city for the development of a park. (And we didn't even have to vote for them!)

Well, politics aside, **Harbourfront** was soon born. Right now, the complex is ninety-two acres of shoreline that stretches from just west of the Toronto Hilton Harbour Castle complex for nearly 2 km (a mile) to Bathurst Street.

For nearly a decade now **Harbourfront** has been the scene of fabulous entertainment. And by 1987, if all goes well, there will be housing for more than eight-thousand water lovers, plus offices, restaurants, more parks and marinas, and a continuous walkway the length of the quays. And this time most of the quarter-billion bucks is coming from smart developers instead of crafty politicians.

We could tell you more, but there are newspapers down at **Harbourfront** that list all the doings that day or week or month, and there are listings in Toronto's major dailies as well. Anyone who has experienced Pier 39 in San Francisco or Inner Harbor in Baltimore knows what can be done when

37

creative minds and wallets get together with a piece of water-front land.

For the children: In addition to special events, from magicians to singers to plays, there are year-round supervised play areas at the Bathurst Quay, and a "make a mess" room at the York Quay centre, which should not be missed. And they are all free – another good reason for them not to be missed.

Antique Market: Every Sunday and holiday antique dealers from rural Ontario to Quebec to backyard Toronto set up stalls overflowing with treats, treasures, nostalgia, and nonsense.

Eateries: Although packing a picnic lunch is always a joy – **Harbourfront** is right on the water, remember – there are snack bars and kiosks on Queen's Quay and the always satisfying **Amsterdam Café**, which offers homemade soups, cabbage rolls, quiches, sandwiches, and desserts. **Pier 4**, between Queen's Quay and Spadina Quay, has restaurants that offer seafood and burgers. The renovated **Queen's Quay Terminal Building** at the foot of York Street opens in the summer of 1983, with seven new waterfront restaurants, three floors of shops, stores, and boutiques, and a 450-seat dance theatre.

Special Events: There are special events almost every day or weekend at **Harbourfront**, but they are still special: classic and contemporary films (there have been a Japanese series, a Swedish series, and a Katharine Hepburn series) and art exhibits, from fibre and photography to children's book illustrations.

The **Canadian Opera Company** performs excerpts from some of the great ones each summer, and in August there is an annual **craft fair**. It lasts three days and attracts artisans who not only display but demonstrate their talents.

There is a **jazz festival** in August, **dance festivals** at various times throughout the year, **theatre festivals**, **skating rinks** in the winter and **sailing** and **canoeing** in the summer. There is even **dancing** under the stars. Any visitor will not regret a day here; hundreds of thousands of Torontonians spend many of them.

Harbourfront is open year round, seven days a week. There is no charge to enter the site, and there are always several free events. For information phone 364-5665. It may be a good idea to begin your first visit by going to the **information centre** on York Quay, 235 Queen's Quay West, close to York Street and the Hilton.

How to Get There:
Harbourfront is quite easy to get to by public transportation. Take either the Yonge or University subway line to Union Station, then the Bay bus (6 or 6A) to the foot of Bay. You can also take the 77B bus from Union Station or the Spadina subway. If you drive, there are parking areas along Queen's Quay West, but they tend to fill up quickly, especially on weekends and on days when major events are on. It will also run you up to $4 for a few hours, which you might find steep. Unless your group or family is quite large, you might be wise to take the subway or bus.

THE METRO ZOO:
BORN FREE, AND LIVING PRETTY FREE, TOO

"It's fantastic," said the supervisor for the Busch Gardens Zoo in Williamsburg, Virginia. "It's something for everybody else to shoot for in the years to come."

"Yeah, I guess we want to copy it. We're not proud," said the zoologist and curator for the up-and-coming Syracuse zoo.

Maybe he's not proud, but thousands of Torontonians are. And their pride in the zoo is not because it's the biggest or the tallest or the oldest. Theirs is the warm-hearted, generous pride of people who have a zoo built for animals, not people. No more animals shut up in small cages like so many furry criminals. Indeed, some animals might be inside a cave or too far in the distance to see or photograph – and you can jolly well wait or come back later.

The zoo's open concept is unique and aims to show off the animals in their native environment. And the visitor is requested to share the environment. And with the zoo spread over 710 sprawling acres, there is a lot of environment to share.

Being housed in an ecology-minded zoo pays off for the animals. These are some of the babies born on the premises during one six-week period in May and June 1982: six wood bison, five reindeer, six mouflon wild sheep, one Indian fruit bat, five Bactrian camels (unofficially declared to have the worst breath of any animal alive), five Arctic wolves, four aoudads (Barbary sheep), two gemsbok (African antelopes), one European bison, two mara (South American rodents), one patas monkey, eleven white-tailed deer, nine mandarin ducks, three Barbary apes, two South African fur seals, six mute swans, two Himalayan tahr, one sacred ibis, three beavers and, surprisingly, not a single partridge or pear tree.

It wasn't always thus. For nearly a century the main zoo of this city was squished into nine acres near the Don Valley. Between 1887 and 1973, the tiny park served a city population that was growing a lot more rapidly than the animal population – although, to be fair, the old Riverdale zoo did manage to breed tigers, chimpanzees, orangutans, and to hatch some king vultures.

In the 1960s came the inspired choice of site, the Rouge Valley, which was worth a visit even before the zoo was there. With a varied terrain, from river valley to open landscaped areas to dense forest, the area was perfect for what is rapidly becoming the perfect zoo. The **Metro Zoo** has been ranked as one of the top ten in the world (by *The New York Times*, yet), and at the end of a new five-year development plan, which includes building thirty new exhibits at a cost of over $5 million, it could edge toward number one.

But whatever the ratings, the animals are happy – largely because they are truly at home. Most of the mammals, birds, reptiles, fish, trees, and shrubs in the **Metro Zoo** have been grouped according to where they live in the wild. This concept is called zoogeography: the zoo is divided into six zoogeographic regions: Eurasia, North America, South America, Africa, Indo-Malaya, and Australia. And in most regions, you'll find remarkable botanical exhibits in climate-controlled, enclosed pavilions. More than five hundred species of plants make the animals feel more at home than you probably do in your home town. A three-ton Banyan tree is in the **Indo-Malayan Pavilion**, along with giant rubber, mango, and umbrella trees. The **African Pavilion** has a gorgeous fan-shaped Traveller's palm from Madagascar. And the jasmine vines with their perfumed flowers in the **Eurasian Pavilion** are beyond description.

The zoo has charted a number of walking tours, and the trails are clearly marked with brightly coloured sasquatch-size footprints that are fun to follow. The "round the world tour" takes you to the major pavilions and exhibits. Taking about three hours, it's suitable for any kind of weather, as much of your time will be spent inside the pavilions.

It has been estimated that it would take four full days to see everything in the **Metro Zoo**, so study the map given out at the entrance and decide in advance what you want to see most.

In case you haven't learned anything new today, here are some zoo facts. Since the anteaters would each devour more than 10,000 ants a day, they are fed pellets, instead. Tantor the elephant is almost three metres (nine and a half feet) tall, weighs nearly four tons and holds the record for biggest beast at the zoo. On any one day, Tantor will devour more than 45 kilos (100 pounds) of beet pulp, 147 kilos (325 pounds) of "concentrated elephant cubes" and four bales of hay.

During the 1970s, the zoo's chief veterinarian became the first person to set a broken giraffe jaw. A 170 cm (68 in) tracheal tube was lowered down the critter's throat for the duration of the surgery.

By 1981, the **Metro Zoo** grocery bill was more than a third of a million dollars. The premise that food has to go somewhere, led to a tale of capitalistic ingenuity. Two million pounds of animal waste was being dumped annually at a landfill site. Then someone thought up the brilliant idea of marketing the stuff. The zoo sells thousands of bags a year, and it is also available at plant nurseries around Toronto.

Everyone has his or her own favourite things to see, but the orangutans in the **Indo-Malaya Pavilion** bring the most joy to people – probably because they act so much like we do. The gorillas in the **African Pavilion** are especially hilarious at meals. Call the zoo ahead of time or ask when you arrive exactly when feeding time is. (Human feeding time is anytime. Picnicking is welcome, and there are tables scattered throughout the site.)

In **Littlefoot Land**, located just north of the main gate, children can touch and feed carrots to rabbits, sheep, goats, donkeys, and even camels. And while rides on the lumpy backs of camels Amy, Casey, and Piglet should thrill the children, the family admission price – under ten dollars for four – will please their parents.

There is an electrically powered train that moves slowly and silently through the **Animal Domain** without frightening the animals. It runs frequently, costs one dollar, and is an excellent way for first-time visitors to get a sense of the vast layout. The train is air-conditioned and can accommodate wheelchairs. A one-dollar Zoomobile ride in an open vehicle will also cover much of the zoo.

Free wheelchairs are available inside the main gate. All the pavilions have ramp access, and there is an elevator in the **African Pavilion**.

The zoo may seem far away, but, in fact, it is only a half-hour drive from downtown, and even closer from hotels along the 401. And when you consider that Africa, Asia, and South America are so near, you shouldn't wait.

How to Get There:

The **Metro Zoo** is located in northeast Toronto, at Highway 401 and Meadowvale Road, about 16 km (10 miles) east of the Don Valley Parkway. The closest exit from Highway 401 is clearly marked. Then just follow the signs. There is parking for 5,000 cars; the cost is two dollars. But if you are up for a ten-minute walk, you can pocket that money and use the free lot just across Meadowvale Road. All parking is free in winter. If you are going by bus, take the Scarborough 86A bus that leaves the Kennedy subway station (at the east end of the Bloor-Danforth line). Call the TTC (484-4544) for more information. And remember – the zoo is open all year round. You can even see it on skis. For recorded information about the zoo, call 284-0123. Zoo administration is 284-8181.

CANADA'S WONDERLAND: AMERICAN INGENUITY

It's hard not to be cynical. When Canada, whose children can recognize presidents of the United States but not their present prime minister, finally got its first major theme park, it was built by the Taft Broadcasting Company of Cincinnati. Like the rest of the world, Toronto would be made safe for those Canadian cultural giants Yogi Bear, Fred Flintstone, and Scooby Doo.

The neighbours weren't thrilled. Nearly a decade before **Canada's Wonderland** finally opened on May 23, 1981, area residents heard of the plans to build the park, and they lobbied hard against it. We don't want another Disneyland, they said. This is the richest farm land in the world – why cover it with concrete?

But those guys at Taft are no fools. As they already owned and operated three other theme parks, they worked hard to overcome objections. A Canadian partner, Great West Life of Winnipeg, was sold some of the stock, and the Ontario government was almost promised that lots of jobs would be created. (Besides, there are nearly two dozen theme parks in the United States, so the American market is saturated.)

Well, Canada's Wonderland is here, at the cost of more than $130 million. The fears of congestion on Highway 400, the major road to cottage country, have vanished, thanks to nearly $5 million of local road and highway improvements.

Is it good? It will depend on whether you've been to Disneyland, Disney World, or the other American parks – and whether you like this sort of thing. Your response will also depend on the ages of your children and whether they enjoy brassy entertainment, stomach-churning rides, and little restaurants named Yee Ribb Pytt that serve French Fryes and Shrymps.

Yes, it can be a lot of fun. And yes, it is expensive. A family of four would be hard-pressed to spend less than $100 – more than $60 of that would go for four "one-day-unlimited-use-passports." But there are many discount promotions each summer, and the public can often save a fair amount on admission.

Another way to save money, although the nice folks at Canada's Wonderland won't appreciate this recommendation, is to pack a lunch. The park has kindly provided some fairly pleasant picnic areas outside the site proper and you need not spend all your dollars on paella, pizza, and chicken teriyaki, just like mother never made.

There are five theme areas: **Medieval Faire, Grande World Exposition of 1890, International Street, International Festival**, and **Hanna-Barbera Land**, which is best suited to children under eight. There are frequent live shows, most of them free. As you enter the park you get a free sixteen-page guidebook and a souvenir book, which include a park map and information on rides, restaurants, first aid, and services for the handicapped, so there's no need to list all that here. Line-ups are shortest after midday on weekdays.

Canada's Wonderland opens weekends in early May and then daily from early June through Labour Day. Then it's weekends only until Canadian Thanksgiving, which is the first Monday in October. As you can see, one of the problems of a northern climate is that you just can't run a theme park year-round.

You can buy Ground Admission for $10.95, and an adult book of twelve coupons for the rides and entertainment costs $13.95. (The same coupons cost $11.95 for seniors and children under 8.) Anyone who plans to hit a lot of rides should buy the one-day-unlimited-use passport, which runs $15.95. There is a very good deal for those who expect to return a few times during the summer: A season pass costs $29.95. It's sold until late June and is good for the entire, hundred-plus days of the summer and fall run.

And a further pleasant thought. There is a new, ten-thousand-seat music theatre at **Canada's Wonderland**, where big-name entertainment will perform seven days a week.

One more thing. My nine-year-old son is furious because I haven't raved about the fantastic rides. Okay, I just raved.

How to Get There:
Canada's Wonderland is probably closer to a major city than any other theme park in North America. It is only about 30 km (19 miles) northwest of downtown Toronto. If you are driving, take Highway 401 to Highway 400; take 400 north for about ten minutes to Rutherford Road, where the exit is clearly marked. You can't miss the park's symbol, a huge, man-made five-million-dollar mountain. GO transit buses leave regularly from the Yorkdale and York Mills subway stations; Gray Coach also has a service to the grounds; and many of the hotels around the airport provide regular bus service and discount prices.

MARINELAND:
DON'T DRINK THE WATER

Ever hear of Kandu and Nootka? How about Nemo and Bubbles? They are killer whales and dolphins, respectively, and you'll never hear the end of them should you choose to take this short detour from Niagara Falls. **Marineland**, founded back in 1961, is second only to Niagara's famous falls in popularity, and with good reason.

The one admission price covers all attractions, which is a pleasant surprise, as is the free parking. And it's open year-round. **Marineland** is undergoing a $100-million development program during the 1980s, to make the thousand-acre complex one of the best of its kind anywhere.

Be sure to see the killer whales, two giant black and white beauties who are about 7 metres (22 feet) long and weigh 3600 kilos (8,000 pounds) each. They do spirals, back flips, and hurdle jumps in a display of competition that would turn Montessori teachers grey.

The dolphins soar gracefully out of the water, bounce balls, and leap in unison over hurdles. They are a lot more agile and probably considerably brighter than most people.

The sea lions stand on one flipper (can you do that?), juggle balls, and even play music.

The tigers and elephants perform only during the summer. Elephant rides are available for children.

In 1983, they are opening the world's most amazing ride. (Who are we to argue?) It includes a mile of steel roller-coaster track, three coaster trains, large replicas of both the Canadian and American Falls, spirals, loops, a boomerang, tunnels, a volcano pit, and a river, all built around a mountain landscape. It sounds like the Canadian economy.

How to Get There:
Marineland is located less than one and a half kilometres from the Canadian Falls. Coming from Toronto, take the QEW (Queen Elizabeth Way) west and south into Niagara Falls, then turn left on McLeod Road. The exact address is 7657 Portage Road. Phone 1-356-8250 for more information.

AFRICAN LION SAFARI:
IN DARKEST SOUTHERN ONTARIO

With the cost of flights to Africa nowadays, it sure is a relief to have a place like the **African Lion Safari** just an hour west of Toronto. The experience of driving your car slowly – you wouldn't want to run over a monkey, would you? – through a wildlife park full of wandering animals is really very exciting.

When a six-metre (eighteen-foot) giraffe sticks its graceful and absurdly long neck into your car window and licks your child's face with its long, sticky tongue you will not soon forget it. (Nor will your sticky-faced child.)

But if the antics of friendly giraffes or monkeys scare you, there are air-conditioned trams that can carry up to 3,000 visitors a day over a ten-kilometre (6-mile) safari trail, and charming guides make the journey all the more pleasant. And even if you do choose to drive your car through the six reserves filled with lions, tigers, cheetah, black bears, elephants, white rhinos, elands, and zebras, few of the animals get too friendly. (Although come to think of it, that bear that decided to hang onto our trunk did cut down on our gas mileage, if not on our laughter.)

Although there are parts of the complex that are commercial – the International Bazaar, the cafeteria, the Safari Oasis Bar – it is pleasantly surprising to find how uncommercial most of the Safari is.

That's probably because, back in 1969, the owners, like Noah, wanted to save as many endangered species of animals as possible. So they bought five farms, which were not being worked because of the poor quality of the land, and they have been growing animals ever since. We mention this because highways, buildings, and entertainment complexes around Toronto have had an unpleasant tradition of tearing up some of the best farmland outside the Ukraine for their nefarious purposes. The Safari, we are pleased to report, did not follow that tradition.

The place is really quite remarkable. It has the world's first peregrine falcon born in full public view (proving that

Canadians know no shame). It is fascinating to see how many animals from warm climates thrive in our cold one. The Safari has sent Bengal tigers to Japan and a rare mandrill monkey to the Peking zoo. (When Ontario starts sending antelope to Africa, we'll know that man has finally succeeded in destroying his environment.)

More than eight million visitors from around the world have visited the **African Lion Safari**, and the only ones who have regretted it were those who forgot to bring a camera.
How to Get There:
The **African Lion Safari** is just outside Cambridge, Ont. Phone 1-519-623-2620 for further information. From Toronto, it takes about an hour to get to where the wild things are. Take Highway 401 west to Highway 6 south; turn right on Safari Road. It can also be reached by taking the QEW southwest to Hamilton, then 403 west to Highway 6 north, and then left on Safari Road. Should you prefer to go by bus, there are package tours provided by Gray Coach (979-3531).

In March (spring break excepted) and November, the Safari is only open on weekends. It closes completely from December to February. After all, animals need privacy, too.

GREAT BUILDINGS

OLD, NEW AND BOTH

More than in most cities around this shrinking globe, Toronto
has witnessed profound passions raised over its buildings.
Yes, many great ones have been torn down in the name of
Progress (or is it Mammon – we forget); but nearly as many
have been saved, often after ferocious fighting between citizens' groups and developers. In your wanderings about our
fair town, you will find a remarkable number of "living
museums," where costumed men and women bake bread,
wait on tables, knit (one purl two), shoe horses, pass muster,
dip candles and do various other things that we Torontonians did a century or more ago.

There are countless buildings and streetscapes worthy of
note, but we simply don't have space to comment on them
all: the beautiful and moving Soldiers' Tower on the University of Toronto campus, the many gargoyled walls about the
city, the mirrored towers that reflect the images of smaller
historical buildings nearby and catch the changing lights of
days and seasons. But the ones listed in this chapter should
give you lots to see and savour – with the hope that you might
pick up one of the many recent books on the architecture of
Toronto, and discover even more.

TORONTO'S CITY HALLS:
THE TWENTIETH CENTURY CUDDLING UP
TO THE NINETEENTH

For a city only a century and a half old, Toronto seems to
have more than its share of city halls. The first one, built for
£7,000 in 1844, is part of the south St. Lawrence Market. The
second City Hall, now affectionately called **Old City Hall**,
stands on the northeast corner of Queen and Bay, sweetly
coexisting with the futuristic **New City Hall** across the
way. Although the old one was opened in 1899, its construction was approved way back in 1880, which suggests that
some things, except perhaps the mail, were a bit slower in the
last century.

A design competition was held, and the winner was
Edward James Lennox, the Frank Lloyd Wright of his
time. (He would later design Casa Loma.) In 1891 the cornerstone was laid, into which were placed copies of Toronto's

newspapers of the day (the *Globe*, *Mail*, *Empire*, *World*, *Evening Telegram*, *News*, and *Monetary Times* – a lot more competition back then for a lot fewer people). And they put in a copy of "The Maple Leaf Forever," some coins from the first City Hall's cornerstone, an American dime, probably worth more than Canadian coins even back then.

The **Old City Hall** is such a beautiful building – it was one of North America's most impressive municipal halls at the turn of the century – that one recalls with shock that Eaton's urged its demolition in the 1970s to allow even more room for the Eaton Centre. But it was not torn down, thanks to the howls of outraged Torontonians who rallied to the defence of its hallowed walls; and since the opening of the **New City Hall** in 1965 it has been used to house the provincial courts, county offices, and thousands of brief and cheap marriages. It is also the place where most people fight their parking tickets, which makes some Torontonians feel less nostalgic about it.

Above the front steps of the **Old City Hall** are hideous gargoyles, Lennox's way of mocking certain politicians of the time. The architect also surreptitiously carved his name under the eaves on all four faces of the building: E. J. Lennox, Architect AD 1898. You've got to look carefully, but it's there – a cry for recognition from nearly a century in the past.

Don't miss the great stained-glass window (how could you?) facing the main entrance to the **Old City Hall**. It depicts the union of commerce and industry, which one hopes will never undergo a divorce. The rising sun is the emblem of activity, and the city's coat of arms runs across the top panels, with the motto INDUSTRY. INTEGRITY. INTELLIGENCE, flanked by the symbolic figures of Peace and Honour. Not bad for a building full of civil servants.

The **New City Hall** took just as long to erect as its 1899 predecessor; nineteen years passed between the 1946 vote to permit the acquisition of the land and 1965, when the $31-million structure opened. So much for progress. The **New City Hall** is daring and unique. In the spring of 1958, an international competition was held, and some 520 architects from 42 countries submitted designs.

Imagine the controversy over the winning design by Finnish architect **Viljo Revell**. Two towers of differing height – and curved, yet! An aerial view of the **New City Hall** shows a circular council chamber sitting like an eye between the two tower "eyelids." In Finland, the centre of a subject is referred to as the "eye," much like the centre of a hurricane – an apt image of some of the exchanges that have gone on in the Toronto council chamber.

The **New City Hall** became a symbol of a thriving city with a silhouette as recognizable as, say, the Eiffel Tower. Unfortunately, architect Revell died before his masterpiece was opened to the public.

The **New City Hall** is a living, breathing environment. **Nathan Phillips Square**, named after the mayor who served the city the longest and who initiated the project, spreads across a nine-acre plaza in front of the building. It has become a true gathering place for the community – a perfect area for a Royal visit, a protest rally, a picnic lunch, a concert, or toe dipping in the reflecting pool. In winter, office workers armed with skates pop down to the pool-turned-rink for a lunch-time constitutional.

The bronze sculpture in the square, created by British sculptor **Henry Moore**, is known as **The Archer**, although its family name is **Three Way Piece No. 2**. And inside the main entrance to City Hall is **Metropolis**, a remarkable mural put together from 100,000 common nails that sculptor **David Partridge** had lying about his shop.

The library, on the street level, is a pleasant place to stop and rest and browse through a few magazines before you take a free tour.

These thirty-minute guided tours leave Mon.-Fri., 11:15 a.m. and 3:45 p.m. Phone 947-7341 for details. And special aides for the disabled can be obtained by calling 947-7732.

You may not be able to fight city hall, but you can skate there and get a free view of the city, which is more than you can say for any other city hall we can think of.

How to Get There:

Take the Yonge subway to Queen and walk west one block to Bay, or the University subway to Osgoode and walk one block east. The Queen streetcar travels past the city halls a hundred times a day from both directions. There is a huge underground parking lot directly beneath the **New City Hall**, but it is not cheap and fills rapidly every morning. And you can find a decent cafeteria and licensed dining-room in the basement of the **New City Hall**.

QUEEN'S PARK:
BETTER LEGISLATURE THAN NEVER

Queen's Park, as with most things in this world, has a number of meanings. To the tired Torontonian or visitor, it is a charming circle with a park that provides much needed rest and relaxation after a long day around Bloor Street. It's just south of the **Royal Ontario Museum**, on University Avenue below Bloor, and its many trees and green grass (when not covered with cold, white stuff) provide a delightful place for lunch and people or pigeon watching. But **Queen's Park** also means the **Ontario Legislative Building**, where it all happens or doesn't happen, depending upon your political persuasion.

Opened on April 4, 1893, the building is extraordinary, with dozens of square windows, rectangular towers, tri-angled roofs, and circular and oval glass. Like the **New City Hall**, it was the product of an international contest among architects. And in the classic Canadian tradition of looking elsewhere for guidance, the winner was a thirty-two-year-old Briton who, naturally, was living in Buffalo, New York. His much-used passport read "R. A. Waite."

Many people find the residence of Ontario's government to be rather eccentric, with its pink exterior and heavy, almost Romanesque quality. (Some refer to its style as "Early Miami.") But, in fact, there is beautifully complex detail carved in its stone, and inside there are enormous, lovely halls that echo of five hundred years of English architecture. (By the way, the pink exterior in no way reflects its politics, but rather the colour of Ontario sandstone.)

The long hallways are hung with hundreds of oil paintings by Canadian artists, most of which capture scenes of our province's natural beauty. One of the most famous paintings, if not the finest, is that of Canada's Fathers of Confederation. The original was destroyed in a fire, but this copy is report-edly the best in existence.

Should you take one of the frequent and free tours, you will see the chamber where the 125 elected representatives called MPPs, Members of the Provincial Parliament, meet and decide our fate. The **Ontario Legislative Building** is filled with history. There are two heritage rooms – one each for the parliamentary history of Britain and Ontario – and each is filled with old newspapers, periodicals, and pictures that help visualize the growth of this province from a colony to an important part of a new country.

In the **1812 Gallery**, paintings depict the life, times, and battles of **John Graves Simcoe**, the first governor of this province when it was still called Upper Canada.

The lobby holds a large collection of minerals and rocks, which you may well wish to pick up and throw at the giant paintings of former political leaders. Restrain yourself.

On the lawn in front of the Parliament buildings are a number of statues. There's Queen Victoria in all her stiff-upper-lip glory, who appears unamused by the shenanigans going on inside. And there are statues of two giants of Canadian history: George Brown, editor of Canada's first great newspaper, *The Globe*, and founder of the Liberal Party, which has run Canada for sixty of the past eighty years yet has never been able to get a handle on Ontario. The Conservatives have been in charge here since 1943, which beats Haile Selassie, and almost every other political leader outside of Franco.

Nearby physically but very far away politically is a statue of the remarkable Sir John A. Macdonald, Canada's first prime minister, a Scot who almost singlehandedly tied this country together with railroad track, bullying, adhesive tape, and brilliant debating, all through a smoke-screen of booze.

By the way, should you choose to take a tour, you'll get pamphlets and handouts on the legislature and the government of Ontario, which may or may not help junior's next social science project. And you'll also receive a souvenir medallion showing the Ontario coat of arms and the trillium, which is our province's official flower. Tour times vary, and are thirty or sixty minutes long, depending on whether the House is in session. Tour guides inform us that three or four ghosts have been seen in the building, over the years. Scholars will be pleased to learn that documentation of these ghostly visits are in a special file in the library, presumably under "G." For information on when the House is sitting (and yelling and compromising) call 965-4028. Tours take place weekly throughout the year as well as on weekends during the summer.

How to Get There:

Take the University subway to College Street and walk north one block. If you drive, park on one of the side streets above College or in one of the hospital lots on College east of University. There are also meters around Queen's Park Circle if you want to stay less than an hour or risk a parking ticket.

UNION STATION: TAKE THE TRAIN, EH?

It seems almost presumptuous to call an edifice barely seventy-five years of age an historic building, but that is certainly what **Union Station** is. But when you consider that it was designed back in 1907, when trains were as exciting as Concorde is today, you'll understand why.

As writer Pierre Berton has noted, the care that went into its planning recalls "the love lavished on mediaeval churches." But the cathedrals of Europe took centuries to build, and our shrine to steam power took little more than a dozen years to put up.

Put up? More like erect. Establish. Create. Imagine the awe of the immigrants who poured into Toronto by the thousands, staring up at the towering ceiling of Italian tile and leaning against one of the 22 pillars each 12 metres (40 feet) tall and weighing 75 tons. Walk along the lengthy concourse. See the mellow reflection in its walls. Sense the beauty of the light flooding through the high, arched windows at each end of the giant hall.

When you look up, you might expect to see a rose window or the names of saints. What you do see is the names of the towns and cities of Canada served by the two railroads that used **Union Station** when it opened in 1927. Many of those towns and cities, spread across this "geographically absurd" land, are no longer served by trains, which take too long in a world travelling at the speed of light.

That **Union Station** remains, its trains still running back and forth beneath its glorious canopy, is no thanks to many politicians of the 1970s who wanted it torn down. But once again, Torontonians rallied and petitioned, and won the day.
How to Get There:
It's on Front Street, between Bay and York across from the Royal York Hotel. Both north-south subways stop there, and there are lots of parking lots in the area. Just look up. You can't miss it. Nor should you.

BLACK CREEK PIONEER VILLAGE: MEANWHILE, BACK AT THE RANCH
Less than a half-hour's drive from downtown Toronto is a village out of the early- and mid-1800s. You walk through a time barrier.

The buildings and fields of pioneer farmer Daniel Stong are still there, and more than twenty-five period buildings have been moved to the site to create the village: a town hall, weaver's shop, printing shop, a blacksmith's shop, and a school with its dunce cap waiting for a new generation. The mill, dating from the 1840s, has a four-ton wooden waterwheel that can, and does, grind up to a hundred barrels of flour a day. And as you and your children watch, men and women in period costumes go about the daily routine of mid-nineteenth-century Ontario life. You'll see them shear sheep, tend their gardens, fix horseshoes, bake bread, string apple slices, and dip candles. They will also explain what they're doing and how they do it, and answer any questions you can think of about pioneer farm life.

A free wagon ride, a decent restaurant, and lots of farm animals make Black Creek a delightful outing. And even though the buildings are closed in the winter, you can still skate, toboggan, and have a sleigh ride.

Special seasonal events are held at **Black Creek Pioneer Village** throughout the year: making maple syrup, Easter egg hunts, woodworking, sheep-shearing, corn fests, apple harvesting and, of course Christmas. Phone 661-6610 for more information.

How to Get There:

Take 401 to Highway 400, then 400 north about 5 km (3 miles) to Finch. Go east on Finch to Jane Street, then north until you see the signs on your right. Call the TTC (484-4544) for information about public transportation. And do note: a family of four can enjoy many pleasurable hours here for less than ten dollars. Maybe we *are* back in the 1850s, after all!

FORT YORK: DAMN YANKEES

Where were you on April 27, 1813? You can take your time answering, because that date goes on forever in a living time capsule known as **Fort York**. While you're thinking we'll give you a painless history lesson.

When Quebec was divided into two provinces (Upper and Lower Canada) in 1791, the seat of government for Upper Canada (Ontario) was established at Niagara. But the lieutenant-governor, John Graves Simcoe, soon realized that the provincial capital was far too exposed to the Americans, just a long spit across the river. So in July 1793 he moved his regiment, the Queen's Rangers, to York, a.k.a. Toronto.

There he established **Fort York**. His original barracks soon grew to accommodate seven hundred soldiers, all keen to defend the town of about six hundred civilians when the War of 1812 broke out. The Yankees landed, a fierce battle ensued (you guessed it – on April 27, 1813) and the British soon decided to hightail it out of there. In the classic tradition of "don't let it fall into enemy hands," the British set fire to the magazine filled with hundreds of barrels of gunpowder. Well, the blast was so successful it took a number of Yankee hands (and legs) with it. Chunks of stone rained down like hail, and 38 Americans were killed, and 222 wounded.

This Canadian version of the shot heard 'round the world was, alas, not enough to save the tiny town of York. In a five-day spree, the Americans looted private homes (it was slim pickings; there were only about a hundred houses in York at the time, mostly poor), burned the legislative buildings, ripped off $8,000 from the provincial treasury, and stole dozens of books from the provincial library. These were later returned – overdue fines must have been stiffer back then.

Fort York was also torched, as you can imagine, and the few militia installations left standing were burned when the Americans hopped over the border again a few months later.

What the Americans did get the first time around was the thirty-ton *HMS Sir Isaac Brock*, a sitting duck in the York drydock. Had the **Brock** survived, it is likely that the British would have had superior naval forces and the War of 1812 would have lasted only a few months rather than dragging on to 1814.

So what is left of **Fort York**? Plenty. More than enough to provide you and your children with a fascinating 1816 day (1813 being rather violent, as you will recall). For in 1816, the fort was rebuilt – stronger and bigger than before. There are eight buildings, and their brick, stone, and log frames should give you a good sense of what it was like to be a British soldier stuck out in the boondocks nearly two centuries ago.

The centre blockhouse housed 160 men and the east blockhouse housed 124. When you see how barren they are, you'll understand how dozens of men froze to death in their beds over the years. (The record snow drift at Fort York in the nineteenth century was as high as a two-storey barracks.) There's the officers' quarters where the senior officers of the garrison were billeted – a world away from the men's barracks. In the mess, twentieth-century serving women bake bread in the giant stone fireplace. Have a nibble, but don't expect samples of pounds or shillings in the vaults in the basement where the troops' pay was stored.

The centre blockhouse has a model of the famous battle scene and a tedious film about army life in the last century that will have you longing for reruns of *Gilligan's Island*.

All year round, men get rigged out in the uniforms of the era, call themselves the Fort York Guard, and perpetuate the memory of the soldiers who fought back in 1813 and blew it, in more ways than one. They perform nineteenth-century infantry drills daily, and artillery salutes with muzzle-

loading cannons occur frequently. Children will love to climb over and around, if not in, the many cannons, and the tour guides are both knowledgeable and helpful. If you need more information, phone 366-6127. A tip: each year there is a Fort York Festival on Victoria Day, which is the fourth Monday in May. There are lots of activities including a mock military tattoo, and a mock battle between groups in period uniforms firing blanks. All in all, a lot safer than April 27, 1813.
How to Get There:
It's quite complex. We recommend you take the Bloor subway west to Bathurst and then the Bathurst streetcar south to the entrance on Garrison Road off Fleet Street, between Bathurst and Strachan. It's east of the Canadian National Exhibition Grounds.

If you insist on going by car, here goes! Get on Lakeshore Boulevard West. (Do not take the Gardiner Expressway by mistake; thousands did and have never been heard from again.) Follow Lakeshore Blvd. until you reach Strachan Avenue. You are now directly in front of the Princes' Gate of the CNE. Turn right onto Strachan, then right again on to Fleet Street. Make a quick left, go underneath an archway, and you are at **Fort York**. (We warned you!) Have fun, and be thankful you were not a soldier in the early nineteenth century.

MACKENZIE HOUSE: IN THE LYON'S DEN

Just a few blocks from Yonge and Dundas is a deceptively modest row house. Its owner, **William Lyon Mackenzie**, was born in Scotland at the end of the 1700s. He came to Canada in 1820, began a newspaper, and so enraged the big shots of the time (known as The Family Compact, which is not a Japanese car) that they broke into his print-shop and dumped his type into Lake Ontario.

Undismayed, Mackenzie became the first mayor of Toronto, and designed our coat of arms. When he wasn't re-elected in 1836, he gathered about seven hundred supporters and marched down Yonge Street to overthrow the government.

As you may have guessed, he and his troops were roundly defeated, and Willie escaped to the States with a price on his head. When the Canadian government granted amnesty to all concerned in 1849, Mackenzie came back, was promptly elected to the legislative assembly, and began to publish another newspaper. But the poor fellow was so down and out by 1858 that some friends passed the hat and bought him and his family the house we recommend you visit.

Mackenzie only enjoyed the place for three sickly and sad years, dying there in 1861. But it has been beautifully restored, and you can enjoy it for a pleasant few hours, in the heart of 1980s Toronto. If possible, drop in during December, when a Victorian Christmas is staged, complete with oatmeal cookies, cider, and cranberry punch. Your kids will stare at the antique toys and wonder where the batteries go. But all year round, afternoon tea is served 2:00-4:00 p.m. Phone 595-1567 for further information.

How to Get There:

Mackenzie House is located at 82 Bond Street, just two blocks east of Yonge and a few feet south of Dundas. Take the Yonge subway to Dundas and then walk east to Bond. If you drive, there is parking north or south of the area.

THE GIBSON HOUSE: LITTLE HOUSE IN THE SUBURBS

You don't have to travel out to Black Creek Pioneer Village to experience the mid-nineteenth century in Toronto. Up in North York, on Yonge Street above Sheppard, is a large brick farm home that once belonged to a supporter of William Lyon Mackenzie's 1837 rebellion.

Sad to report, **David Gibson**'s original home was burned to the ground by anti-Mackenzie men, while Gibson was sitting out a decade-long exile in the U.S. But when he returned to Toronto in 1848, he built what you can visit today. The wood you see was cut down on his farm and the bricks were fired in a neighbouring kiln.

As at Fort York in the summer and Black Creek nearly all year 'round, you'll encounter men and women in nineteenth-century costumes who demonstrate the cooking and crafts of the pioneers who lived in the area before house prices skyrocketed. It is beautifully restored, and it's fun to encounter such a charming "living museum" in suburban Toronto.

How to Get There:

Gibson House is located behind a post office at 5172 Yonge Street, about a mile north of Sheppard. Phone 225-0146 for more information. Try and catch Hogmanay, a Scottish New Year's Eve celebration, which they hold each Dec. 30.

THE ENOCH TURNER SCHOOLHOUSE: ONE GOOD TURNER DESERVES ANOTHER

Most people forget that the idea of free schooling is really a product of the mid-nineteenth century. Back in the 1840s, Toronto parents paid two-thirds of teachers' salaries and the government picked up the rest. But public school was such an important issue that the right to universal free education was even one of the demands in Karl Marx's 1848 manifesto.

Well, Karl won. But when the Ontario legislature passed an act in 1848 that authorized cities to provide free schools (by hitting mommy and daddy in the property taxes), the Toronto city council refused to go along with the radical idea and shut down every public school in town.

One response was the kindly act of a brewer named **Enoch Turner**, who was shocked by the reactionary policy of our city elders, and created this city's first free educational institution. It's called **The Enoch Turner Schoolhouse**, at 106 Trinity Street, near the corner of King and Parliament, just a few blocks east of Yonge.

You will be relieved to hear that our cheapo city council relented three years later, and Mr. Turner's generosity was absorbed into the public school system of Toronto. But the people of Toronto recognized the historic importance of the unassuming building and they restored it in the 1970s. It now sits, modestly, in its original state, behind Little Trinity Church.

There is a slide show on nineteenth-century Toronto, and mock-teachers in period costumes, armed with slates and surrounded by ancient desks, often strut their Dick and Jane stuff. These serious, well-researched re-enactments are usually booked months in advance by Toronto teachers who wish to show their students just how far (or little) we've travelled pedagogically since. Admission is free, but call 863-0010 first to check hours and possible nostalgia.

How to Get There:

Take the King streetcar east from the centre of the city to Trinity Street, past Parliament. If you drive, there is limited parking in the area.

TODMORDEN MILLS MUSEUM: REPAST IN THE PAST

Not far from the Don Valley Parkway and Bayview Avenue, is a trip into the past. A number of the city's oldest buildings have been restored on their original sites, and it's all in a parkland, which makes it especially appealing for a snack or a picnic, weather permitting.

The name **Todmorden Mills** comes from England, as did the settlers who built these places. You can see two pioneer houses (the **Terry House**, restored to 1837; the **Helliwell House**, restored to 1867); a **brewery** that unfortunately no longer produces its demon drink but is now an exhibit hall; a **paper mill**, which has housed an **art gallery** since the mid-1970s; and the old **Don Station**, built in 1891 to serve the great railroads, the Canadian National and the Canadian Pacific.

If you are lucky, you just may walk into one of the programs often put on here for Toronto school kids. But the park and the buildings are enjoyable anytime. It's a 19th Century-Fox production.

How to Get There:

Todmorden Mills Museum is located at 67 Pottery Road, just east of the Don Valley Parkway. Access to the museum is from either Bayview or Broadview Avenues. Take any northbound bus from the Broadview Station, get off at Mortimer, and walk south to Pottery Rd. For further information, phone 425-2250. The museum is open every day except Monday.

MONTGOMERY'S INN:
THE INNS AND OUTS OF THE 1800s

Go west, young person, to west Toronto, where you can experience more of the nineteenth century. Built some 150 years ago, **Montgomery's Inn** has been restored to the late 1840s, and is a good example of the Loyalist architecture of the time. Once a popular hotel and gathering place for *hoi polloi*, it is now a lovely living museum. If you've been staying in a modern Toronto hotel you'll enjoy the way the costumed staff re-create what it was like to stay in a hotel 135 years ago – except you won't be able to sleep there.

How to Get There:

Montgomery's Inn is located at 4709 Dundas Street West at the corner of Islington Avenue. For more information, phone 236-1046.

CAMPBELL HOUSE:
GEORGIAN ON MY MIND

Just steps from the heart of downtown Toronto is the stately, handsome, Georgian house of **Sir William Campbell**, the sixth chief justice of Upper Canada. It was built in 1822 and has been wonderfully restored with elegant eighteenth- and early-nineteenth-century furniture. (It is now owned by a group of lawyers called The Advocate's Society.)

Costumed hostesses will tell you about the social life of an upper-class family like the Campbells, and you can see a model of the town of York as it was in the 1820s.

The kitchen has been restored to its original state. Stand in awe and wonder how on earth these people managed without a Cuisinart.

How to Get There:

Campbell House is on the northwest corner of Queen Street West and University.Take the University subway to Osgoode. There's really not much free parking, but if you insist on driving there are lots a couple blocks west on Queen Street, a few hundred feet west of University and meters on University Avenue. Phone 597-0227 for more information and to book a tour.

SCADDING CABIN:
THANK GOD FOR MODERN PLUMBING

The oldest house in Toronto can be viewed just west of the band shell on the Canadian National Exhibition grounds. It is a log cabin, built by pioneer **John Scadding** around 1794, when this town was no great shakes as a tourist centre. Scadding managed the estate of John Graves Simcoe back in England. When the guv'ner was shipped off to Upper Canada to be everybody's governor, Scadding dutifully followed to risk life, limb, and terminal boredom in the York of the late-eighteenth century.

Scadding's little cabin stood by the lakeshore for most of its first century and was moved to the Exhibition grounds in 1879, when that durable institution began. It can only be viewed on the outside, but then, so can most people.

How to Get There:

Drive or walk into the Exhibition grounds, find your way to the band shell, and walk west (away from the CN Tower).

SCADDING HOUSE:
LITTLE HOUSE BY THE EATON CENTRE PRAIRIE

Yes, it is related to the **Scadding Cabin** down at the Exhibition grounds. The youngest son of pioneer John, **Henry Scadding** was a cleric in the Anglican church (which proved one had "arrived" in nineteenth-century Toronto), and he wrote a number of histories of the early decades of this city. For years, his 1862 residence was used as a community centre for the **Holy Trinity Church**, just behind the Eaton Centre. When the giant complex went up, the building was handed over to the Inner City Angels (who are not a street

gang). This fine group moved it about fifty yards, restored it, and turned it into a children's centre for the arts. You can reach it via a passageway from the Eaton Centre.
How to Get There:
Scadding House is just a few steps west of Yonge and south of Dundas. Drop over while visiting the Eaton Centre. Call 598-0242 for information.

HOME, HOME ON THE GRANGE

In 1911, **Mrs. Goldwin Smith** donated her historic house, **The Grange**, and its 3½ acre parkland to the Art Museum of Toronto, aged eleven. It stands on the south side of the **Art Gallery of Ontario** (the original museum was renamed in 1966), and, in many ways, it is more satisfying to visit than the AGO itself.

The columned Georgian front and the delicately balanced wings that flow from the sides of its porch only hint at the joys within. Built in the second decade of the nineteenth century by the Boultons from Yorkshire, the charming two-storey home suits a family that ruled what passed for society in Upper Canada.

The Grange has been restored to its original elegance and carefully refurnished in English Regency style. The large, stained-glass window surrounded by black-walnut wood-work is a pun: a crossbow arrow ("bolt") thrust into a barrel ("tun"), symbolizes the name of the original owners.

The large music room on the upper floor and the beautifully carved four-poster in the master bedroom are fascinating, but the biggest thrill may well be the freshly baked bread from the brick ovens of the nineteenth-century kitchen. You'll never want to touch supermarket bread again. **The Grange** and its hostesses exude hospitality rather than museum mustiness and provide a relaxing break from your wanderings in the **Art Gallery of Ontario**.

Since The Grange is part of the AGO, admission to one will admit you to the other. And it is free on Thursday evenings. See the **Art Gallery of Ontario** listing for How to Get There. Phone 977-0414, ext. 356, for information on hours and prices.

COLBORNE LODGE:
HOWARD'S HAVEN

The style was called "cottage ornée," and it was very big in England when **John Howard** built his handsome home on a hill in **High Park** overlooking Lake Ontario, in 1836.

On his death in 1890, Howard bequeathed his 165 acres of land to the city on condition that it remain park and public. The house itself fell into disrepair, and it was falling apart by the mid-1920s when **The Women's Canadian Historical Society** begged some money from the ungrateful city of Toronto to open the lodge as a living museum in 1927.

Colborne Lodge is open to the public all year. The Regency-style cottage with its quaint triple chimneys and low, broad veranda is a delight to the modern eye. You'll see the original fireplace, bake oven, and kitchen, as well as some of the hundred or so drawings and paintings by Mr. Howard himself.

On the first Sunday of every October there is a Harvest Festival, with demonstrations of nineteenth-century domesticity, apple butter made over an open pit outside the lodge, music, games, and lots more.

How to Get There:

Colborne Lodge is located on Howard Road at the south end of High Park. Take the Bloor subway line to the High Park station. If you drive, parking is available around and near High Park. No vehicles are allowed in the park on weekends, between May 1 and Sept. 30. Phone the Toronto Historical Board at 595-1567 for more information.

THREE WAYS TO GO DOWN THE DRAIN:

THE R. C. HARRIS FILTRATION PLANT (694-3238) is fascinating, honest. Since people once paid their water bills in person, the designer decided the place should be impressive. And it is. The stair rails and door handles are gleaming brass; the corridors are marble. It was built in the late 1930s; and when you see the marble clock tower and the domed glass skylight, 11 metres (33 feet) above you, you'll never take a glass of clean water for granted again. Apart from its art deco beauty, there are a free film and a walking tour on weekends. And there's a spectacular view of Lake Ontario. The plant is at 2701 Queen Street East, at the foot of Victoria Park Avenue.

"THE EXCHANGE" (THE TORONTO STOCK EX-CHANGE) moved to its new location in May 1983, in the newly constructed Exchange Tower, at 2 First Canadian Place at King and York Streets. The TSE, one of the world's major stock exchanges, occupies the third-to-seventh floors of the tower as well as the highly automated trading pavilion behind the tower. Phone 947-4670 for tours, which take place weekdays at 4:00 p.m. There is a Visitors' Centre and a presentation gallery for the tours.

ECOLOGY HOUSE, 12 Madison Avenue (967-0577), one block east of Spadina at Bloor Street West, might fill you with more hope or fear than any other building in Toronto. Here you'll see demonstrations of water and heat conservation, waste management, solar greenhouses, and solar water heaters. The friendly staff of **Pollution Probe** will show what an ecological wastrel and spendthrift you are. It's free, so you can conserve your money as well as energy.

THE UNIVERSITY OF TORONTO & YORK UNIVERSITY:
A COLLAGE OF COLLEGES

The city of Toronto has grown too large to be labelled a "university town." But with a staff and student population of more than fifty thousand, an annual operating budget of close to a quarter-billion dollars, and 225 buildings on three campuses, the **University of Toronto** is almost a city in itself. It has its own newspapers, post office, fire marshal, police, infirmary, sports teams, restaurants, theatres, bookstores, libraries, workshops, chapels, clubs, and residences.

It all goes back to 1827 when King George IV signed a charter for a "King's College in the Town of York, Capital of Upper Canada." The Church of England had control then, but by 1850 the college was proclaimed non-denominational, renamed **The University of Toronto**, and put under control of the province. And then, in a spirit of Christian competition, the Anglicans started **Trinity College**, the Methodists began **Victoria**, and the Roman Catholics begat **St. Michael's**; by the time the Presbyterians founded **Knox College**, the whole thing was almost out of hand.

Not to worry. The seventeen schools and faculties are now united and welcome anyone who can pass its entrance exams and afford the tuition, which, thanks to government funding, is only about $1000 per year.

It's architecturally fascinating, if uneven – you would be too, if you'd been built in bits and pieces over 150 years. We recommend a walking tour. Enter the campus just behind the Parliament buildings where Wellesley Street ends. Go under the bridge, past the guardhouse (whose keeper will not let you pass if you are in a car), and right, around King's College Circle.

At the top of the circle is **Hart House**, a Gothic-style

student centre built during the teens of this century by the Masseys – the folk who brought you Massey-Ferguson farm equipment, Massey Hall, Vincent Massey, a governor-general of Canada, and Raymond Massey, the actor. Once an all-male enclave, today even *women* may visit the Great Hall and the library, self-conscious imitations of Oxford and Cambridge! You'll love getting lost in the labyrinthine lower level of Hart House, not to mention the music room, where concerts are sometimes held at lunchtime, and a splendid view of the back campus is always to be had. Check out the dining hall, for its amazing stained-glass windows as well as the food, which is cheap and rather good.

As you continue your walk around King's College Circle, you'll spot, on your left, the **Old Observatory**, now the headquarters of the Students' Administrative Council. And on your right as you round the corner, is the Romanesque **University College**, built in 1859.

Next is **Knox College**, whose Scottish origins are evident in the bagpipe music that escapes from the building at odd hours. It's been training ministers since 1844; but the building went up in 1915. **Convocation Hall** is where they graduate the lucky few; but between giving out diplomas they have lectures, concerts from lieder to punk, and public gatherings.

You might well wish to tip your hat to the **Medical Sciences Building**, no beauty, but where, in 1921, Drs. **Banting** and **Best** discovered the insulin that would save the lives of more than thirty million people.

It's well worth walking west a few hundred yards to St. George Street and visiting the **Robarts Research Library**. It's by far the largest university library building in the world, and it is unfondly called Fort Book by intimidated students. After spending more than forty million dollars on the building, the university ran out of money: note the eerie, periscope-like structure that stands there doing nothing – it was supposed to contain a clock. Don't miss the **Thomas Fisher Rare Books Library**, where you can view tomes and manuscripts going back to the early Middle Ages.

There is lots more to see and do around the main campus of the **University of Toronto**. Visit **Information Services** (978-2021) at 45 Willcocks Street, east of Spadina and south of Harbord, and pick up free maps of the university grounds. Guided one-hour walking tours are held on weekdays in the summer. They set out from the map room of Hart House at 10:30 a.m., 12:30 noon, and 2:30 p.m. For information phone 978-5000 or 978-2452.

THE SCARBOROUGH CAMPUS

The University of Toronto has two satellite campuses. **Erindale campus** is out west of the city in Mississauga and, quite frankly, you can give it a miss. **Scarborough College**, in the east end, is very different indeed.

The **Scarborough campus** has generated raves and ohs and ahs ever since it opened in 1965, mainly because it is built in a 300-acre forested ridge and ravine. There are two large wings, for sciences and humanities, respectively. They are linked by offices and a meeting area within a four-storey atrium. One critic described it as "not only a building" but "an event," and indeed it is. The 32 km (20 mile) drive out to the campus is pleasurable, and the massive structure worth seeing and walking through.

How to Get There:

Take Hwy 401 east from the city to Morningside Avenue. Drive south along Morningside to Military Trail, and turn east (left) past Ellesmere Road, to the campus on your right.

An easier way is to board one of the buses that leaves the main campus of the University of Toronto for the Scarborough Campus regularly.

YORK UNIVERSITY: LITTLE SISTER GROWN BIG

York was founded in 1959 and began accepting its first students in 1960; but did not become completely independent of its mama, the University of Toronto, until 1965. The main campus is a 600-acre Siberia in the northwest corner of Metro at Keele and Steeles. It is like something out of George Orwell: giant, poured-concrete structures dropped hither and yon across a treeless, barren void. It's not very welcoming to the eye, but there are more than 10,000 students up there.

Just so no one thinks that York is an oversized sensory deprivation tank, we must mention two things. First, there is **Glendon Campus**, a beautiful, wooded, 84-acre ex-estate at Bayview and Lawrence, that seems full of not-quite bilingual diplomats-to-be. Second, whatever its appearance, York's main campus holds terrific cultural and social events. Check *The Globe and Mail* any Monday for that week's happenings, particularly at **Burton Auditorium**. The main phone number is 667-2100.

How to Get There:

Drive west on the 401 to Keele, and then north a few kilometres to the campus, just above Finch.

SCARBOROUGH:
THE CIVIL CIVIC CENTRE

"Scarberia," some call it: boring houses, endless shopping plazas – Toronto's version of Jersey City. It's not quite fair, but the image remains.

There is one amazing complex that overwhelms the firmest Scarborough hater: its civic centre, another jewel in the very sparkling crown of architect **Raymond Moriyama**.

The **Scarborough Civic Centre** tries to do it all, and it does it very well. There is the government office building, all striking diagonals and gleaming glass; a shopping centre with more than 130 stores, boutiques and eateries; **Albert Campbell Square**, with its large reflecting pond that serves as both wading pool and skating rink, much like the one at the New City Hall. It's a perfect example of architecture that works – form and function blend with physical beauty to serve the people at all levels – governmental, community, and social. And if you want your children to become architects, this is the place to take them. Well, one of the places.

There are guided tours every half-hour, 9:30 a.m.-5:00 p.m., Mon.-Fri., weekends 11:30 a.m.-5:00 p.m., and an audio-visual show about the borough of Scarborough. Phone 296-7216 for further information.

How to Get There:

Drive east from the city along Highway 401 to McCowan Road. Go south a few yards, and there you are. You'll see its glowing beauty from the highway.

ANNUAL ANTICS AND SEASONAL SEASONINGS

TO EVERY SEASON THERE IS A THING
You can tell a great deal about a culture by its language: the Inuit have dozens of words for snow; the Fijians have none. You can also tell a great deal about a city's culture by its traditional events–or lack of them. The following listing tells a lot of good things about Toronto.

Let's be blunt: how many cities in North America could hold gigantic picnics, parties and dances in the parks, day and night, for thousands of people without mishap?

Toronto can. For all its incredible ethnic mix, our citizens seem to get along with each other, even to the point of partying together, a number of times each year. It's a wondrous thing to see, and to participate in. So check your calendar, and then check out the following:

THE CANADIAN NATIONAL EXHIBITION: EX MARKS THE SPOT
To millions of divorced, separated, and single folks around the world, "Ex" means a former spouse or lover. But to millions of Canadians, the Ex is something absolutely loyal: the Canadian National Exhibition, which takes place every year from mid-August until Labour Day.

To many, the Ex, or CNE, is just as much fun as those other old reliables, death and taxes. But three million people pour through its gates each year.

It began back in 1879 as an agricultural show, and remnants of that tradition can still be found in the livestock exhibitions. But the *Ex* in the 1980s can also be a noisy, crowded, entertaining collection of carnies pushing four-dollar balloons, try-your-luck-for-only-a-quarter, stomach-turning midway rides, beauty contests, live bands, horticultural and technological exhibits, and occasionally superb entertainment. The french fries are always greasy, the cotton candy sweet enough for ten thousand Harlequin Romances. But it goes on year after year, and the Ex didn't become the world's longest-running annual fair without *something* to attract the people.

Is it possible to visit the Ex with the family, have a charming time, and not get ripped off or poisoned? Of course. Do it by catching at least a few of the following events:

Every year there is the CNE opening-day parade, which starts at noon at Queen's Park, just above College Street on University, and makes its way downtown along University to the Exhibition grounds. There are colourful floats, bands, entertainers, and sports personalities. Even if you never plan to go to the CNE, the parade is a very cheap and entertaining way to spend a few hours in August.

The 1936, art deco Bandshell on the CNE grounds, has free concerts, usually lasting two hours, every evening during the Ex. Jazz, country, and general nostalgia prevail.

In 1983, the Annual Film Competition celebrates its tenth anniversary: films produced by Canadian post-secondary school students are shown in early September, usually on the last day or two of the Ex. Discover the Cukor or Capra of the 1990s.

The dog swim (K9-H_2O) is hilarious: more than one hundred of Toronto's most daring, athletic, and moist canines rush in where men and women fear to tread. The great dog dunk usually takes place during the first week of the Ex and attracts tens of thousands of spectators to the waterfront. Free horse shows go on for the full three weeks, and include a parade of champions and the National Grand Prix. The mayors' bathtub race features nearly two dozen mayors from across Ontario dressed up in crazy costumes, looking like a wet version of *Let's Make a Deal*.

Miss CNE is crowned in the first week of the Ex, disappointing the other hundred entries, thrilling thousands of viewers, and enraging millions of feminists.

The CNE water show is dazzling entertainment for the entire family, and the Canadian National Air Show, also on the waterfront, is considered a highlight of the Ex with wing walkers, parachutists, the world's fastest aircraft, the air-force precision flying teams, and more. To air *is* human.

The **Grandstand** shows cost a hefty amount, but are usually well worth it for such performers as Paul Anka, Rod Stewart, the Beach Boys, Bob Hope, Burton Cummings, Kenny Rogers, and Dionne Warwick. There is a fireworks display each evening, following the grandstand show.

Traditionally, the **Food Building**, in the centre of the Exhibition grounds, was the perfect place to fill up on freebies – soft drinks, nickel hot dogs, dime yoghurt. The days of filling up for less than a buck are long gone, but there are still lots of surprises at the Food Building: cheap drinks, occasional free samples, and lots of coupons that can save you money back in the real world.

The **Midway** is raucous, with rock music blaring out of every monster ride, but the teenagers love it. Be warned: the average ride lasts less than ninety-five seconds and costs at least a dollar. More than an hour on the midway with children over nine years old will set you back $25, easily.

If you live in Toronto, have your kids cut out coupons for free rides or free tickets from the newspaper (usually *The Sun*, occasionally the *Star*), and let *them* buy their fun.

Each year, a supermarket chain offers free tickets to the **Exhibition** if you buy a certain amount in groceries. Check it out and save $10 or more for the family. And every year get in free on children's day, which helps the family budget.

Because the **Ex** is down at the lakefront, the breezes can get chilly and the temperatures can drop precipitously, even in August. Take a sweater and wear comfortable shoes.

The carnies and junk-food-pushers are going to hate us for this, but you'd be wise to pack fruit or juice in a shopping bag, and even better, a picnic, if you have the strength to carry it.

The Toronto Star and *The Sun* carry maps and daily lists of what's happening at the Ex during its three-week run; you'd be wise to map out your day before you go.

Admission was $3.50 for adults and teens in 1982, less for kids and senior citizens. Entrance to the Ex also includes free admission to Ontario Place, the superb entertainment complex and playground just south of the Exhibition grounds.

How to Get There:

Do not – we repeat – *do not* take your car. If you are coming in from out of town, leave the car near a subway stop. It will cost you a ton of money to park anywhere near the CNE grounds (and you won't be that near), and you'll be exhausted by the time you get to the entrance.

Take the bus or streetcar from the Dundas and Bay bus terminal, or from most any of the major shopping centres in Metro Toronto, or grab any one of the dozens of streetcars labelled "Exhibition" that run all over the city (especially down Dufferin), from mid-August until Labour Day. You'll bless us when they drop you off right in the Exhibition grounds. Call the TTC (484-4544) for further information. Phone 593-7551 a day in advance to find out about what's happening at the *Ex* on the day you plan to visit. Over 350 acres (143 hectares in fluent metric), await your presence, tummy, and wallet.

INTERNATIONAL PICNIC:
EATING ETHNIC

Being listed in the *Guinness Book of World Records* should not be our idea of glory, and Toronto is not so hungry for fame that it fights for inclusion, like some rotter who plays hop-scotch for 36 hours, 28 minutes straight. Well, we made it in spite of ourselves – for the CN Tower, yes, but also for "the world's biggest free picnic." This celebration is so much fun, Anglo-Saxons have been known to change their names to sound more exotic.

Celebrating its seventeenth anniversary in 1983, the International Picnic usually begins on Canada's birthday, July 1st, at the CNE bandshell down by the lake. It moves to Nathan Phillips Square at the New City Hall on July 2nd, and returns to the Exhibition bandshell on July 3rd and 4th.

Highlights include karate exhibitions, polka and limbo competitions, some two dozen ethnic dancing and singing groups. And eating contests! Baklava-eating contests, pizza-eating contests, yoghurt-eating contests, knackwurst-eating contests.

Sports activities, arts and crafts displays, and countless other attractions make the picnic one of the more interesting happenings of its kind. And that doesn't include the professional entertainment – a series of outdoor concerts featuring literally thousands of Canadian and international artists. The concerts in 1982 included such diverse talents as Italian tenor Giuseppe de Stefano and Duo Ouro Negro, a pop rock group from Lisbon.

Admission is free. Phone 531-9991 for more information.
How to Get There:
It takes place all over town, so check the papers for exact locations and events.

CARAVAN:
AROUND THE WORLD IN NINE DAYS

Eat your heart out, Phileas Fogg. Each June in Toronto you can go around the world any number of times, eat and dance and be entertained from Amman (and Ankara and Athens) to Zagreb (and Zakopane and Zurich), and still sleep in your own home or hotel.

It's called **Metro International Caravan**. Started back in 1969, **Caravan** thrives in the very city that epitomized WASP rectitude, right up to the Second World War.

Toronto is now a city of 500,000 Italians, 170,000 Germans, 130,000 Portuguese, 90,000 Greeks, 80,000 Chinese and

40,000 Hungarians, and there is something wonderfully – how can we say it – ethnic – about the major groups that organize pavilions filled with song, dance, food, and great cheer.

The surprise is, it works remarkably well in this world of strife and war. Not that Caravan hasn't had its diplomatic problems. The question of whether the Arabs or the Israelis got to name their pavilion "Jerusalem" arose in 1979.

But it all seems to be humming along much better than the United Nations. The fourteenth annual **Caravan**, which ran for nine days in 1982, was considered the most successful yet, and organizers hope that the 1983 **Caravan** will include a pre-Caravan parade and new pavilions.

The forty-four pavilions of the 1982 Caravan included such world cities as Belgrade, Budapest, Helsinki, Kiev, Krakow, London, New Delhi, Manila, Port of Spain, Tokyo, and Vienna, and such Canadian towns as Dawson City, the Yukon, and L'Orignal, named after a predominantly French-speaking town in northern Ontario.

And one more thing: it is surprisingly authentic. Some of the entertainment is highly professional and a lot of the food is superb. Whether won ton, perogi, paprikash, baklava or schnitzel, it might be served on plastic, but it will rarely taste like it.

Line up the two or three (or more) "cities" you wish to visit each night and hit the road on special buses that run between the various pavilions. Although they are sprinkled across the city, there are often up to a dozen pavilions within a square mile or two, and within walking distance.

In 1983, a passport, good for all nine days, costs $10. A one-day passport costs $5. Children twelve and under are admitted free with an adult. If you buy your passports a week or more in advance, you can save twenty per cent. Call 977-0466 for information.

MARIPOSA FESTIVAL:
THE OLD FOLK (MUSIC) AT HOME

Since it began in 1961, the **Mariposa Folk Festival** has undergone more changin' than Bob Dylan ever dreamed of.

In its youth, Mariposa, often held on the Toronto Islands, attracted such Canadian youthful talents as Gordon Lightfoot, Bruce Cockburn, and Joni Mitchell, all of whom became major stars. In more recent years, the folk festival itself became international, attracting such personalities as the great god Dylan Himself.

After a two-year intermission, the festival reappeared in

June 1982, at Harbourfront, with its first all-Canadian list of entertainers since 1963, when it lacked the money to hire anyone but its own. It is hoped that the festival, now into its third decade, will bring acoustical guitars, autoharps, and fishing, sealing, and logging songs to a new generation.

The **Mariposa Festival** is held in early summer in a Toronto park. Phone 363-4009 for more information or write The Mariposa Folk Foundation, 525 Adelaide Street East, Toronto, M5A 3W4.

CARIBANA: BLACK MAGIC

The first **Caribana** was in 1967, the West Indian community's salute to Canada's hundredth birthday. Since then, the annual festival has become a major tourist draw. It is a project of the Caribbean Cultural Committee, which represents more than 160,000 West Indians in Metro Toronto. In the 1980s, more than a quarter of a million spectators come from across Canada, the United States, and the West Indies to view, enjoy, and participate in the remarkable parades, balls, and "floating night clubs" in Toronto harbour.

On July 31, 1982, the fifteenth annual **Caribana** parade took over downtown Toronto: fourteen "bands" (groups of between one hundred and four hundred participants dressed in elaborate costumes) danced to calypso, soca, steel band, and reggae. The four-hour-long parade went from Queen's Park, down University, and ended up at Harbourfront's Bathurst Quay.

But the visual and musical spectacle of the parade was only one highlight of the nine-day festival, which always runs the week preceding and including Civic Holiday, the first Monday of August.

Other events include a floating Caribbean "night club," four nights of ferry-boat cruising. A pre-Caribana dance is usually held the Saturday before festivities begin. A Miss Caribana Ball is held on the Friday night of each **Caribana** week, at the Royal York Hotel (100 Front Street W. across from Union Station). An informal dance is held at the Royal York on the evening of the giant Saturday parade.

And Centre Island is miraculously transformed into a Caribbean paradise, with music, dance, drama, West Indian handicrafts and food, and calypso limbo dances. All this takes place on the same Saturday as the parade. It is an experience you won't find anywhere else – culturally, musically, gastronomically. And you haven't seen a costume until you've seen what the West Indians of Toronto create for Caribana: giant butterflies, massive pirates, and strange creatures of the deep.

How to Get There:

The **Caribana** parade always begins at 10:00 a.m. on the Saturday of the August Civic Holiday weekend, so just hop a subway to the St. George stop on the University line and then walk to Varsity Stadium on Bloor at Bedford Road. Call 925-5435 for information after July 1. Buy your ticket early and get your dancing shoes out.

MOVIE MADNESS

The **Festival of Festivals** is Toronto's world-class film festival, held annually since 1976 in a dozen different theatres around town. It runs during September and includes everything from director retrospectives to big previews, foreign films, and forgotten classics. Prices are not cheap, but they are standard for a festival of this type. Besides, it is an experience to rub shoulders, if not popcorn, with Robert de Niro or Bette Midler. From June to September every year, the newspapers overflow with articles and press releases. The phone number is 967-7371.

FALL FAIRS IN THE VICINITY: SO FAIR A FALL WE HAVE NOT SEEN

The **Niagara Grape and Wine Festival:** At the end of September in St. Catharines, about 145 kilometres (90 miles) southwest of Toronto, Ontario's version of the Dionysian festival of ancient Greece takes place. The Niagara region is famous for its vineyards, and the festival sponsors some 175 different events in the area: concerts, parades, vineyard tours, and – best of all – wine tastings. Call the Niagara Grape and Wine Festival (1-688-0212) in St. Catharines for more information.

The **Binder Twine Festival** in Kleinburg, just north of Toronto, can be traced back to the turn of the century. Local farmers used to come into town to buy their binder twine for the approaching harvest. While they were there they'd sit around, chew the fat, and have a good time. Since 1967, thousands more have joined in the fun. It's held annually on the first Saturday after Labour Day in September. There is a charming fair, with local residents dressed in period costumes, games, competitions, and – need you ask? – the crowning of the Queen. A fine time will be had by all. Watch for ads in the newspapers and magazines.

Oktoberfest, in Kitchener, Ontario, west of Toronto, is the largest party of its kind apart from its famous Munich predecessor. Two dozen beer halls, some seating almost three thousand, are packed during this ten-day drink-a-thon each October. More than half a million people come from across Canada and the United States to drink beer, dance, drink beer, eat sausage and sauerkraut, drink beer, and sing, and drink beer. The **Oktoberfest** parade, on Thanksgiving Monday, is televised across Canada. To be fair, there is more to **Oktoberfest** than beer drinking; you can see sports competitions, an operetta, German brass bands, bavarian dancing, and arts and crafts exhibits. Buy your tickets early. Kitchener is about 90 minutes west of Toronto along the 401. Call 519-576-0571 for further information.

The **Royal Agricultural Winter Fair**, held at the Canadian National Exhibition grounds each November, is the world's largest agricultural fair under one roof. Now that may not excite you, if the closest you've ever been to a pig or cow was in the meat section of the grocery store. True, the world crop championships, paying tribute to the best corn, wheat, and soybeans of the year, can be less than thrilling. So, too, the poultry trophy presentations. Or the royal Canadian dairy-goat sale.

But to see some 12,000 beasts of different varieties filling the 27 acres of the coliseum; to snicker at humans in black tie and full-length mink coats picking their way very carefully through the stalls; to gawk at the butter sculptures; to stare in awe at the sheep-shearing contest – now *that's* entertainment. And the prestigious **Royal Horse Show** is exciting, even if all you know about show jumping is National Velvet. And wouldn't you want the chance to milk a cow? What? You wouldn't?

The week-long winter fair runs during November each year. Admission is reasonable, especially for students and kids. Phone 366-9051 for further information.

PARKS, PICNICS AND PLAYING

Toronto is rich in parkland. It has a lot to do with the way Toronto grew and the way Torontonians think. The city used to be a series of little villages, each treasuring its tiny common or huge park. As we grew, we found ourselves close to three million strong, living in boroughs, but often thinking in the old village way: saving from development as much park or common land as possible.

But our parks are more than grass. They are great places to bird-watch; there's a delightful farm smack inside the city; there are good places to pick-up a picnic and beautiful places to eat it. There are dozens of sports available to both visitor and resident – baseball, football, hockey, tennis, of course, but also others, from cricket, lacrosse, and field hockey to darts, polo, and *bocce*.

THE TORONTO ISLANDS: EIGHT MINUTES TO HEAVEN

Just a short ferry trip away from downtown Toronto is one of the world's great parks: the Toronto Islands. Every year more than one million wise people flock to these remarkable havens where a person can step back into another century all for the price of a boat ride. The Islands – **Centre**, **Ward's**, **Algonquin**, and **Hanlan's Point** – have been attracting people since 1833, four years before Victoria became Queen and a year before York became Toronto.

The 552 acres of parkland are irresistible, especially during those hot summer months when Toronto seems to be melting as rapidly as your ice-cream cone.

Be warned: the crowds go to **Centre Island**, as that's where most of the amusements are. Indeed, it gets so crowded there that no bicycles are allowed on the ferry to that island during summer weekends. Take one of the equally frequent ferries to Ward's or Hanlan's, quiet, glorious places to picnic, sunbathe, read under a tree, or simply escape the city. The beaches on Ward's tend to be the cleanest and least crowded. On Ward's and neighbouring Algonquin Island, there are about a hundred homes that some politicians have been trying to tear down for more than a generation. (That people living in a public park makes it safer, seems to be lost on them.) But, as so often happens in Toronto, public outrage is keeping the politicos in line, and island homes have been saved at least until the end of this century.

If you have kids, **Centre Island** is certainly the one to check out first. Signs everywhere read, "Please Walk on the Grass," but you are unlikely to be fined, should you be unable to bring yourself to do it. A few hundred yards from the ferry docks on Centre Island lies **Centreville**, an amusement park that's supposed to be a turn-of-the-century children's village. The concept works. Oh, sure, the pizza, french fries, hot dogs etc. are barely edible, but on main street there are delightful shops, a town hall, a little railroad station, more than a dozen rides, and no entrance fee for the fourteen-acre amusement park – Walt Disney, eat your heart out. There is an antique car ride (when was the last time you were in a 1907 Ford Tourer?), a scary flume ride (you'll get wet, but who cares), and a restored carousel from the turn of the century that has more than four dozen hand-carved animals to ride on. Perhaps most enjoyable is the **Far Enough Farm**, which is near enough to walk to. It has all kinds of animals to pet – piglets, geese, cows, and other gentle barnyard beasties.

If you hadn't noticed it by now, all transportation comes to you compliments of your feet. No cars are allowed, although you can rent a bike or bring your own (but not directly to **Centre Island** on a summer weekend, remember?). Your nostrils will rejoice at the lack of exhaust fumes, and your feet will probably enjoy the 2.4 km (1.5 mile) walk along the boardwalk from **Centre** to **Ward's Island**.

Next to the **Gibraltar Lighthouse** there is a pond, stocked with rainbow trout. You can buy bait and rent rods there, but your catch may be limited to two fish. Beginning in 1983, there is no charge to fish. (In the past it cost $3.50. This is one reason why we love Toronto.) By the way, check out that lighthouse. It was built way back in 1808 and is the oldest monument in the city that is still sitting on its original site.

Sandy beaches are all around the Islands; the most enjoyable ones are on the southeast tip of Ward's, the southernmost edge of Centre, and the west side of Hanlan's, which was occasionally denuded of clothes, if not (nowadays gay) people. There are free changing rooms near each of these areas, but there are no facilities for checking clothes. No swimming in the various lagoons and channels is allowed.

What we haven't mentioned is the astonishing view of

downtown Toronto: the magnificence of the CN Tower; the golden gleam of the Royal Bank Tower; the silver-blue and black majesty of the other odes to Mammon known as our other major bank buildings. It is truly a sight to behold. And if it makes you feel beholden to the banks, you can save some money by packing a picnic lunch. Call 947-8193 for further information.

How to Get There:

All ferry boats leave from the foot of Bay Street, just behind the Harbour Castle Hilton Hotel. The best way to get there is to take the subway down to Union Station (both north-south lines will get you there). Then hop on a southbound Number 6 Bay Street bus, or walk the short jaunt to the docks.

Yes, there are some parking lots near the docks, but the private ones are expensive and the cheaper municipal lots usually fill up rapidly in the summer. Leave your car at home or uptown somewhere, and take the subway.

There are guided boat tours of the Toronto Harbour and islands from early May until late October. The tours run from three dock locations: the main dock is at the foot of Yonge Street and Queen's Quay, just east of the Harbour Castle Hilton; the second dock is next to the Queen's Quay Terminal Building at Harbourfront; the third dock, which is open only until mid-September, is at Ontario Place. Phone **Boat Tours International** (364-2412), 5 Queen's Quay West.

HIGH PARK:
LOOKING A GIFT PARK IN THE MOUTH

High Park is the northern equivalent of New York's Central Park and the New World equivalent of London's Hyde Park, but with fewer muggings and no political lectures. Nearly all 399 acres of it was a gift from a talented architect whose life is almost as remarkable as the park he so generously gave to his adopted city.

John Howard was born in 1803 in a town north of London. He became an architect, and came to Toronto in 1832, when the building boom went bust in the old country. After suffering through a dreadful Toronto winter, Howard met the new lieutenant-governor of Ontario, **Sir John Colborne**, who appointed our hero as drawing master of a new boys' school, Upper Canada College.

Howard was soon building churches and shops, and was made city surveyor by our first mayor, William Lyon Mackenzie. Four years after his arrival in our frozen land he was able to purchase 165 acres of land west of the city (you guessed it, **High Park**), where he built a home. He called it **Colborne Lodge** in honour of the benefactor who gave him his first break in the new country.

Meanwhile back at his ranch, he cleared away some of the forest, built paths and roads, planted more than ten thousand flowers. In 1873, he kindly thanked his chosen city by deeding his 165 acres as a public park. Unlike many great men since, Howard did not insist that it be named after him, but merely requested it retain the name he had given it – **High Park**. He also stipulated in his will that no alcoholic beverages should ever be sold in the park, which might depress you but it keeps the parties there quiet, a century later.

A few hundred acres were added to the park over the years, in the knowledge that it is one of the better places to visit and escape the city: lots of trees, hills, and little hideaways. One of the delights of the park is **Grenadier Pond**, a little lake in the southwest corner of **High Park**. Named for the British soldiers who used to drill on its frozen surface during mid-nineteenth-century winters, the pond is home and stopover to thousands of migrating birds (and tens of thousands of migrating children and their adults). You can fish in its well-stocked waters, from the shore or a rented rowboat. There are Sunday afternoon concerts in the summer, on its dock; in the winter, skating is welcomed and supervised.

The **High Park Zoo** is known officially as the animal paddocks, but I think only the animals themselves use that term. It's not the Metro Zoo, by any means, but it's convenient, and small enough that even kids won't get tired walking through it. Here you can find spotted and Virginia deer, various bison, yaks, llamas, mouflon and Barbary sheep, white fallow deer, white peacocks, rabbits, pheasants, and the only native Torontonians around – raccoons. You are welcome to feed the animals – they like stale bread and popcorn and the keepers don't seem to mind at all.

High Park has a tiny bird sanctuary, which is off-limits unless you happen to have feathers. But you can throw crumbs to the birds at the stone-fenced pond near the children's playground, at the southeast corner of the park. Other highlights include a large swimming pool, open during the summer; tennis courts (wait your turn); fitness trails; hillside gardens, where you can find beautiful rose gardens, hanging plants, and wonderfully sculpted hedges. The park is a great place for transcendental meditation – necking. **Col-**

borne Lodge, John Howard's city/country villa, is described in detail in our Sites and Sights section.

High Park – hundreds of acres of footpaths, trails, bike paths, and roads – a perfect way to spend a leisurely day in Toronto, in any season.

How to Get There:

Take the Bloor subway west to the High Park station, or the College streetcar (506) along College to the eastern end of the park. There is parking along Bloor Street just north of the park and along the side streets on the eastern side. But on crowded days parking may be a problem. The park is closed to cars on weekends May through September. But for the elderly and handicapped the Lambton bus, out of the High Park subway station, does go into the park on those crowded, carless weekends in the summer.

NATURE WALKS THROUGH TORONTO'S RAVINES:
TARZAN, EAT YOUR HEART OUT

Most Torontonians refuse to discuss the matter, but at quiet moments they will reluctantly admit that their city does not have the natural beauty of Montreal, Vancouver, or San Francisco. We are not built on a mountain or over seventy-seven hills, nor do we have an ocean lapping at our shores.

But we do have the **Toronto Islands** and **High Park**, and we do have 450 acres of ravines spread throughout the city, some only yards from the most hectic parts of Toronto.

It is surprising how little residents know about some of the nature walks, but now they have no excuse:

The **Rosedale Ravines** are only a few minutes walk from the shopping at Yonge and Bloor in the very heart of the city. They are a series of peaceful ravines that cut through the luxurious, heavily treed neighbourhood of Rosedale.

Start in **Craigleigh Gardens**. Walking north from the Castle Frank subway station along Castle Frank Road to Hawthorn Gardens. There you will find a short footpath to the park. Suddenly, the tiny, quiet park gives way to a ravine, and paths wind steeply down through a tangle of underbrush.

Decisions, decisions. From here you can go west, up Balfour Creek across Mount Pleasant Road and through **David Balfour Park** to St. Clair Avenue. Or you can walk northeast, past the Don Valley brick works to **Chorley Park** to Mount Pleasant Cemetery, by way of the still-undeveloped Moore Park marshes. The marshes remain an excellent breeding ground for wildlife, even though they lie within a bustling city.

Another way to tackle the ravine is to start at Yonge and St. Clair. Walk east along St. Clair a few blocks until you come to the bridge. On the north side of the street is a sign marked "nature trail." Believe what you read.

Following the path below St. Clair, you are promptly in dense brush. This leads to an asphalt drive winding down to the ravine and a small stream. By crossing tiny bridges and going under some larger ones, you'll eventually arrive at a parklike setting, with manicured grass (and washrooms). You can continue on to Mount Pleasant Road, cross it, and in another few kilometres reach the Don Valley.

Edwards Gardens, a 35-acre retreat of beautiful hillside gardens, flows into one of the city's best ravines. Located on the southwest corner of Leslie and Lawrence Avenue East, you can walk along the winding paths beside colourful floral displays and gorgeous rock gardens. There is a genuine, ever-turning water wheel and a Civic Garden Centre, where you can get information on gardening. Refreshments are available, but there are picnic facilities, and leave Rover at home.

The great ravine walk begins from **Edwards Gardens** as you head south through **Wilket Creek Park**. Follow the path through the winding Don River valley, walking southeast under the Don Valley Parkway and continuing along Massey Creek. After hours of walking through almost uninterrupted parkland, you'll end up at the southern tip of **Taylor Creek Park** on Victoria Park Avenue, just north of the Danforth. Not bad, when you consider that you began way up at Lawrence and Leslie.

Sherwood Park remains a secret to most Torontonians until they send their kids to the camps that use its facilities each summer. Drive or take a bus north on Mount Pleasant. A few blocks south of Lawrence Avenue East go east along Sherwood, a dead-end road turning into a steep hill. Some dead end! This is where the living begins, especially for children (see p. 83).

The ravine begins at the bottom of this hill. You can either follow the stream or head up to the hill, which backs on to Bayview Avenue.

You'll eventually cross Blythwood Road, as the ravine winds its way under the Mt. Pleasant bridge all the way to Yonge Street and Lawrence. There a subway and buses await you – and, more satisfying, the beautiful rose gardens in **Alexander Muir Park**, named after the man who wrote one of Canada's anthems, "The Maple Leaf Forever."

The **Nordheimer Ravine** can be approached from a path leading from Boulton Drive, in the shadow of Casa Loma, running northwest from Poplar Plains Road, or by driving or taking the subway/bus to the St. Clair West station, between Bathurst and Spadina.

If you enter from Boulton Drive, you can view some of the great mansions of Forest Hill on your right, and to the left, Casa Loma, above a steep bank of trees. At this point the ravine opens up, and you are soon at **Churchill Park**, which has the best tobogganing in the city.

Humber Valley, in Toronto's west end, is well worth a hiking tour. It is almost continuous parkland, stretching along the Humber River ravine from north of the city limits (Steeles Avenue) all the way down to where the Humber pours into Lake Ontario.

A lovely formal garden, **James Gardens**, can be reached from Edenbridge Drive, east of Royal York Road. Adjoining it to the south is **Scarlett Mills Park**, one of North America's only wildflower reserves. (Both parks are open every day of the week until sunset, with lots of free parking. But get out and walk, instead. And try and visit in spring, when the flowers are really spectacular.)

You can follow the road through the park from Dundas Street West through **Home Smith Park** and **Etienne Brûlé Park** to **King's Mill Park** below Bloor, passing the historic **Old Mill** as you go. Made of stones from the Humber Valley, the mill dates back to 1849, and its ruins can be seen on the crest of the western slope of the ravine. In the north-central part of the city, there's the **G. Ross Lord Park**, running north from Finch up to Steeles, along Dufferin. There are cricket pitches, soccer fields, a large dam, and an open meadowland park.

Highland Creek is to the east side of Toronto what the Humber is to the west. Two parks follow the route of Highland Creek: **Colonel Danforth Park** and **Morningside Park**. Colonel Danforth Park can be reached south of Kingston Road on the east side of Highland Creek bridge at Colonel Danforth Trail. And Morningside Park is accessible off Morningside Avenue, between Kingston Road and Ellesmere Avenue. Both parks can be entered from the grounds of Scarborough College (part of the University of Toronto), at 1265 Military Trail in Scarborough.

Since the Highland Creek ravines are almost in their natural state, they are considered the most beautiful of all of Toronto's ravine parks. And like the Humber and Don ravines, they are excellent for cross-country skiing, biking, and jogging. The **Toronto Field Naturalists** (488-7304) take about 150 outings each year, mainly within these ravine systems. There are just plain hikes, plus sketching, star gazing, and bird-watching walks.

Farther north and east is the only campground for trailers in Toronto. Go along Sheppard Avenue East to Twin Rivers Drive (just east of Meadowvale Road and south of the Zoo), to **Glen Rouge Park**. Within its wide-open twenty-five acres are horseback riding and facilities for tent camping – a rarity for a metropolitan area.

For more information on the many conservation areas and parks in Toronto, call 947-8186. Remember, these parks are free and offer leafy respite for residents and tourists alike, and year-round to boot. No, Toronto may not be beautiful but certainly *parts* of it are, and most are within walking distance of every hotel, apartment, and house in the city.

PARKS FOR THE TIMID

Many parks are intimidating: they seem to go on forever, turn into ravines, threaten to take up your whole day, if you're not careful. But not these. While not postage-stamp size, they are manageable. And each is located in a different part of the city, to allow you to escape the madness for a few minutes and rest those weary feet and sensible shoes.

Queen's Park: A very short walk from all the shopping around Bloor and Avenue Road is this charming, disarming, unalarming park, ringed by the buildings of the University of Toronto. It sits there quietly, with its trees, pigeons, war memorial, and equestrian statue of King Edward VII, right behind all the hot air of the Parliament buildings. You can see it from the Royal Ontario Museum, calling for you to come down the hundred yards and have a rest. It's not worth taking a subway to, but it is worth visiting on the way to or from something bigger.

Allan Gardens is exactly what its name declares: a giant greenhouse, only a few blocks east of Yonge on Carlton. The park itself is nothing much, but that greenhouse is well worth a visit, especially in the winter. It's open 10:00 a.m. to 5:00 p.m. every day, but children younger than fifteen are requested to bring along an adult to accompany them amongst the flowers and plants.

Sir Winston Churchill Park is located at Spadina, running south from St. Clair into a ravine. There is a sweet playground, a sandbox, a jogging track, tennis courts – and the hill. In summer it masquerades as one of the best kite-flying hills in town, but its true nature emerges in winter: it is the most terrifying toboggan run in the city. We've gone down it in cardboard boxes. We are therefore qualified to recommend that you get a sled, toboggan, or family-size insurance policy.

Sherwood Park is one of the best-kept secrets in Toronto, and we are reluctant to let it out. Head up Mt. Pleasant north of Eglinton until you get to a little street called Sherwood. Go right (east) a long block and there you have it – one of the best children's playgrounds in the city, a lovely wading pool (filled with the proper wading material in the proper season) and a beautiful hill that seems to go on forever. **Sherwood Park** is the best cure for cranky children under ten.

PARKS BY THE LAKE

Although Torontonians are renowned for not taking advantage of the natural beauty of Lake Ontario, there are some parklands that you should check out.

First the east end. **Scarborough Bluffs** drops 90 metres (300 feet) to the lake. It's often in the news because an intrepid but incompetent rock climber or a slightly inebriated teenager hangs from a bush until a sure-footed rescuer saves his hide.

Geology buffs should study the way the various levels of clay deposit, recording five different glacial ages, are demarcated by the layers of sand that once formed the floors of ancient lakes. The bluffs are beautiful from a boat on Lake Ontario, but you can get a landlocked view from **Cathedral Bluffs Park**, at the foot of Midland Avenue. Drive east along St. Clair to Midland, and then south to the park.

As part of the eastern beaches, there is **Kew Gardens**, which runs from Queen Street East to the Lake, between Waverley and Lee. It has a bandshell, walkways, a baseball diamond, shrubbery, flower gardens, and you, if you want a pleasant break.

In the west end, check out the strip of open beach along Lakeshore West. It stretches from the grounds of the Canadian National Exhibition, near Bathurst, all the way west to the mouth of the Humber River with only the occasional private club intervening. At the west end of this strip, you can find **Sir Casimir Gzowski Park**, which has a marvellous view of the Toronto Islands, Ontario Place, and the downtown skyline. You can swim at **Sunnyside Park** (unsupervised) and in the free Sunnyside Pool at the foot of Parkside Drive (very supervised). It's only a few blocks east of Bathurst, easily accessible by streetcar.

THE LESLIE STREET SPIT:
SO FAIR A FOUL YOU HAVE NOT SEEN

Much of Toronto, from the museums to the CN Tower, is man-made but there are few attractions more strange than the Leslie Street Spit. It's a peninsula that juts out more than 4 km (2.5 miles) into Lake Ontario, built up from sand dredged for a new port entry and the landfill of a hundred skyscrapers.

It has been suggested that it become a giant park, a kind of Ontario Place east, but what it is, in fact, is a home (or stopover) for the largest colony of ringbilled seagulls in the world, and for dozens of other species of terns, ducks, geese, snowy egrets, and lots more feathered creatures.

A bird-watcher's paradise, the spit is a cycler's paradise too. Automobiles are banned and must be parked at the foot of Leslie. Closer to downtown than the Toronto Islands, it has been open every weekend for hiking, bird watching, and picnicking since 1974.

How to Get There:
Drive east along Queen Street to Leslie, then south to the lake. Or take the Queen streetcar to Leslie. Buses to the spit leave hourly from Queen and Leslie and at twenty minutes past the hour every Saturday and Sunday during July and August.

THE RIVERDALE FARM:
COW DO I LOVE THEE

Where can you find Herbie and Hughie Clydesdale, Flo and Eddie Mule, Max, Morley and Honey Pony, Buttercup, Daisy and Star Cow, Alfalfa, Jasmine, Sonny and Cher Goat?

Of course you want to know. At the **Riverdale Farm**, smack dab in the middle of Cabbagetown.

The **Riverdale Farm** is quite charming, and its existence is an example of Toronto thinking at its very best. It stands where the zoo was located for many years. When the upwardly mobile apes and tigers moved to the **Metro Zoo**, a number of acres were left tenantless. Developers moved in for the kill – and were foiled. Build high-rises? Never! So the Riverdale Farm was born.

The old bird house on the grounds is the last remnant of the old zoo, so the city started afresh – but not necessarily anew. The most interesting structure is a Pennsylvania bank barn, built in 1858 and moved to the farm in 1975. Inside are various farm implements: a light sleigh from the turn of the century and an exact replica of a Conestoga wagon, the kind used by German-speaking immigrants to this country in the early nineteenth century.

The twelve staff members, labourers, farm attendants, and tour guides are friendly and pleased to answer your – and your children's – questions about the mules, ponies, cows, calves, pigs, piglets, chickens, geese, and turkeys. They have to be friendly, as thousands of schoolchildren from nursery school to grade four come and visit each year.

In the bird house, there is the remarkable trio of Jerry, Ricky, and Jack Crow, and at least one of them talks incessantly, at least early in the morning and at feeding time (around 4:30 p.m.). Its total vocabulary consists of "Hello!" and "Oh, boy!" But when you see the ecstasy on your kids' faces as they hear a silly-looking ruffled crow screeching, "Oh, boy!," "Oh, boy!," "Oh, boy!," you'll know the pleasures of parenthood.

The "pony lady," comes into the farm every evening with scraps to feed the ponies. It is a farm ritual to watch her pull out carrots, peel and cut them, and then purposefully slide them into the mouths of the animals.

There is a "farmhouse kitchen" on the grounds, where you can get a snack, but you'd be wiser to bring your own picnic. (Or, hop over to **Jeremiah's Ice Cream Store** on the southwest corner of Sumach and Winchester on the edge of the farm. They have quality ice cream and a nice selection of nibbles, snacks, and lunches.) And don't forget to take a bathing suit for the very little ones, weather and season permitting; there's a wading pond in the lovely park adjacent to the farm.

In September 1982 a new tradition began at the farm: a fall festival, which lasted several days and included a pancake breakfast, milking and blacksmith demonstrations, storytelling, spinning, weaving, a horseshoe pitch, and other events that Torontonians have always assumed only happened out at Black Creek Pioneer Village.

Riverdale Farm is a real, working farm, right in the middle of the city and less than 2 km (a mile) from the corner of Bloor and Yonge. For that reason alone – although talking crows help – it is a marvellous place to visit.

Dogs and bicycles are prohibited; admission is free. The farm is open from 9:00 a.m. until dusk daily. And when they say daily, they mean it – 365 days a year, 366 in leap year. It is the only place we can think of other than milk stores that is open on Christmas and New Year's.

How to Get There:

Riverdale Farm is located a few blocks south of Bloor Street East, a few blocks east of Parliament Street. If you drive, go east on Bloor to Parliament Street, and then seven blocks south to Winchester Street. Drive east a few blocks to Sumach, and there you are. From the south, follow Carlton to Parliament; then go north two blocks to Winchester and then east. By public transit, take the Carlton streetcar to Parliament, then walk north to Winchester and east to the farm. Trust us, it's easier than it sounds.

PICKING UP A PICNIC

Tired of waiters hanging over your shoulder, unctuously suggesting a more expensive wine? Or maybe you have fantasies of a real *déjeuner sur l'herbe*? Well, there are a few places in town that provide everything but the squirrels and ants, should your heart and credit be big enough.

We've already suggested the Toronto Islands and the parks that are great for a picnic. Here are the places who will pack it for you.

Mullen & Cie (481-8889), 2615 Yonge Street above Eglinton, **La Cuisine** (484-0661), 417 Spadina Road above St. Clair. If you've got two people and $25, or four people and $50, or 30 people and $375, this is the place. They will pack you gazpacho, zucchini and almond soup, vichyssoise. They will give you some of the best vegetable or chicken pâtés you have ever tasted. Their Waldorf salad is wonderful, as are their marinated vegetable salad, ratatouille, and vegetable curry. And those desserts! Go commune with nature. **Mullen & Cie** will give you plastic cutlery, although their food really deserves silverware and china.

Daniel et Daniel (968-9275), 248 Carlton Street, west of Parliament. Perfect soups, fine salads, sliced beef tenderloin in Dijon mustard, fresh salmon in dill, brie, and amazing desserts. About $20-25 for two, but you won't regret it.

Mövenpick (366-5234), 165 York Street below Queen. A dozen canapés for $6, or a picnic of four kinds of cheese, a salad, rolls, and an assortment of meats for around $6 per person. Slices of cakes will be delicately tossed in for around $2.50 a person. Call a day or two in advance.

Patisserie Patachou (782-1322), 875 Eglinton Avenue West at the corner of Bathurst and (927-1105), 1095 Yonge Street, below St. Clair. Sinfully good ham and cheese, spinach, mushroom and zucchini, and tomato quiche for less than $4 each; wonderful Danish pastries; good baguettes and croissants. This is French food at its best.

Emilio's (366-3354), 127 Queen Street East near Jarvis. Tall and juicy sandwiches: roast beef, ham, Brie, Emmenthal, a good French or rye bread – all at around $4 a sandwich. Salads run from $2 to $4, and huge brownies at $1 complete the meal.

Kensington Kitchen (961-3404), 322 College Street west of Spadina. A Middle Eastern picnic: fresh pita, a salad of tomatoes, cucumbers, and garlic called *fattoush*, lemon-flavoured eggplant called *baba ghanouj*, plus *tabbouleh* and *hummus*. Under $15 for two.

Gryfe's Bagel Bakery (783-1552), 3421 Bathurst Street above Lawrence. Considered by mavens to be the best bagel place in town – they have a crispy crust and a light texture inside. You can get them with poppy seeds or sesame seeds. With some cream cheese and smoked salmon picked up at Daiter's just a few blocks north you'll have a picnic fit for a king. Be warned – Gryfe's is often sold out of bagels by noon. With very good reason.

Village by the Grange, on McCaul Street between Dundas and Queen (next to the Art Gallery of Ontario). Good ethnic "fast food" places, where you can pick up some very fast, very ethnic food at very reasonable prices. Grab a Greek salad from **Elina's Fine Greek Food**, *tabouli* or *falafel* from the **Falafel Hut**, little skewers of grilled chicken or beef at **Saté Saté**, and fresh fruit from the **Apple Core** grocery. Eat, drink, and be merry, and rejoice that Toronto is a multicultural masterpiece.

Taiko Sushi Restaurant (921-6408), 607A Yonge Street above Wellesley. Picnic baskets for under $9 will feed two very hungry sushi eaters.

That's just a taste of what you can grab for a few dollars on your way for a perfect day at the island, beach, or park.

There is a nosher's paradise around Bathurst and Eglinton – **Daiter's**, **Goldy's**, **Chapman's** will provide goodies to be spread on and over the bagels and ryes and pumpernickels you can pick up at the **Bagel King**, **Bagel World**, **Harbord Bakery**, **Lottman's Imperial Bakery**, **Health**, **Haymishe Bagel**, **Bregman's**, and other fine bakeries around the city. Have a good time.

CROSS-COUNTRY SKIING IN TORONTO: THERE'S NO BUSINESS LIKE SNOW BUSINESS

We are not going to say that Toronto is a Canadian Aspen. But when there is snow on the ground, many of our parks, ravines, bike trails, and even golf courses are open for cross-country skiing. Here are some of the best places to go, most of them free:

Toronto Islands: For the cost of the ferry ride, you may use most of the six hundred acres of this island park for skiing. The islanders who live there have even been known to offer free coffee to visitors, which beats a mugging any day. For information on winter ferry times, call 367-8193.

Earl Bales Park: This was a golf course for many years before the City of North York and Metro Toronto generously bought it for the people. It runs east from Bathurst, just south of Sheppard – north of the 401. There are 150 acres with marked trails, you can rent skis and even take a lesson. Enter at Bainbridge Avenue and keep to the left until you get to the pro shop. Phone 638-5315 for information.

Metro Zoo: One of the best ideas in years is *Zooski*, where people can head off in their Duofold long johns to talk to the animals. There are groomed trails, snack bars, ski rentals, and as many exotic animals as healthy people. But watch it – the hyenas have been known to laugh hysterically when you fall.

Central Don Valley is worth a full day. There are nearly ten km (6 miles) of bridle trails and footpaths just made for you. You can start just a few blocks south of Lawrence on Yonge and ski southeast in the valley, which will take you over to Bayview Avenue. Hike north about a football field to Sunnybrook Hospital (it's good to know it's so close); then head east and ski through **Sunnybrook Park**, **Wilket Creek Park**, **Serena Gundy Park**, behind the Inn on the Park and the Ontario Science Centre, through **Ernest Thompson Seton Park** and **Taylor Creek Park** (laughing at all the silly people snowbound on the Don Valley Parkway above you), and on to Victoria Park Avenue near Danforth. Grab a great Greek dinner and think of us. Phone 947-8186 for information.

David Balfour Park, in the centre of the city, has two hundred acres of ravines. You can't rent skis or take lessons here, but it's handy. Enter the park from St. Clair a few blocks east of Yonge or at Mount Pleasant and Roxborough Drive. For further information phone 947-8159.

High Park has 399 acres waiting for you. No lessons or rentals, but lots of trees and people and freezing pigeons. Take the Bloor subway to High Park, and it's right there.

Centennial Park is out west in Etobicoke. Four acres have been designated for cold-and-fresh-air fiends. Right behind the Nancy Greene Ski Chalet is a rare grouping of Shagbark Hickory trees. Take the Anglesey bus from the Royal York subway station. For further information, phone 626-4161.

Humber Trail is the western equivalent of the Don Valley trek we just described. There are lots of marked trails that go from Dundas Street west of Jane Street, all the way through **Magwood Park**, **Home Smith Park**, **Etienne Brûlé Park**, and down to **King's Mill Park**. You can also enter at Old Mill Drive on Bloor Street West. Phone 947-8186 for more information.

Beaches and **Woodbine Parks** have more than one hundred acres of parkland along Lake Ontario. You can enter anywhere south of Queen and east of Woodbine. Just take the Queen streetcar to any stop between Woodbine and Silverbirch. Phone 947-7251 for further information.

And there are still more places for cross-country skiing in our fair city:

Thomson Memorial Park in the east end has 2 km (over a mile) of marked trails, lessons, change rooms, and refreshments. Enter at Brimley Road north of Lawrence. Phone 296-7406.

The **Highland Creek Park System** between Kingston Road and Ellesmere Avenue in Scarborough, has nature trails and picnic tables.

Downsview Dells in North York can be reached via Sheppard Avenue West. It's between Keele and Jane.

Rowntree Mills Park in the northwest part of Metro Toronto can be entered from Islington Avenue and Rowntree Mills Road, north of Finch.

For more information, pick up *Cross-Country Skiing in Ontario*, by Iris Nowell, which has maps as well as information on hows and wherefores. And as they say in show biz, break a leg.

SPORTS

PROFESSIONAL AND UN-

Toronto and Chicago have much in common: both sit on Great Lakes; both have fabulous science centres; and both have a history of professional sports franchises that are to winning what Stalin was to social justice.

But let's not be too hard on Chicago. This is a Toronto book, after all. We Torontonians have four major professional teams with our letters spread across their uniforms, but the tendency for our teams to lose, lose, and then lose does get a bit depressing after a while.

And yet, what do Torontonians do? Why, they throw money at them like rice at a wedding. Look at the figures: the disastrous Toronto Blue Jays baseball team drew nearly eight million fans in its first five years of existence. The Toronto Argonaut football team – which began as a rowing club and many insist it still is – hasn't won the Grey Cup in three full decades (although in 1982 they were edging up), and still averages 35,000 fans a game. The Toronto Maple Leafs, forever in search of the Stanley Cup, are one of the most financially successful hockey franchises in the world.

What is important is that the sports fan has much to enjoy in Toronto, whether professional or – in the case of the Blue Jays, Argos, Maple Leafs and the soccer-playing Blizzard – a-mateur. And being a masochist helps.

The Toronto Blue Jays, Canada's gift to the American League basement (like housework, someone has to do it), made their debut in the snow in April 1977. It's been downhill ever since. When the Ontario government finally relented and allowed beer to be served in Exhibition Stadium, fans reacted with the gratitude of a prisoner being released from the Gulag Archipelago. This is a very strange town. The **Blue Jays** season runs the same time as the rest of the league; if it didn't, maybe we'd have a better chance.

Tickets range from about $2 for bleacher seats up to around $9 for the best ones. You can buy your ticket at the box office at the CNE grounds, daily from 9:00 a.m. to 6:00 p.m. and at BASS and Ticketron outlets around the province. For information on tickets and schedules, phone 595-0077. Or call 595-1362 and charge it.

The joke until their fine 1982 season was that **The**

Toronto Argonauts had been so nice to other teams since their last championship in 1952 that they tried to avoid hitting or tackling their opponents. Yet their games in the CNE Stadium continue to be near sell-outs. The Argos play two pre-season games and eight home games from about mid-June until early November. Then snow falls and, usually, so do they. Phone 595-9600 for information.

The Toronto Maple Leafs have, until recently, sold out every home game since 1946, and most of those seats belong to season ticket-holders. Season tickets are literally bequeathed by fathers to sons (mothers and daughters have more sense). Tickets are sometimes available, if you call Maple Leaf Gardens (977-1641) at 9:00 a.m. sharp. Otherwise, be prepared to be scalped outside the stadium or watch it on TV. This is a hockey town, even if the **Maple Leafs** have forgotten how to play it.

Maple Leaf Gardens is at 60 Carlton Street, just east of Yonge and the College subway stop. It is also used extensively for circuses, wrestling, and rock concerts, where no one loses quite as badly except the kids who sit too close to the speakers.

The Blizzard has been playing professional soccer under that name since 1979, and not only tends to lose but doesn't even get many fans. As of the summer of 1982, the team dropped indoor soccer, after attracting an average of only 5,100 fans each game at Maple Leaf Gardens. More recently, like the Argos, they have been doing better – but they still fail to bring out the fans. No, you do not have to read this as a plea to come out. As of 1982, the Blizzard had a new owner, new money, a new coach, and new players, which suggests something. Call the CNE Stadium, or 977-4625 for ticket and schedule information.

Other Sporty Things To Do Around Toronto:
Auto Racing:
The big city not exciting enough for ya? Check out **Mosport** to see the way motorcycle and formula racing is done. The Can-Am is in June and September. **Mosport** is about 100 km (60 miles) northeast of Toronto; take 401 east to exit 75, then north to the track. In the city, phone 665-6665.

Less than a half-hour drive (fifteen minutes if you're speeding) is the **Cayuga International Speedway**, which holds international stock-car races from May through September. Call 1-765-4461, for a calendar of events, which includes a weekend of food, dance, and *vvvvrrrrrroooooom*.

Horse Racing:
All that money burning a hole in your pocket need go no further than to **Greenwood Race Track** (698-3131), 1669 Queen Street East at Coxwell, the closest any North American track gets to the heart of a city. Thoroughbreds race here from mid-March until late April. Then it's harness racing all summer. Phone for track times, and information. When the horses aren't coming your way, there's a fine view of the lake.

The other great track in the Metro area, **Woodbine Race Track** (675-6110), in the northwest at 550 Rexdale Boulevard off Highway 27. Better call first. At certain times during the year the flats move to Fort Erie. Woodbine is exclusively for thoroughbreds. It's quite beautiful, with a stylish grandstand and landscaped grounds. It is home to the Canadian International Championship and the Queen's Plate – the oldest, continuously run horse race on the continent. You bet on the bob-tailed nag; I'll bet on the bay.

Bowling: Almost nine out of ten lanes in Toronto are five-pin, but there are some ten-pin lanes out there. Find them in the yellow pages.

Fishing: Call the Ontario Travel Information office (965-4008) or visit them at 900 Bay, above College, for brochures on seasons, rules, and where to watch the big one get away.

Golf courses are to be found around the city. Check the yellow pages or call Metro Parks (367-8186).

Lacrosse runs (and runs and runs) between May and September. Call the Ontario Lacrosse Association at 495-4230.

Sailing can be a breeze; phone the Ontario Sailing Association at 495-4240.

Skating is big in Toronto all year round. The Department of Parks and Recreation (367-7251) can rattle off where nearly two dozen outdoor artificial rinks, many indoor rinks, and more than a hundred natural ice rinks may be found. And don't forget about the lagoons on the **Toronto Islands**, **Grenadier Pond** in High Park, and the skating rink at **Nathan Phillips Square** at the New City Hall.

Downhill skiing can be found in and around Toronto. Phone the Canadian Ski Association at 482-6067 for the nearest hill. For snow reports call 364-4722.

Swimming is a year-round occupation in Toronto. Call Parks and Recreation (367-7251) for where and when at the many indoor and outdoor pools across Metro.

Tennis can be played outside with the proletariat in two dozen public parks – first come, first served. Call 367-7251 for information. And it may be played indoors, at various clubs, in winter.

You are always safe giving the *"Y"* a call; the Central Y (921-5171) is at 40 College Street, west of Yonge. And **Sports Administration Centre** (495-4000) will tell you almost everything you want to know about who's playing what, where, and when – and how you can join in.

There are also an infinite number of other sports available in Toronto – everything from cricket, polo, and field hockey to darts and shove ha'penny. Most organized sports have associations listed in the phone book.

HOCKEY HALL OF FAME AND CANADA'S SPORTS HALL OF FAME: THE PUCK AS ARTIFACT

Down at the Exhibition grounds, but open all year round, are two sports museums housed in the same building.

Hockey Hall of Fame: For those who think champagne is beer brewed in the Stanley Cup, this is your big chance: Lord Stanley's trophy is displayed here with as much reverence as the Royal Ontario Museum's Ming tomb. Hockey sticks, skates, jerseys, and goalie masks – even the one created by Jacques Plante – are on display.

The **Sports Hall of Fame**, on the right as you swim, jog, or skate your way into the building, displays memorabilia from rowing to cycling to track. There is a nominal fee to enter the hockey hall, but the sports hall is free.

How to Get There:

Drive or bus down Bathurst or Dufferin to the CNE grounds. For more information, phone the Hockey Museum (595-1345) or the Sports Museum (595-1046).

The Rosedale Ravine Expedition Team

FRIENDS, ROAMIN'S AND CREDIT CARDS

NEIGHBOURHOODS, WALKS, AND SHOPPING AREAS

Part of the greatness of Toronto is that it is a city of neighbourhoods. The cliché is that America is the great Melting Pot, while, Canada is the Ethnic Mosaic: tiny bits and pieces of cultures, religions, races, and nationalities that do not "melt" into one another, but maintain their individuality. Like all clichés, there is some truth to it, but some exaggeration and romanticism as well.

Let's just say that this is a very interesting, safe, and often exotic city to live, walk, and shop in. We've listed, in this lengthy chapter, some of our favourite neighbourhoods, walks, and shopping areas. We've also included a critical and affectionate list of the best antique stores and bookstores in Toronto, which are like neighbourhoods in themselves, despite being sprinkled across the city. During the past decade Toronto has become the object of many shopping pilgrimages. You are welcome to worship at the stores of your choice.

A SHOPPING TOUR OF BLOOR, BETWEEN YONGE AND UNIVERSITY: THE GLAMOUR BEHIND THE GLITTER

When Joseph Bloor made his brewery fortune and built his family home on this street over a century ago, how was he to know that his name would become synonymous with success and high fashion? Had he known, he would never have sold an inch of his property; land on Bloor is among the most expensive in the world.

Some call it Toronto's Fifth Avenue. Some smug Torontonians call Fifth Avenue "New York's Bloor Street." In any case, it is packed with high-priced stores specializing in designer clothes, furs, and jewels. Bloor is where classy tourists in the know head first and where residents in the know struggle to avoid until the sales in January or July.

Here's a highly personalized selection of our favourite shops.

Alan Cherry (925-4105), 711 Yonge Street. We'll begin just off the Bloor Street strip on Yonge, but right on, as far as high fashion is concerned. Cherry specializes in formal wear, suedes, leathers, silks, and furs for men and women. He is the exclusive importer of the luxurious Sergio Soldano furs from Italy. And his bridal department has gowns from around the world. Alan Cherry prides himself on personal attention. (Ask him about the time he and his staff raced down to the Harbour Castle Hilton to give fittings of mink coats to a group of Arab princesses.) He worries less about labels, more about you. And with his quality, at these prices, we would hope so.

The Bay (964-5511), 2 Bloor Street East, at the northeast corner of Yonge and Bloor. It's the elegant flagship of the department store chain, much like Bloomingdale's in New York, and far more chic than its namesakes in suburban malls. The Mirror Room for women and the Hudson Room for men carry elegant high-fashion designer clothes with such labels as Jaegar, Izod, Ports, Albert Nipon, Aquascutum, Ralph Lauren, Alfred Sung, Dior, Gucci, Redaelli, Hardy Amies, Warren Cook. Forgive the name-dropping, but in this neighbourhood, it's expected. And all of these names are at lower prices than in specialty shops.

Creeds (923-1000), 45 Bloor Street West, Toronto's leader in high fashion for more than sixty-five years. The store is in the Manulife Centre and is beautiful and relaxing: the merchandise caters to the taste of the discriminating and affluent woman. It is here you'll find up-to-date fashion in furs, accessories, sportswear, lingerie, and shoes that are so beautiful it's a shame to walk in them. Creeds is really a number of designer boutiques – Valentino, Ungaro, Chanel, Krizia, Bottega Veneta, Fendi, Perry Ellis, Sonia Rykiel, Chloë, and many others. Smart shoppers always check the Green Room for sale merchandise.

Zoé (922-9621), 25 Bloor Street West. Before leaving the south side of Bloor, it's well worth peeking in here. Zoé haute couture designs are on a par with those of Europe's top names, and we don't mean Margaret Thatcher. Her evening dresses of exclusive imported fabrics are magnificent. She also carries imported accessories.

Sportables (967-4122), 55 Bloor Street West. Sophisticated sportswear for men and women. They also have high-fashion cocktail dresses and men's jackets and accessories. Some of their labels include Irving Samuel, Ralph Lauren, Albert Nipon, and Anne Klein. The store has a charming, wood-panelled, Ivy League haberdashery atmosphere and helpful staff.

Holt Renfrew (922-2333), 50 Bloor Street West. On the north side of Bloor across the road from Creeds is what may be the most beautiful store in town. Holt Renfrew glitters with marble, chrome, and glass. And its fashions for men and women shine, too. This is a specialty department store with the best clothing, accessories, and gifts that money can buy – although credit cards will do fine, too. Holt Renfrew has Canada's only full-line Gucci boutique of ready-to-wear clothing and leather goods. There are special designer boutiques for the working woman. The children's shop sells exquisite imported Italian clothes and beautiful Elen Henderson dresses made exclusively for Holt Renfrew (you may demand that your kids not grow out of them). There's a new boutique for men, L'Uomo, offering an exclusive line of Perry Ellis men's wear. Holt Renfrew is part of the Neiman-Marcus and Bergdorf-Goodman department store chain and their credit cards are accepted. A solid gold chain it is.

Eddie Bauer (961-2525), 50 Bloor Street West. Sturdily made and cleverly designed clothing, equipment, and accessories for all sports, summer and winter. Their goose-down parkas and sleeping bags are justifiably famous, proudly manufactured under their own label. The staff are outdoors experts, and all merchandise is unconditionally guaranteed, even if you fall off the mountain.

William Ashley (964-2900), 50 Bloor Street West. The finest quality china, crystal, and silver available in Canada at competitive prices. They are especially known for their exclusive Waterford Crystal.

David's (920-1000), 66 Bloor Street West. Still on the north side of Bloor, you'll find David's, for more than thirty years the foremost shoe store in Toronto. The shop carries the world's finest fashion footwear for men and women. The owners import exclusive merchandise from such top designers as Charles Jourdan, Maude Frizon, Bruno Magli, Yves St. Laurent, and Givenchy. You'll find the latest in accessories here, too – handbags, scarves, sunglasses, and jewellery.

Capezio (920-1006), 70 Bloor Street West. Down the street from David's is a very different kind of shoe shop for women. Its style is fun fashion, carrying the latest that the new Italian designers have to offer at more moderate prices than David's.

Georg Jensen (924-7707), 95A Bloor Street West. The

show-place of Danish design. Admire the elegant, hand-made silverware, Royal Copenhagen porcelain, crystal, jewellery, tableware, and beautifully crafted furniture and lamps. A great gift shop.

Bowring (924-5975), 102 Bloor Street West. While we're on the subject of gifts, hop back across Bloor and check out Bowring for affordable and unusual items in linens, cookware, woodenware, china, crystal, and interesting accessories. They carry a good selection of Canadian-made gifts.

110 Bloor Street West is a dazzling new complex of condominiums, offices, and retail space that adds a fresh touch to Bloor Street near Avenue Road. New shops are still being opened, and it's well worth a long browse through its elegant boutiques. **Rodier Paris** (968-9284) offers co-ordinated sportswear, knitwear, and shoes for the young set and well set-up. The **Céline** boutique (928-9393) carries a full range of exclusive French high-fashion items from active sportswear to handsome evening wear. Céline is to Paris fashion what Gucci is to Italian. This top-ranking design house uses only natural fibres such as the finest Swiss cotton, Italian silk, and kid leather. Polyester is shot on sight.

Also at 110 Bloor are **Boutique Quinto** (928-0954), a trendy shoe store with custom designs from Italy; an elegant French men's clothier, **Marc Laurent** (928-9124); **DeLorean Jewellery** (967-6219), with fine quality at reasonable prices; **Bedmates** (928-0202), with high-quality linens; and **Leggings** (964-3907), the best hosiery shop in the city.

Harridge's (962-2030), 131 Bloor Street West. A very pleasant women's specialty store, Harridge's carries current fashions at more reasonable prices than are generally found along Bloor Street. It caters to the career woman who wants the classic good looks of timeless yet up-to-date clothing. Shoppers can mix and match in fashion departments carrying labels such as Anne Klein, Christian Dior, Paul Costello, Ports International, and Lacoste, so watch out for alligators.

Hazelton Lanes, 55 Avenue Road. Just around the corner and up Avenue Road at Yorkville, the magnificently designed Hazelton Lanes boutiques wait to charm, dazzle, and bankrupt you. Plan to spend a good hour or two admiring the top quality merchandise of such world-renowned shops as **KSP Jewellery** (922-4100); **The General Store** (961-3499); **La Petite Gaminerie** (960-3292); **Teuscher of Switzerland** (961-1303); **Hermès** (922-6716); **Courrèges** (967-1785); **Turnbull & Asser** (968-0334); **Bart Leather Fashions** (960-3096); **Chez Catherine** (967-5666); **Giorgio Armani**

(960-3339); **Brown's Shoes** (968-1806); and **Little Lanes** (967-1383).

Take a browser's break and ice skate on their lovely outdoor rink in winter, or dine *al fresco* in the elegant **Hazelton Café** (923-6944).

Maskit (968-2444), 38 Avenue Road. Finally, across the road from Hazelton Lanes is the gift shop of Israel, carrying the finest of Israeli jewellery, antiquities, hand-blown glass, and sculpture made especially for export. It's the only shop of its kind in North America. Duty- and tax-free. It's often closed briefly during winter months, so please call first.

Have lunch or dinner at one of the many fine restaurants in the area, get a good night's sleep, and make sure the mortgage is paid, before you venture into the people-watching scene and fine shopping up and down Cumberland and Yorkville, between Avenue Road and Yonge.

EVER-CHANGING YORKVILLE

During our lifetime in Toronto, we've watched the Yorkville Village area go through many changes – from a conservative middle-class residential district to the gathering place for Ontario's revolutionaries, drug pushers, hippies, run-away kids, and avant-garde artists, to a very chic and very expensive shopping district. (And before our time, back in the 1860s, it was a real village with its own Town Hall, planked sidewalks, and horse-drawn streetcars linking it to downtown Toronto).

The ex-Village is made up of Yorkville, Cumberland, Hazelton, Scollard, and Bellair streets, with fringe benefits on Avenue Road, Bay, and Yonge Streets. It will take you several days of browsing to thoroughly explore the delights of this area, so we'll focus on the two main attractions – Yorkville Avenue and Cumberland Street. Shops come and go, but here are some of our favourites that have been around for a while to get you started. Most shops are open from 10:00 a.m. to 6:00 p.m. Monday to Saturday.

If you're crazy enough to drive to this hectic core of our city, park in the Cumberland Terrace indoor lot or at meters on the side streets west of Avenue Road. Otherwise, get off the subway at Bloor and Yonge and breathe in the rich and heady air.

We begin our walk at the corner of Yonge and Yorkville where one of the city's most delightful specialty stores is located:

Touch the Sky (The Kite Store) (964-0434), 836 Yonge Street. This is our city's great kite centre – kites and accessories for flying and decorating. Also, mobiles, wind chimes, and frisbees.

The Clockworks (961-6341), 7A Yorkville Avenue. Around the corner on Yorkville is a lovely row of ritzy specialty shops. The first is this store crammed with every size and type of timekeeper, some of them priceless heirlooms. Speaking of which, they'll repair and restore your grandmother's mantel clock that is gathering dust in your attic. And you know she would have wanted that.

Irene Dale (929-0552), 9 Yorkville. This is a charming little shop of Ms. Dale's own designs and creations for little ones – exquisite quilts, buntings, bibs, hobby horses, and clothing. How do we love them? Let us count the dollars.

Across the road is a last glimpse of the original Yorkville – the quaint library and old fire hall. On the latter, you will see Yorkville's official coat of arms. On it are carved the initials of the first five elected councillors, along with the signs of their trades: anvil for blacksmith, plane for builder, brick mould for brickmaster, beer barrel for brewer, and a cow's head for butcher – all solid, middle-class occupations. While they'd be impressed by the recently acquired glamour of their old habitat, they would probably shop elsewhere.

Back on the south side of Yorkville is another sort of landmark:

Lovecraft (923-7331), 63 Yorkville. Where you'll find titillating delights for your loved one: sexy lingerie, cards, candies, sex aids, toys, aphrodisiacs, and schlock graphics. (Sure it's dirty – but is it art?)

Meyers Deli (960-4780), 69 Yorkville. Open till 3:00 a.m. for you late-night noshers, they claim they're the deli that made Yorkville famous. Judging from their delicious sandwiches, salad and desserts, they may be right.

At the corner of Yorkville and Bay is the Cumberland Court complex. It's well worth a stroll for such modish stores as **The Soap Box**, **Paper Things** (the fund-raiser for the National Ballet of Canada), **Saint-Germain-des-Près**, **Ye Olde Candle Shoppe**, **The Compleat Kitchen**, **Swimsuits Etcetera**, **Newfoundland Weavery**, the **Bra Bar**, and **The Hosiery Box**.

Across the road is one of our favourite men's stores – **Bill Brady** (922-6600), 104 Yorkville. Here are beautifully made men's designer fashions, even if some of the labels are on the inside.

Madelaine (920-0846), 106 Yorkville. Gorgeous imported children's fashions at equally rarified prices.

Indulge your kids, but save money on yourself at **Miranda's Models' Clothes and Samples** (923-7604), 108 Yorkville. High-fashion items at 30-60 per cent off the retail prices. But don't let the word "Models" scare you off; they carry sizes 5-15.

Across the road is another gold mine (pun intended) of savings: **The Shoppe D'Or** (923-2384), 119 Yorkville. Recycled elegant clothing once owned by the Rosedale crowd, and often only once worn. Also never-worn designer samples.

Finally, at the Avenue Road end of Yorkville – **Lynda's Love, Lace & Lingerie** (968-3004), 140 Yorkville. A spin-off of Lovecraft, offering "unspeakable delights" in X-rated lingerie, if that's your sort of thing.

Upstairs, you'll find a little more class and taste at **The Pottery Shop** (923-1803), 140 Yorkville. Run in conjunction with the Ontario Potters' Association, it has lovely on-going exhibits of local talent.

Right at the corner of Yorkville and Avenue Road is the beautifully designed **York Square** complex, with fine boutiques built around an open courtyard. It's certainly worth a good, close look. And after a rest under the shady trees, walk south on Avenue Road one block to Cumberland, treat yourself to some Swensen's ice cream, and continue your tour:

The Guild Shop (921-1721), 140 Cumberland Street. A must stop for gift hunting. This beautiful store is packed with the finest in Canadian crafts. It's a non-profit retail outlet for Canadian craftspeople and is operated by the Ontario Crafts Council. It has ongoing exhibits, plus stunning ceramics, textiles, glass, metal, wood, and superb Inuit art. The staff is knowledgeable and helpful, and it's kind of nice to know that your money is going to talented, often struggling Canadian artists.

Across the lane is **Trade Winds** (922-2294), 138 Cumberland. Gifts of a more commercial nature, but you'll find a large variety of handicrafts from all over Canada.

Cakemaster Ltd. (921-6353), 128½ Cumberland. You have just arrived at one of the truly magnificent bakeries of Toronto. For years this downstairs shop has been making delicious Hungarian and continental pastry that leaves your mouth watering for more. They have the best Danishes in town (which isn't bad for Eastern Europeans). There's also a small deli counter where you can relax over a cup of specialty coffee and one of their tortes.

Stop in at the two maternity clothing stores up the street if you're in the well-to-do-family way: **Maternally Yours** (922-0636), 120 Cumberland, and **Lady Madonna** (921-3116), 110 Cumberland.

Hot Stuff (961-7687), 124 Cumberland. This is a great place to buy elegant designer lingerie and loungewear for gifts, or better yet, for yourself, you lucky, sexy person you.

Norma (923-5514), 116 Cumberland. Everything in this beautiful store is designed by owner Norma Lepofsky and hand-made by Toronto craftswomen. You'll find gorgeous one-of-a-kind sweaters, coats, suits, scarves, and evening wear. The garments are expensive, but will last a lifetime; they are well worth it, considering the time and talent that went into making them.

The Way to Go (928-9166), 114 Cumberland. Forgot to pack something for your trip? Relax. This shop has every travel accessory you can think of or need. And probably even some you hadn't thought of and don't need.

Fidani (960-8606), 108½ Cumberland. *The* place in Toronto for the latest in designer Italian men's fashions.

After dining *al fresco* (weather permitting, *bien sûr*) at the **Bellair Café** (964-2222), 100 Cumberland, cross Bay Street (heading back to your car if it's parked in the Cumberland lot), and turn north on Bay to:

Henri the Second (928-0961), 1235 Bay Street. For that witty name alone, we love this place. It's crammed with seconds in beautiful kitchenware and gift items at one third to one half off retail prices. They carry ends of lines and over-runs in such items as Copco pots and Boda crystal. How many people check their Boda for seconds, really?

Mr. Smith (961-6320), 1233 Bay. Mr. Smith himself designs many of the classic, yet affordable, woman's fashions in this chic shop. His clothes are well made of fine fabrics.

Finally, **The Toy Shop** (961-4870), 62 Cumberland. One of our kids' favourite places. We have to drag them out, kicking and screaming, while the store's well-behaved patrons look disapproving. The giant rocking horses (at around $1,500, as we recall), models, games, arts and crafts, dolls, and toys are a garden of delights. The staff is a great help in selecting quality toys that any youngster will love and use.

There's much, much more in the Yorkville/Cumberland walk; you'll just have to discover for yourself. But when friends visit from out of town, it is Yorkville, more than any other area except, perhaps, the magnificent Eaton Centre, that has them raving. And in many cases, broke.

BALDWIN STREET:
FROM TOFU TO FROZEN YOGHURT IN A
FEW EASY STEPS

One of Toronto's special neighbourhoods is **Baldwin Street**, especially the short stretch running between McCaul Street and Beverley Street, just two blocks north of the Art Gallery of Ontario. It's murder trying to get a parking place on this two-block stretch. We usually leave the car on one of the cross streets – Henry or McCaul.

Baldwin is a mini-demographer of Toronto and the times: it began as a predominantly Jewish neighbourhood; then the Chinese moved in, who got on fine with the Jews, followed by hippies and American draft dodgers, who horrified the Chinese, followed by the punk-rockers who horrified everyone. Now the street seems to be settling down into a quiet commercial middle-age.

But it's lost none of its charm. Grab a snack at one of its delectable cafés, rest yourself on one (or many) of the wooden benches under the shady chestnut trees, bask in the afternoon sun (or snow), and watch the people go by.

When your feet stop hurting, begin your browsing at **Yet Sing Company** (977-3981), 11 Baldwin Street. This is the largest maker of tofu and soybean products in the city, and supplies most of the Chinese restaurants in Toronto. Pick up some fresh tofu in handy containers for supper, but be sure to tell the kids that it's a new kind of candy.

Next door is **Solomon on Baldwin**, a friendly, well-stocked art supply company, handy for the hundreds of students of the Ontario College of Art, just three blocks south, at 100 McCaul. Solomon (977-7330) is at 13 Baldwin.

Ever tried sleeping on an all-cotton futon mattress? We love ours. They fold up easily, and take up less space than those hideabeds of yesteryear. One of the nicest futon stores in town is **Futon Designs** (977-6412), 17 Baldwin Street. The government insists on chemicals added to make futons fire-retardant. But with a doctor's prescription, they will make a futon without additives for you.

Yofi's Restaurant and Café (977-1145) at 19 Baldwin. This is one of our favourite cafés, specializing in Middle-Eastern and health food. Everything is carefully prepared from fresh ingredients and beautifully presented on fruit-garnished plates. Their falafel sandwiches on whole-wheat pita are delicious, and their frozen yoghurt is among the best in the city. Prices that rarely run more than $10 for two make this café truly special. Licenced, too.

Legacy Art (977-4678), 23 Baldwin Street. This recently opened gallery serves as the agent for the Ojibway artist Norval Morrisseau. They're open till 9:00 p.m. for evening browsers who want to enjoy the bold canvases by the artist whom some consider to be the Picasso of Canada. Their hours vary: they are often open Sundays, so call to verify.

Caffé Italia (593-5376) is a hidden treasure at 27 Baldwin that serves reasonably priced, freshly made pasta and ice cream. It has a charming European atmosphere, where you can relax and play chess or read the newspaper. Check out the espresso and capuccino.

Next door is one of the oldest and greatest dairies in the city – **Mandel's Creamery** (977-4003), 29 Baldwin Street. Their rich, smooth cream cheese is legendary, a must for perfect cheese cakes. Their brick cheese, eggs, and butter are the freshest around. They're usually closed or sold out by 1:00 p.m., so get there early.

Morningstar (977-3976), 31 Baldwin Street. One of our favourite clothing shops in the city, it's smaller, less modern, and more laid-back than its younger sister on Yonge St. south of Bloor. It carries exclusively imported East Indian natural garments for men and women, plus an eclectic assortment of gift items and accessories. The homey, wooden-floored, incense-filled store captures the alternate casual lifestyle of many of those who frequent Baldwin Street. Haight-Ashbury lives.

Ragnarokr (977-1966), 33 Baldwin Street. Another of the Baldwin Street old-timers. The owners handcraft custom-made leather sandals, bags, purses, belts, and sheep-skin mittens and slippers. It's lovely stuff, beautifully made and long lasting.

Le Petit Gaston (596-8270) offers *al fresco* dining and a delicious French menu at 35 Baldwin Street. Have a peek into **Exile** for the latest in recycled far-out clothing for men, women, and others. Then head next door into the new little complex of fabulous Chinese eateries at 41-45 Baldwin Street. **Eating Counter** (977-7028), features barbecue and seafoods; **Dinner King Restaurant** (596-0433) vegetarian and Cantonese dishes; and **Baldwin Garden Restaurant** (593-4035) specializes in Szechuan and Hunan dishes. All three have avid fans and regulars.

Cross the road to the north side of Baldwin. There's the lovely **La Bodega Restaurant** (977-1287), at 30 Baldwin Street, for gracious *cuisine française* and a canopied outside patio.

Letki Designs (979-2821), 26 Baldwin Street. These craftspersons have been specializing in custom-made silver jewellery for many years. This is a good place for gifts because the staff will design pieces to suit any person you describe.

Next door (979-2832) at 22 Baldwin Street, is the **Yung Sing Pastry Shop**. The line-ups stretch down the street at lunchtime, as everyone waits for aromatic, sweet, flaky, meat-filled buns and delectable Chinese pastries. It's a superb take-out place – and at less than 75¢ for a filling bun, an astonishingly cheap one – and a lunchtime tradition for thousands of downtown office workers.

At 20½ Baldwin Street is our favourite health-food store in the city, **Baldwin Natural Foods** (979-1777). This handsome wooden-floored-and-binned store is one of the few places in town where you can get organic produce from Ontario and California, even during the dark, bleak months of winter. And they have an extensive array of health foods, too: organic meats, fresh whole grain breads and baked goods, nuts and beans, cereals, vitamins, and cosmetics--just about everything the health-food enthusiast could want. No smoking, please.

Around Again (979-2822), 18 Baldwin Street. The two low-key, knowledgeable owners, Barbara Eisenstat and Martin Lea, buy, sell, and trade new and used records. They specialize in classical, jazz, and rock music and encourage browsers to listen to a record on the premises before they buy. They have a following of loyal regulars, mostly the college crowd and serious record collectors. And they'll track down rare records for you, including that one your Uncle Harold never returned.

Almost at the end of the block is **The Women's Press** (598-0082), 16 Baldwin Street. For ten years this non-profit collective publishing house has been producing important books with a socialist-feminist outlook for children and adults. They distribute their books in retail stores across Canada, but if you drop in they will allow you to browse around and purchase from their stock.

Finally, at the very end of the block is the only place on the block where you might get clipped: a fine, reasonable, hair-styling joint, **Your Basic Haircut** (979-9790), which tells it like it is, at 14 Baldwin Street. It's highly recommended by the locals.

Baldwin Street. It's two of the best blocks you'll walk in Toronto.

THE YONGE STREET STRIP: THOUGH IT DOESN'T STRIP ANY MORE

Tired of glittering Bloor Street and posh Avenue Road? Want to experience the seedy side of the Big City?

Then head south from Bloor and Yonge to take in The Strip. By the time you reach Dundas, you'll have found the soft-core porn bookstores and movie houses, the pinball arcades, the harmonica-playing vagabonds, the street vendors peddling jewellery, buttons, crests and stickers, the hustlers and whores, the fast-food dives, the occasional future politician, and the ubiquitous patrolling cops.

Times Square this isn't. In recent years, there has been a movement afoot (and ahead) to clean up Yonge Street. **The Strip** no longer radiates the danger and despair it did back in the early 1970s; it has more the air of a tacky carnival. Three million dollars has been spent refurbishing streets adjoining Yonge, adding trees, benches, outdoor cafés, and Victorian-style lampposts to create a fresher look. Within the next decade more than ten thousand people are expected to move within five blocks of the main street, making it a community for the young and old, families and businesses.

Unlike many American cities, the Toronto downtown is safe twenty-four hours a day – more or less. The body-rub parlours, where more than backs were rubbed, are gone, as are the sex shops and heavy drug peddlers. The street is now packed with people enjoying the punk rockers, the far-out clothing and head shops, the raucous music blaring from the shops – and avoiding the panhandlers. Everyone jaywalks.

If you are from a small town and/or have a good sense of history, this part of Yonge Street is not to be missed – it's the hard core of a road that dates back to 1793 and stretches from the Lake to Rainy River 1,896.3 km (1178.6 miles) to the north. Indeed, Yonge Street has been officially recognized as the longest street in the world. The *Guinness Book of World Records*, ah, immortality! It was named after Sir George Yonge, British secretary of war and good buddy of our first lieutenant-governor, John Graves Simcoe. It is interesting, perhaps symptomatic, that Yonge never stepped foot on Canadian soil. And if he saw parts of his namesake today, he probably wouldn't want to, either.

We recommend that you begin your walking tour at the northwest end of the strip at Yonge and Bloor. It's here you'll find the most interesting shops. Now, don't get the wrong idea. We're not going to recommend the latest in video sleaze or the best roach-clip in town. This is a family book, after all.

Like petunias in the onion patch of Yonge Street, are the following:

Alan Goouch (964-6373), 776 Yonge Street. The ritzy branch of the original Brick Shirt House, with plush green-plaid broadloom and designer men's sportswear.

The Locker Room (960-3904), 774 Yonge Street. A great place to buy gifts for the kids: they are agents for NFL team shirts, specializing in jerseys, sweaters, T-shirts, pennants, and baseball hats. Alas, they cannot guarantee that your team will win.

Shirt Factory & Gift Shop (968-7918), 762 Yonge Street. "We print anything while you wait." And indeed they do – every imaginable and unimaginable logo on the shirt of your dreams. A great place for Toronto souvenirs.

The Athlete's Choice (928-9696), 760 Yonge Street. The exclusive agent for Adidas sporting goods, clothing, and equipment sells only that brand.

Curry's Art Store (967-6666), 756 Yonge Street. This is *it*. Since 1911, Curry's has been The Source for local artists. It has every imaginable artist's supply, and some you'll never guess a use for. The racks upon racks of markers and Letraset are mind-boggling.

The Brothers Restaurant & Deli (924-5084), 698 Yonge Street. Stop for a snack at this great deli and take-out joint.

Morningstar Trading, 680 Yonge Street (922-1858), is our favourite of the many Indian-Oriental clothing and gift shops that line the Yonge Street strip. Their clothes are fashionable and well made, and they have delightful knick-knacks and accessories. This is the smartest looking of their three branches.

AA Sweets (922-5346), 602 Yonge Street. A delectable candy and bake-shop specializing in European marzipan and tortes. Their hand-made chocolates are out of this world; just sniffing in here can send you into diabetic shock.

Take a detour west one block, along Wellesley. You'll find **Sweet Rosie's Cookies and Muffins** (923-9112) and **The Falafel Hut Lebanese Food** (923-5099), serving delicious, nutritious, unsuspicious Mid-East fare. **Directions East** (967-6920) sells oriental silks, jewellery, rugs, and gifts. **Hobbit, "The Comfort Store"** (967-7115), offers the most reasonable Birkenstock footwear in town, plus natural-fibre clothes, gifts, and futon mattresses. **Goldberry Natural Food Supermarket and Bakery** (921-4057), 17 St. Nicholas Street. California-style health-food shopping and eating – a warehouse full of every wholesome edible imaginable. Buy in bulk and save money as well as your life.

Back to Yonge, still heading south. You'll pass the newly renovated and elegant **College Park** shops, 444 Yonge Street, many of which are magnificent. This building on the southwest corner of College and Yonge was a major Eaton's department store until the late 1970s. Eaton's chose the unfortunate time of 1928-1930 to build their College Street store, complete with marble walls, brass railings and a jewel of an auditorium on the top floor. In spite of the odds, however, the store survived the Depression and thrived thereafter. Today the building has been renamed **College Park**, and is filled with dozens of beautiful stores and eateries – a magnificent example of how cities can preserve their pasts while they march proudly into the future. And now you hit the real sleaze, or what's left of it, south from College to Dundas – leather shops, head shops, sex-aids stores (did you ask for help?), dirty flicks, and dirtier magazines.

But there's one bright spot: **The World's Biggest Bookstore** (977-7009), at 20 Edward Street, just a few feet west off Yonge. This central branch of the Coles chain brags that it has the largest selection of books anywhere and the best stationery and art supplies department in downtown Toronto. Well, one thing is for sure: if you can read or look at pictures, you can spend happy hours in this former bowling alley.

From here south to Queen, the west side of Yonge is dominated by the Brobdingnagian **Eaton Centre**, so cross to the east side to begin the trek north to Bloor, just a mile and a half up the street. You immediately run into the two great record-and-tape stores of Toronto, all these years still almost next door to each other, vying for customers, each with its own loyal fans: **Sam the Record Man** at 347 Yonge, and **A & A Records and Tapes** at 351 Yonge – both with unlisted phone numbers. We hope you are duly impressed.

Great Chocolate Chip Cookie Machine (977-2447; 977-7878), 355½ Yonge Street. Delicious, giant cookies from natural ingredients. No preservatives allowed, so you don't have to feel too guilty about all those empty calories. This is a fun shop in keeping with the Yonge Street spirit. They'll make three sizes of chocolate chip cookie for you, and they'll put whatever zany message you want onto a cookiegram or giant birthday cookie. A great, offbeat, and tasty way to tell someone you care. They deliver too. But does your dentist make house calls?

Lou Myles (977-1290), 363 Yonge Street. A haute couture men'swear store that has been an oasis of good taste on the tasteless Yonge Street strip for years. The gorgeous, pricey and custom-made suits, shirts, and shoes attract such international celebrities as Bill Cosby, Vic Damone, and the greatest entertainer of them all, Lee Iacocca. The shop itself is stunning: beautiful carpets (made to measure, no doubt) and rich, dark wood.

Hercules Department Store (924-7764), 577 Yonge Street, is a super place for fun clothes–they specialize in army surplus and all sorts of camping equipment. Take home a Canadian army shirt or an Australian army slouch hat, and confuse your neighbours.

Aida's Falafel (925-6444), 597 Yonge Street. Even if you're not hungry, this Middle-Eastern eatery and take-out is a must stop. We think they serve the best falafel in town, fresh and deliciously spiced in warmed whole-wheat pita bread. They cater too, which is more than mom ever would do.

The Brick Shirt House (964-7021), 601 Yonge Street. Clothes as cute as its name–fashionable men's clothes at decent prices.

Mr. Gameway's Ark (925-3434), 675 Yonge Street. A three-storey trip into fantasy for the whole family: adult toys, family games, electronic games, Dungeons & Dragons, science kits, Trivial Pursuit, model trains, games, and toys. In this ark, you hope the rain never stops.

Le Chateau (920-6734), 719 Yonge Street. Here's a potpourri of the latest fashions for the young and Yonge at heart.

Finally, cool your feet and warm your insides at **The Goulash Spot** (920-1705), 727 Yonge Street, a cheap, cheerful, and delicious Hungarian eatery.

Cheat, cheat, cheat. As we cunningly parked the car at the Cumberland Terrace (east of Bay), we couldn't resist going next door into the aromatic and delectable **Dinah's Cupboard** (921-8112), 50 Cumberland Street, for some sinful (in keeping with Yonge Street), home-made chocolate truffles. This is an exquisite gourmet food shop. Take home some of their fabulous pâtés, coffees, quiches, kumquats in brandy, rose water, pink pepper, caviare–you name it. Strictly medicinal, of course, to help you recuperate from all this walking!

Hey mister! Just walked Yonge Street, eh? Do you feel dirty all over? Are you worried we won't respect you anymore? Not at all. Just feel a bit nostalgic. After all, you just walked the street where Canada's first streetcar line was inaugurated in

1861; where the first section of road in British North America was macadamized and tested in 1833; where (under where?) the first subway line in this entire country was built in the early 1950s. Feel better now?

THE ANNEX:
A REAL NEIGHBOURHOOD JUST A STROLL FROM THE CITY CENTRE

In world affairs, annexation is never pleasant and rarely peaceful. It is somehow fittingly Canadian then that the Annex, which is relatively peaceful, has been described as the nineteenth and twentieth centuries at war.

The origin of the name is hardly the stuff of romance. It was born when the burgeoning town of Toronto annexed the area between Bathurst and Avenue Road, north from Bloor to the Canadian Pacific railway tracks, alias Dupont Street. The year was 1887, and during the following century many changes have been made. And many more have not. That's where the war comes in.

The Annex was still country in 1887, so it soon became an enclave for the well-to-do. **Timothy Eaton** (of department store fame) and the **Gooderham** family (of liquor fame) escaped the masses and built north of Bloor. Eaton built a handsome structure at 182 Lowther Avenue; the Gooderhams erected a lovely red castle at the corner of St. George and Bloor, now the proud home of the exclusive York Club.

Even today, nearly a century later, many examples of the Romanesque style of architecture can still be spotted and enjoyed on Admiral Road, Lowther Avenue, and here and there on Bloor. Round turrets, pyramid-shaped roofs, conical and comical spires – a walk through the Annex provides many such pleasures.

As Queen Victoria gave way to King Edward, the old rich gave way to the new rich in the Annex. The Eatons headed further north, but the Annex was still home for others, such as philanthropist Sigmund Samuel, whose name is now etched on a major library on the University of Toronto campus, not far from his Annex home.

Ethnic groups came and went, until the arrival of the ultimate neighbourhood wrecker – the developer. And here is where the war began and might never end.

A brief example: At the foot of Admiral Road is Taddle Creek Park. A residents' association organized to prevent the construction of a multi-storey building that was to fill two full blocks. Only one block was built, and the remaining land was expropriated by the city to create the park. A dozen such battles have been fought and, occasionally, won.

Alas, much of St. George Street has been lost to high-rises, and as you near the Spadina subway entrance along Lowther and Walmer, many Edwardian mansions have given way to apartment buildings whose architecture will forever remain 1960.

More than twenty thousand Torontonians live in the Annex – university professors, students, writers, and folks, who rightly find the area a vibrant place to live.

A charming, if unglamorous, walking tour would be to stroll west along Bloor from Spadina to Bathurst. In many ways, it is Hungarian town as much as Dundas is China-town. Some of the city's finest Hungarian restaurants – the **Continental**, the **Tarogato**, **Country Style** – can be found along this ethnic strip, compliments of the 1956 revolution.

Hardware stores, electric appliance stores, excellent fruit stores, some of the cheapest single and double bills in the city at the Bloor Cinema – and, best of all, **By the Way** (967-4295), 400 Bloor W.

By the Way, as thousands of Torontonians know, has a giant sign above it that declares "Lickin' Chicken." But it also has smaller neon letters in the window that announce "Out of Chicken." Apparently, the landlord refuses to allow the sign to be taken down, expecting the restaurant some day to go chicken once more. It can be counted on to serve some of the finest Israeli food and fabulous yoghurt in a dozen flavours including, every March 29 – the anniversary of its founding – fried chicken.

May the Annex never die.

EVERYTHING'S COMING UP ROSEDALE

Morley Callaghan, the Toronto author who used to box with Ernest Hemingway and quarrel with F. Scott Fitzgerald, called the neighbourhood "a fine and private place." Others have called it blueblood alley, millionaire row or more stately mansions. But let's face it – the people there have just as much trouble getting their kids away from the TV as we do.

The place is **Rosedale**, *the* residential area of Toronto, symbol of inherited money, established money, money begetting money. For *hoi polloi* like us (and perhaps like you), Rosedale means a nice place to visit – lovely place to walk, bike or drive and to admire the wonderful, oversized, handsome houses, and to weep – however slightly – for the folk who have to pay to heat them.

It's bounded by Yonge Street on the west, the Don Valley on the east, St. Clair to the north and the Rosedale Ravine (just above Bloor Street East) to the south. It is as if nature, herself, planted ravines around the area to keep out the riffraff.

"Rosedale Ain't What It Used To Be" was the title of a pithy article written some years ago by a child of the privileged – and indeed, it ain't. Many of the old families have gone, and their mansions have been chopped up into expensive flats. And, Lord preserve us, pseudo-Georgian townhouses have sprouted up in side gardens.

And speaking of gardens, that's where the original suburb of the very rich got its name. **Rosedale** began as the country estate of Sheriff William Jarvis, one of the powers that were, back in the 1820s. He brought his wife Mary to settle on the two hundred acres, and she labelled her home **Rosedale** because of the wild roses that blossomed in profusion.

Most of the roses are gone now; so are the magnificent elms that once lined Elm Avenue – including the famous Rosedale elm, planted by Mary Jarvis herself back in 1835. Dutch elm disease hit even the very rich during the last generation.

Yet, there is surely not another metropolis in North America that maintains such an upper-class neighbourhood just steps from the heart of the city – a jumble of Edwardian, Victorian, Georgian, and Tudor, and massive maple trees cast their heavenly shade upon it all.

The best way to enjoy **Rosedale** is to walk or bike – or even drive through it. The heart of Rosedale is just a few yards north of the Castle Frank subway station on the Bloor line. Walk up Castle Frank to Hawthorne Gardens. On the northeast corner of the two streets stands the old **Seagram** (as in booze) mansion, which has recently been – horror of horrors – converted into five condominiums. Two doors north, along Castle Frank, is the impressive **Thomson** home, belonging to the family that brought you *The London Times*, some three dozen papers across Canada and the Caribbean and, more recently, *The Globe and Mail*.

Just keep walking, biking, driving along Elm Avenue, Milkman's Road (really!), Craigleigh Gardens, South Drive, whatever – you really can't lose. And if you do get lost, you are in very good company, indeed. Just follow that Rosedale bus, like everyone else does – it'll show you the way out.

Another way to get to **Rosedale** is via Roxborough Street or Crescent Road, just eight blocks north of Bloor, east of Yonge. It is easy to find because there is actually a Rosedale subway stop on the Yonge line. Just follow the streets down and around all the ravines.

Or drive south from St. Clair, down Mt. Pleasant (a few blocks east of Yonge), until you come to Roxborough. Make a left turn and drive around until you run out of gas. You can also come down (or up) the Don Valley Parkway, and exit at Bloor/Bayview. Pick up the Bayview Extension heading south, then make a right, onto Rosedale Valley Road, just north of Bloor. It's a beautiful sight in any season, but it's breathtaking when the leaves turn in autumn. Take Rosedale Valley Road about a mile to Park Road, then turn right. You are soon in the heart of Old Rosedale.

And listen carefully. You just may hear the delicate clicking of tea cups as they are set down on their Wedgwood saucers.

FOREST HILL:
UPHILL ALL THE WAY

In the autumn of 1982, there was a great controversy in the city of Toronto: would the former village of **Forest Hill** continue to have backyard garbage pick-up, or would the villagers have to (gulp!) drag their rubbish out front like everyone else? Toronto city council finally voted to continue the special service, on the principle that invisible garbage was one of the unwritten terms of Forest Hill's amalgamation with Toronto, back in 1968.

This tempest in a teapot (and if the teapot is cracked, leave it in the backyard with the garbage) illustrates the special nature of Forest Hill. The golden square of about 940 acres is bounded by Bathurst Street on the west, Avenue Road on the east, Eglinton Avenue on the north, and St. Clair West on the south. Today Forest Hill is home to approximately 25,000 rather well-heeled people, although it numbered some 2,100 souls back in 1923 when it chose to become a village on its own. Its first reeve passed a by-law requiring that a tree be planted in front of every house; you can see the shady results of his campaign today. At that time, there were no paved streets. Eglinton was a wagon trail, and Old Forest Hill Road was part of an old Indian path that meandered from the Humber River to Lake Ontario.

It remained its own little village with its own police and fire departments and school system, until it was incorporated into Toronto. Today, apart from the green street signs and the right to leave the garbage where it belongs, **Forest Hill** is mainly a state of mind.

You don't need a car to see **Forest Hill**. Either bike or walk along some of the streets, and you are in for an enjoyable hour or two. It does not have the gorgeous ravines of Rosedale, but you'll see some of this city's grandest homes and gardens. A good place to start would be Forest Hill Road, just west of Avenue Road and St. Clair. You are entering the thick of Forest Hill, with its handsome English manors and splendid Georgian homes. Just up the street is **Upper Canada College**, one of the country's most prestigious private schools. Here the cream learn to use the old-boy network the way we peasants use calculators. It has educated the likes of Stephen Leacock, Robertson Davies, the Eatons, bankers, mayors, premiers and the finest of the fine establishment since the 1820s.

A few blocks west of Upper Canada College, is **Bishop Strachan School** ("Strachan" rhymes with "yawn"). It is one of the select private girls' schools in the city (others include **Havergal College** and **Branksome Hall**). BSS is much admired, much attended and much paid for, and it is fitting that it shares a Forest Hill with UCC; they both conjure up other initials: M.B.A., MP, MPP, and, in general, VIP.

Walk along Old Forest Hill Road where you'll see some of the most impressive homes, then head up and down the streets that run north and south: Dunvegan, Warren, and (our favourite) Russell Hill. South from St. Clair, Russell Hill Road is a winding masterpiece of mansions.

There is only one tiny strip of stores and services in **Forest Hill**, on Spadina Avenue a few blocks north of St. Clair on both sides of the street. It still retains a feeling of a small village, which seems proper for the proper people of Forest Hill.

It's a special part of Toronto and, like Rosedale, a rare example of tranquil beauty within a few kilometres of Bloor and Yonge. Come to think of it, a lot of Forest Hill's inhabitants own *stores* at Bloor and Yonge, don't they?

CABBAGETOWN: FROM RAGS TO RICHES

Cabbagetown. The name doesn't quite roll off the tongue. Or smell quite as good as Rosedale. Or sound as elevated as Forest Hill. But during the 1970s, Toronto woke up one morning to discover that **Cabbagetown** was one of the most desirable places to live and the old houses a few blocks away from College and Yonge were valuable.

Exactly where is **Cabbagetown**? No one is quite sure, but it seems to be bordered by Parliament Street on the west, the Don River or Broadview on the east, Gerrard or Danforth on the north and Queen Street on the south. These were the mean streets, where people kept pigeons and poor Irish immigrants grew cabbages in their front yards. (You figured it out, didn't you.)

A century ago, little one-storey homes were workers' cottages for employees in the local glue factory. Back then, the houses up and down Wellesley Street, Amelia Street, and Sumach Street were bought and sold for around $300. In the 1960s, you could buy one for $10,000. You should have bought ten, you fool. In the 1980s many of them now sell for $125,000 and more.

As you can imagine, many "real" Cabbagetowners resented the trendies and speculators and "white-painters," who bought cheap, tore the guts out of these old houses, and sold high. Some feel they pushed out the poor. Others are angry because some of the renovations destroyed the original gingerbread architecture.

To explore the neighbourhood, drift in and out of the tiny streets and cul-de-sacs off Parliament Street, no relation to the government buildings over at Queen's Park. At the east end of Wellesley Street is Wellesley Park. And at the east end of Winchester Street, at the corner of Sumach, is the **Riverdale Farm**.

But best of all – and don't think we're being morbid – stroll by the charming Victorian chapel and gatehouse on the northeast corner of Winchester and Sumach and into the **Necropolis**. This is the resting place for some Torontonians who got little rest above ground: two patriots, **Peter Matthews** and **Samuel Lount**, who were hanged for their part in the 1837 rebellion against the privileged classes; **William Lyon Mackenzie**, the first mayor of Toronto and the leader of that 1837 rebellion; **Ned Hanlan**, whose family named a point of Toronto Island and was a world-champion oarsman; and **George Brown**, who was nearly the first prime minister of Canada and who founded *The Globe* newspaper, which you probably read this morning.

Cabbagetown was once described as "the largest Anglo-Saxon slum in North America" by its native son and chronicler, the late novelist Hugh Garner. Some feel it was never a slum – and it certainly isn't one now. But if you want to get a sense of what Toronto looked like when large drawings and photos of Queen Victoria on her Jubilee were plastered on every wall and window in town, then you could do no better than to wander around **Cabbagetown**. Most of the cabbages are gone, as are the $300 houses. But, for thousands it's still home.

THE JOYS OF GREEK TORONTO: FROM THE MEDITERRANEAN TO THE DANFORTH

The **Danforth**. A strange name for a street; but stranger still is its crazy-quilt ethnicity: once English-settled (although it was named after **Asa Danforth**, an American contractor who cut a road in the area in 1799), it is now Italian, Greek, East Indian, Latin American, and more and more Chinese. But it is still called Greek town, with its late-night taverns, all-night fruit markets, and lots of the most exciting restaurants and stores in Toronto.

There are now a quarter-million Greek Canadians; more than 150,000 live in Ontario, half in Metro Toronto. They created such major Canadian enterprises as Devon Ice Cream and Diana Sweets restaurants and gave the world internationally acclaimed opera star Teresa Stratas. For more than a decade Toronto provided a home and a professorship for exiled Andreas Papandreou, now Greece's socialist prime minister.

In the summer of 1982, fifty street signs in the "Little Athens" area of the Danforth between Logan and Woodycrest avenues went bilingual: English and Greek. When you've had too much souvlaki and wine they can help you find your way home.

The Danforth is a treat for the eyes, ears, and nose. The mile-long stretch from Broadview to Pape is a noisy, crazy marketplace of fishmongers, coffee houses, bakeries, nightclubs, poolrooms, and all-night fruit stores.

Take the subway to the Broadview exit or drive over the bridge from Bloor Street East, enjoying the view of the Don Valley below you and thanking the builders who were prescient enough in 1918 to include a tier for the subway trains. Walk along the Danforth for a few blocks, on either side. And now you are ready to begin.

The Hellenic Place (463-6785), 124 Danforth Avenue near Broadview. Fine moussaka, lamb in lemon sauce, and lamb stew, all for $5.95. It's dark and romantic with lots of wood and fine food.

The Neraida Tavern (463-9442), 129 Danforth Avenue. Open from noon to 1:00 a.m. seven days a week. There is dancing each evening to a mixture of live bouzouki and North American music. A group of singers and a belly dancer perform every night. Food includes shish kebab, pork tenderloin, and the ever-popular Greek Salad.

The Motorcycle Factory (465-7777), 358 Danforth. Filled with monster-sized bikes such as custom Harley Davidsons for $10,000 and more.

Parthenon Jewellery & Gifts (469-2494), 371 Danforth. Overflowing with statues of Greek gods, Greek tiles, Greek glassware, and Greek cassette tapes and records.

Omonia Shishkabob Restaurant (465-2129), 426 Danforth. Busy, crowded, and very reasonable. A delightful little barbecued quail is only $2.75; pork souvlaki, broiled over charcoal and served on pita bread, is $2.50; barbecued lamb $6.00. A pleasant mural of a ship at sea completes the picture.

The Danforth Fruit Market (463-2370), 479 Danforth. One of a number of wonderful, twenty-four hour fruit stores within a few blocks. The others include **Sunkist Fruit Market** (463-3727), at 561 Danforth and **Greenview Fruit Market** (466-9437), at 607 Danforth. You don't have to be pregnant to get a hankering for fruits and vegetables at 4:00 a.m. Milk, oil, vinegar, yoghurt, snacks, and other goodies are also available.

All the fruit stores reflect shoppers' various ethnic tastes. Some stock over half a dozen kinds of pepper: sheppard, sweet banana, hot banana, chili hot, pimento, roma, and cubanelle. And rapini, a second cousin to broccoli. And escarole, flat beans, pole beans, and okra, and other things not found at your local supermarket.

The Seven Stars Bakery (463-9524), 544 Danforth. Four different kinds of feta – Greek, Romanian, Bulgarian, and domestic. Smile and say "cheese."

And what of the bakeries along the way? The **Acropol Bakery** (465-1232), 458 Danforth, the **Pallas Bakery** (461-1248), 629 Danforth, and **Acropolis Pastries and Pies** (465-8175), 708 Danforth, supply fine baked goods to Greek restaurants about the city. And the **Pallas** is renowned for its tyropites, a filo puff pastry filled with feta cheese.

Olympic Gift Shop (469-2223), 573 Danforth. Greek gifts, baptismal clothing, and religious paintings, as well as silk flowers, linens, crystal, and china, much of it imported from Europe.

Panorama Restaurant and Tavern (463-5276), 634 Danforth. Open seven nights a week from 8:00 p.m. until 1:00 a.m. Greek singing (three women, two men) and bouzouki music starts about 9:00 p.m. Food includes shish kebab, squid, octopus, and shrimp. The seafood is widely admired, and the crowds of Greek and non-Greek customers dancing to the music make it a lively place.

The Round Window (465-3892), 729 Danforth. Bare brick walls and lots of fish nets, which makes sense, as this place specializes in fish. The Mediterranean touch is in the sauce – olive oil, tomato and garlic – in which the shrimps and scallops are sautéed. Try the *tzatziki*, which is a spectacular glob of yoghurt and cucumber tinged with garlic, usually served as a dip with warm homemade rolls.

Hellas Music Company (461-3082), 450 Danforth. It's a gift and variety store with merchandise ranging from Greek tapes and records to vases and items for baptisms.

Georgina's Tea Room (691-0100), 2171 Danforth Avenue. Not Greek at all, but a fortune-teller's establishment. **Katherine Wilkes** has been there for thirty-eight of her eighty years. Tea leaves, tarot cards, palm, and crystal-ball reading; you name it, this place has it.

And on the way back to the car or subway, do not miss two of Toronto's top herbalists, next door to each other on the Danforth. At **Thuna Herbalist** (465-3366), 298 Danforth, a landmark on the block for nearly seventy years, you can get anything from *wahoo* ($2.85 an ounce) to *tonga root* (a south-seas potion for rheumatism sufferers at $4.45 an ounce), to rosemary or wormwood for as little as 45¢ and 85¢ an ounce. **Ottway Herbalist** (463-5125), at 300 Danforth, has similar goodies and has been in the area for more than a half-century.

This is only a honey-drenched taste of the Danforth. But before you leave, check out the beautiful old three-storey brick houses just north of the Danforth on such streets as Playter, Jackman, and Browning, built by the WASP gentry early in this century as summer homes on the other side of the once almost-impassable Don Valley.

THE WORLD OF THE BEACHES: THE STIFF UPPER BEACH

"Where do you live?" you occasionally ask a new acquaintance. "In the Beaches," is the occasional reply. **The Beaches.** Really called The Beach, but it's easier to say The Beaches. Bounded by Kingston Road to the north, the Greenwood Raceway to the west, Victoria Park Avenue to the east and the lake to the south, the Beaches is an attitude as much as a neighbourhood. The chance to live in a small town outside Toronto with easy access to the city via the Queen streetcar and even easier access to Lake Ontario, has attracted thousands of residents, and many more visitors.

A soldier from London, **Joseph Williams**, first settled the area back in 1853, having arrived in Toronto with the 2nd Battalion Rifle Brigade, five years earlier. His twenty-acre grant was named Kew Farms after London's Kew Gardens, and it was there that he raised vegetables, selling them along with pies and pickles at the St. Lawrence Market on Saturday morning. When Williams chose to turn his property into a park in 1879, he called it **Kew Gardens**; it was soon flooded by hundreds of hot and sticky Torontonians attracted by the advertisements for "innocent amusements," and the prohibition of "spiritous liquors."

The youngest son of the *paterfamilias*, suitably named **Kew Williams**, built a stunning house of stone with a circular staircase and tower. It still stands in **Kew Gardens** today, the Beaches' own Casa Loma, serving as home to the park's keeper.

A century ago, when the Beaches became the Cape Cod of Toronto, a horse-drawn streetcar went only as far as Kingston Road. From there, you either walked to your resort or you were met by a horse and carriage.

The settlers who developed the Beaches into a year-round suburb were primarily British or of British descent, like our pioneer Mr. Williams. And the street signs prove that the sun has not set on the Empire: Scarborough Beach, Waverley, Kenilworth, Hammersmith.

The cottages that once dotted the lakeshore vanished with the waves in 1932 when **Kew Gardens**, **Scarborough Beach Park**, and **Balmy Beach** were incorporated into one large park. But on a leisurely walk up and down the charming streets that run north from the lake to Queen Street you will still find hundreds of New England-style clapboard and shingle houses, often next door to formal stucco mansions in the Edwardian tradition.

The **Balmy Beach Canoe Club**, reeking of Oxford and Cambridge, still stands on the lakeshore, but its facilities are open to all those who have become "Beachers" since the British gave way to flower children, who gave way to the doctors, lawyers, city planners, and professors.

July and August are the only months when you do not risk frost-bite dipping a toe into Lake Ontario: but the sunbathing is magical beside the boardwalk graced by huge, shady trees. When you get too warm, there's the free Olympic-size **Somerville Pool** at Woodbine Avenue.

Most of all, the Beaches is the glory of the lake, the charm of the mixed architecture, and wandering up and down Queen Street until you get hungry for food or trinkets. Here is a nibble of both:

The Palm (690-0052), 1959 Queen Street E. Famous for its bacon cheeseburgers and all-day breakfasts of eggs, bacon, sausages, home fries, mushrooms, baked beans, tomato, peanut butter, jam, and toast for only $5.75.

Licks Ice Cream Parlour (691-2305), 1970 Queen Street E. Possibly the best $1.95 hamburger in town, magnificent chips, and eighteen flavours of St. Clair ice cream, one of Canada's best. Pay cash, grab, and run.

The Balmy Arms (699-8467), 2136 Queen Street E. A real, live Edwardian pub with imported beer, steak and kidney pie, shepherd's pie, not to mention steaks and burgers, which we just mentioned.

Nova Fish and Chips (699-1885), 2209 Queen Street E. Are they the best in town? A choice of white, cider, or malt vinegar is a hint.

Enough of eating. What of aesthetics?

Nostalgia Villa (691-1320), 1923 Queen Street E. Leans heavily on ad antiques, from Coca-Cola memorabilia to neon beer signs, for designers, decorators, dealers, or collectors.

Miracles (694-1954), 2014 Queen Street E. A browser's paradise with soap, posters, mirrors, games, jewellery, cards, toys, and novelties. They're hard to resist.

Queen's Comics and Memorabilia (698-8757), 1962 Queen Street E. Movie mags, Mad magazines, comic books, bubble gum cards, and buttons: trivia madness.

Full Moon Teahouse (690-2086), 2010 Queen Street E. The best of the Beaches' many health-food stores. Honeys galore, grains, granolas, and nuts of every variety, including many of the clientele.

How to Get There:

The Queen streetcar takes only about twenty minutes from Yonge Street. You can also take the Bloor subway east to Main and the Main bus south to Queen and Wineva, in the 2100 to 2200 block of Queen Street East. And if you have a bike or can rent one, the bike paths along the Beaches are a glory to ride. And welcome to jolly Olde England.

QUEEN (STREET) FOR A DAY: A ROYAL YET PLEBIAN WALK

In the 1980s, Queen Street West has become the new-wave area of Toronto. It's a great counterpoint to a morning tour of

Toronto's spectacular New City Hall just up the street. After a couple of hours with the bureaucrats, take off your tie and go west, young man, to the *real* Queen Street.

Just west of Simcoe Street to Spadina Avenue, Queen Street is lined with second-hand and second-rate antique stores, sleazy new-and-used furniture stores, second-hand clothing stores, and even a Goodwill outlet. These few mean streets are a section of Toronto's dispersed red-light district. Yet there's a sense of real community among the shopkeepers and residents of this area; they're all struggling together, and they support each other like family.

Amid the tainted and tawdry are some excellent restaurants and arty, chic stores. (We hope our favourite browsing-shopping-noshing spots stay in business until you read this book.)

Most shops seem to be open 10:00 a.m. to 6:00 p.m., and carry free copies of NOW. It's a weekly guide to the Toronto entertainment scene, exploding with huge advertisements, trustworthy listings of entertainment, competent articles on theatre, music, film, and lots more.

We begin at a landmark on the north side of Queen Street W. at Simcoe, **George's Italian Café** (598-3020), 180 Queen Street W. They serve mediocre pizza and good jazz. Upstairs, there's the **Basin Street Cabaret** (598-3013), which has housed everything from superb black jazz, *Indigo* to schlock, soft-core nudie shows, *Let My People Come*.

Dragon Lady Comic Shop (596-1602), 200 Queen Street W. A kid's paradise. Leave yours here to peruse the new and used comics. Slip them some spending money so you can wend your way west to **Early Canadian Furniture Shop** (598-2412), 204 Queen Street W. Although there are two other branches in the city, this is the original, carrying beautifully made pine and oak reproductions of early Canadian furniture: beds, desks, rockers, rocking horses, dining-room sets. We bought an oversized rocking chair here when our first child was born a decade ago, and we still put it to good use, soothing many a troubled neighbourhood youngster.

The Queen Mother Café (598-4719), 206 Queen Street W. Real funky Queen Street, a cosy, cluttered dive of a café and take-out. Soups, great salads, entrées, and decadent desserts are served with style, and can never be mistaken for its styrofoam containers. The human soul needs human hangouts like this. A new art show is hung every month.

Gold's Luggage Shop (598-3469), 212 Queen Street W., is

one of the best luggage shops in the city. They provide expert, same-day repair service. In fact, most of the airlines patronize **Gold's** for this service after they finish bashing around your favourite suitcase. (We warned you not to label it fragile; it only excites the baggage handlers.) **Gold's** carries all sorts of leather goods: purses, wallets, briefcases, umbrellas – and they'll monogram them, too. All at reasonable prices. Many of Toronto's top executives shop here; maybe that's how they got to be top executives.

There are bookstores galore on both sides of Queen Street; get the details in Toronto's Bookstores, pp. 150-156.

Now we hit a row of cool, unusual shops, beginning with **North East West South Trading Co.** (no phone), 288 Queen Street W. A handsome shop selling quality leather handbags, travel accessories, and fine silver jewellery. Even with a name like that, you could get lost in here.

The Brass Collection (593-2765), 290 Queen Street W. As its name implies it carries every imaginable brass item, from house numbers to candlesticks, from umbrella stands to coffee tables, from jewellery to mirrors. The stuff glitters, and as we all know, all that glitters...

Zephyr (593-0795), 292 Queen Street W. A breath of fresh air. This attractive and unusual gift shop carries a large selection of crystal, coral seashells, and natural rocks, minerals, and fossils. There's imaginative hand-carved wooden toys, and even a folk-art rocking duck that holds parent and child at the same time.

Mood Indigo (593-0643), 310 Queen Street W. The first of the funky clothing shops. It's crammed with nostalgia, and 1940s music accompanies you as you browse through ladies' and gents' recycled clothing from the first decades of our dubious century. If you are going to catch a glimpse of Jay Gatsby, this is where he'll be.

A.O. White Supply Ltd. (593-0636), 318 Queen Street W. They have been supplying Toronto's restaurants with equipment since 1934. But the browser is welcome to take advantage of the low prices and enormous selection of kitchenware: some top-of-the-line French merchandise, hotel-weight English china, old-fashioned soda glasses, European knives, and every conceivable woking utensil.

The Second Story (593-0849), 320 Queen Street W. A feast for the senses. You're sure to find a gift here for everyone on your list. You'll even find a list, should you need one: soaps, candles, stationery, kitchenware, a potpourri of novelties, and, quite probably, the kitchen sink.

The Allery (593-0853), 322½ Queen Street W. A tasteful gallery of seventeenth- to nineteenth-century fine prints and maps.

Le Select Bistro (596-6405), 328 Queen Street W. It's one of our favourite casual meeting spots in town – good food in a relaxed atmosphere. Excellent soups, fine entrées, delicious desserts at a *prix fixe* of under $12.

The Queen Street Flower Market (596-0318), 330 Queen Street W. A charming pick-your-own, self-select flower bar. They deliver, but won't send anything by wire, probably on principle.

Cross over Queen at Spadina, and start heading back east along the south side. You'll soon encounter **BJ's Used Records** (593-0548), 427 Queen Street W. Perhaps the best of the used-record shops along Queen. They stock a fine selection of used albums and cassettes in top condition.

Kops (591-1282), 421 Queen Street W. Another used-record store, specializing in hits of the 50s, 60s, and 70s. Now don't you wish you'd kept all your old Bomp-Che-Bom-Che-Bomp-Bomps?

Barney's Open Kitchen (593-0713), 385 Queen Street W. Nothing more nor less than its name. It's a dump, but renowned for its superb French toast and real, honest-to-goodness pulp in the orange juice.

Peter Pan (593-0917), 373 Queen Street W. It really does fly. This classy hamburger joint has enough nostalgia in its decor to send anyone over fifty into apoplexy: incredibly high ceilings made of embossed sheet tin, dark mahogany booths with tall backs, a hardwood floor – all left over from this place's previous incarnation as a 1930s very greasy spoon. Not so the extraordinary salads, huge hamburgers, and magic home-made cheesecake. We *do* believe in you, Peter Pan.

Paradox Studio (591-1537), 351 Queen Street W. The one-man gallery of Yugoslavian-born Vasilise Bukcev, and his bold, geometric, colourful abstract canvases.

And now a row of fine restaurants, our favourites being:

Chives (593-0897), 339 Queen Street W. A winning example of how *cuisine minceur* can be more cuisine than mincing. From astonishing carrot and orange soup to chicken livers dancing on spinach and fennel salad to chicken breasts in watercress sauce, to.... Let the old cuisine choke on its cream sauces.

Madcaps (593-1110), 335 Queen Street W. Its silly name comes from the silly hats around the room. But it gets its excellent reputation from the pastas, soups, veal, shrimp, crab, and lamb. Even the desserts are worth tipping your hat to.

Barrett's Yesterday Antiques (593-0898), 331 Queen Street W. A shop well worth a visit. It has some beautifully carved Victorian armoires in walnut, mahogany, and other fine woods, and quite a bit more. But no food.

The Parrot (593-0899), 325 Queen Street W. A superb veggie place, we gave it an honoured place in our restaurant guide. (See page 198.)

Stardust (593-0887), 321 Queen Street W. A men's and women's clothing store typical of the spirit of Queen Street West: new-old vintage merchandise, meaning they bought up surplus factory stock and are now selling as nostalgia and punk what no one wanted before. If you crave 1955 army uniforms and pointed-toe spike high heels, this is the place for you.

Harlequin & Columbine (593-0882), 309 Queen Street W. Run by one of the original free spirits of Queen Street, Kris Blok-Andersen, this offbeat, colourful, women's vintage and new clothing store has got to be seen to be believed. Newly renovated, it is now also a designers' collective. Like similar enterprising shops in New York, **Harlequin and Columbine** will carry original clothing from some of the exciting, new, young designers, some still in school, who are starting to emerge in the Toronto high-fashion scene – and at budget prices. Kris quips, "This will be couturier clothing for the new class, the professional, independently poor woman." Poor women unite: you have nothing to lose but your Eaton's credit card.

Ms. Emma Designs (598-2471), 277 Queen Street W. All clothing is beautifully handcrafted of cotton, wool, silk, and rayon. There is not a single polyester in sight. Some are hand-painted. The styles are soft, feminine, and flattering. A batik artist, silk painter, and silk-screen artist work exclusively for this shop to create fabrics that are truly unique.

Prime Canadian Crafts (593-5750), 229 Queen Street W. A lovely gallery displaying top Canadian artisans who produce exquisite sculptures, ceramics, glass, wall hangings, and jewellery. The shop is all white, bathed in a clean, pristine light. It's a pleasure to enter after the dingy charm of Queen West.

Zaidy's (977-7222), 225 Queen Street W. A delightful and delicious end to our Queen West walk. Once a tailor shop run by the *zaidy* – Yiddish grandfather – of the owners, it is a most impressive little restaurant. Fine house pâté, delicious hamburgers, fabulous pastas, excellently cooked sole, home-made desserts, and Haagen-Dazs ice cream.

You've had your queenly walk; now get on home, start that diet, and figure out where you will wear the 1930s blouse and spiked heels, and where to put the books and records. Nobody said browsing in Toronto was easy.

THE ST. LAWRENCE WALK: THE PAST IS THE FUTURE

When the city fathers divided up this city in 1834, they gave each district a saint's name. Very wise. The area that lay far-thest to the south, extending from King Street down to the lake and from Yonge, east to Parliament, they labelled *St. Lawrence*.

For years it was St. Elsewhere: a depressing, tacky section of old, dirty buildings, factories, and railway tracks. But like so many parts of this amazing city, it has been Born Again – as any area with a saint's name should be.

During a long, leisurely walk through the St. Lawrence area you will, in typical Toronto fashion, move rapidly from the middle of the nineteenth century to the edge of the twenty-first; from strikingly beautiful, old buildings to the new St. Lawrence project being built south of The Esplanade, designed to house more than seven thousand people. It's part of our city's genius: to create a healthy mix of classy condominiums right next door to co-op and low-cost, or sub-sidized houses. Who says downtowns have to be dead, dirty, and dangerous? Not Toronto.

This area is really where it all began, as the village of York in 1793. So you start there too, at the corner of Front and Yonge streets. Take a look at that wonderful beaux arts exterior of the Bank of Montreal building, put up in 1885. On King east of Yonge, is the **King Edward Hotel**, built in 1903 and recently refurbished in grand fashion. Drop in for a drink or at least a look – the architect was **E. J. Lennox**, the man who designed Old City Hall, Massey Hall – and yes, Casa Loma.

North from King, on the west side of Toronto Street is the understated head office of **Argus Corporation**, built in 1853 as a post office. And still farther to the north is the **York County Magistrate's Courthouse**, built in 1852 and re-stored in 1982. How the years fly.

Walk east, away from Yonge, until you come to Church

Street, where, fittingly, there stands the tallest building in the area – **St. James Cathedral** (Anglican) with its noble, gothic spires. The steeple is the tallest in Canada, and its illuminated spire clock once guided ships into the harbour. We morbidly note that this is the fourth St. James Cathedral on the site; the third one burned down in the great fire of 1849.

Keep walking along until you get to Trinity Street and walk south. There is the first distillery in Canada – **Gooderham and Worts** – which celebrated its 150th in 1982. The massive limestone building is still used today to make rum spirits from molasses. The brothers-in-law began their company as a flour mill, but soon began making alcohol out of the surplus grain.

Walk back along Front Street until you get to the corner of Jarvis. And there it is: the **St. Lawrence Market**. Built in 1844, it was Toronto's first city hall. The upstairs art gallery was the original council chambers.

But don't fight city hall – eat it. The **St. Lawrence Market** is renowned for its food – from kiwi fruit to Ontario cheddar to home-made bread to conch meat. It originated at the turn of the century when a market grew around the first city hall. Who *says* governments don't produce anything?

Renovated in 1978, the market is now the home of nearly four dozen stalls, a restaurant, and the art gallery. On Saturdays, there is the famous farmers' market, where you and the city's fine restaurants can buy fresh as early as 2:00 a.m. But be warned: by late morning, the best goodies in the market are pretty well cleaned out by the hordes of shoppers.

Just immediately north of the market on Jarvis is the **St. Lawrence Hall**, built in 1850 for musical performances and balls. **Jenny Lind** sang here the year after it opened, and **Tom Thumb** once did his tiny strut within these very walls.

Back along Front Street, heading west toward Yonge, you will encounter a building that has relatives in pie-shaped lots all over North American cities – the **Flatiron Building**. There it sits, on the little triangle at Wellington, Church, and Front. Once the head office of the Gooderham and Worts distilling company, now a prestige office building, it was built in 1892. You can still ride inside the original elevator.

Now walk west along through the park to the corner of Yonge, and look back at the wonderful mural by Derek Besant on the **Flatiron Building**: It's a giant painting of a painting of windows drawn around real windows; it looks like it's been tacked up on the wall and is about to peel off. It plays tricks with your eyes, makes children giggle, and it's a nice way to end your St. Lawrence walk – almost.

Trot around the block down toward The Esplanade, and then west, and you'll come upon a row of innovative restaurants, including two for kids – the **Old Spaghetti Factory** and **The Organ Grinder**. Welcome back to the twentieth century.

WOK, DON'T RUN:
THE FAR EAST ON DUNDAS STREET

The Dundas streetcar has been nicknamed the "Orient Express," and with good reason. In area, Toronto's Chinatown is the largest in all of North America (yes, that includes San Francisco). In numbers, there are more than eighty thousand Chinese living here, which is not bad considering that just over a century ago, there was only one – Sam Ching, who opened a hand laundry on Adelaide Street.

One of the best times to explore **Chinatown** is on a Sunday. Even in the 1980s, the Lord's Day Alliance (recently renamed "Sundays for People") has successfully lobbied to keep most major stores closed on that day, save in designated "tourist areas." The famous (or infamous, depending upon your point of view) Blue Laws – attempting to keep Sunday still the "Lord's Day" – are alive but regularly challenged in Toronto.

But have they closed down **Chinatown**? Not on your sweet fortune cookie! Here, Chinese music blasts from store-fronts, cash registers ring, abacuses clack, and bakeries, fish and meat markets, herbalists, and restaurants do their best business of the week. It has been estimated that more than $2 million change hands in **Chinatown** on any given Sunday, and we have eaten meals there that are worth at least that.

Let us start our wok walk. Begin on Elizabeth Street, just north of New City Hall, and walk north to Dundas, then briefly east to Bay, and then leisurely west to Spadina.

If you begin directly just north of New City Hall you can see Hagerman Street on your right. At the far end, near Bay, is **Shing Wah Daily News**, where visitors are welcome to see some of the ten thousand Chinese characters being typeset and printed. **Shing Wah Daily News** (977-3745), 12 Hagerman, is one of seven Chinese dailies distributed in Toronto, four of them sent up from the States. Did you know Blondie and Dagwood spoke Cantonese?

At the **Mon Kuo Trading Co. Ltd.** (977-3461), 120 Eliza-

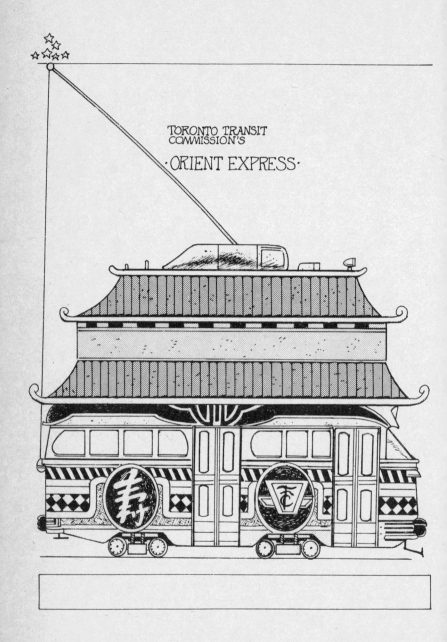

beth Street, you can see endless piles of dried mushrooms that sell for $24-$40 per pound (no kilos here!). In the basement, a sprinkler system cultivates thousands of little bean sprouts on their one-week growth to maturity. More than a thousand pounds of shrimp are prepared here each week for **Lichee Garden** (977-3481), a restaurant that had been a landmark on Elizabeth Street for more than thirty years before moving to its present location in the Atrium at Bay and Dundas.

You are now at Elizabeth and Dundas. Turn right and go east toward Bay Street and the **Pink Pearl** (977-3388), 142 Dundas Street W., which has some of the finest authentic Hong Kong-style cuisine in rather elegant surroundings: brown-and-gold wallpaper, white tablecloths and, orange napkins. See **Toronto's Restaurants** (page 197) for further raves.

Sai Woo, (977-4988), 130 Dundas West. A favourite of many; enough to fill the seven hundred seats on two floors, and renowned for putting on its semi-annual sixteen-course Peking banquet. They fed the Chinese circus while the latter was in Toronto – that must say something.

James Imports (977-3415), 124 Dundas West. The biggest Chinese gift shop in eastern Canada, overflowing with fans, slippers, and happi coats.

Dragon Arts (977-3437), across the street at 119 Dundas West. Elegant and reasonably priced silk blouses and antique porcelain.

Great East Trading Co. (595-0275), 121 Dundas West. Silk kimonos for less than one-third the price at most other stores. And how about that saki set you've always wanted?

The Kowloon Restaurant (977-3773), 187 Dundas West and **Hong Kong Bakery** (977-3760), 179 Dundas West, are believed by many to have the best *dim sum* in town. **Gee On Won Kew** (no phone), is a pharmacy where you can buy either aspirin or sea lizard to help your rheumatism.

Phoenix House of Oriental Arts (977-3770), 120 Chestnut (which runs south from Dundas). They sell beautiful ladies' suits made from silk.

Cross University Avenue. Do not jaywalk in front of the large building with huge Chinese characters over its entrance. As it says – in both Chinese and English – it is 52nd Division police station.

The Karwah Art Gallery (598-0043), 289 Dundas West near McCaul. You cannot only buy the paintings and art supplies, but receive lessons in Chinese art, too. Just to the north is St. Patrick Street, and the **Chinese Catholic Church**, and over on D'Arcy Street is the modern **Chinese home for the aged**, with charming crafts rooms, hydroponic gardens, and lots and lots of goldfish – an Eastern tradition has it that every goldfish that dies guarantees a nearby human being long life.

Take a slight detour to the **Ontario College of Art** (977-5311), 100 McCaul, half a block south from Dundas on the west side. It is one of the major colleges of animation, design, advertising art, tapestry, glass-blowing, sculpture, and painting in Canada, and if you visit during class hours – all year-round – you will be very impressed, indeed.

Directly across the street from the Art College is **Village by the Grange**, 89 McCaul, an apartment-shopping complex that contains more than a hundred shops, from ethnic fast food to chocolate treats to playful and serious art shops. It is a perfect example of what cities need in their downtown areas: a wise blend of commercial and residential.

Past Beverley Street you are back in Chinatown again. The **Dragon Mall** will fascinate, with its Chinese hair stylists, bookstores, and photographers.

Drop in to **Far East Food Products** (977-2482), purportedly Canada's largest fortune cookie factory. It's at 70 Huron Street just north of the Dundas strip. And what of **Champion House** (977-8282), at 478 Dundas West, reputed to have the best Peking duck this side of the Great Wall?

As you walk, wander in and out of all the stores. Be amazed by all the foods and condiments: dried shark, peanut pudding, green heart, enormous Chinese yams and frozen cuttlefish balls. Note the bilingual street signs everywhere ... and stay tuned for more Chinese thrills, as we move on to Spadina, which has its own history, Kensington Market, and is a walk in itself.

YOU SAY SPADINA, I SAY SPADEENA: A WALK ON THE JEWISH/CHINESE/PORTUGUESE SIDE

What other city can't pronounce the name of one of its most important streets? Do New Yorkers say, "Broodway."

Toronto's widest street, Spadina, has been pronounced "Spad-eye-nah" for a century and a half, and it's been too polite to point out that it is really "Spad-ee-na."

And how, you may ask, did Spadina/Spadeena get to be 48 metres (132 feet) wide, double the width of almost every other vintage street in town? The answer goes back nearly 150 years, when a wealthy family decided to do a little landscaping. They cut a path through the forest from Queen Street uphill to Bloor, so they could look down – literally and socially – on Lake Ontario from their home at the top of the hill.

The man who built Spadina Avenue was William Warren Baldwin, an Irish physician who came to Muddy York in 1802 when he was twenty-seven. He soon married a very rich young woman, built a pleasant home where Casa Loma now sits and, since he owned all the land down to Queen, decided to cut that giant swath through the non-urban jungle. Alas, the best laid plans of rich and powerful men gang oft agley: the garden that Baldwin hoped to build from Queen Street (then called Lot Street) up to Bloor (then the city's boundary) was never planted. To add insult to injury, his view of Lake Ontario disappeared in 1874 when a granddaughter sold the land at the crescent just above College Street, for the site of **Knox College** (which moved to the University of Toronto campus several decades later).

Now covered with vines, that Victorian building still sits in that crescent; and a number of the chestnut trees planted by Dr. Baldwin still stand on the west side of the island crescent just above College Street. Little else remains of Dr. Baldwin's *Spadina* except for a handful of Victorian mansions gracing one of the most exotic and fascinating areas of the city.

Spadina from Queen north to College – including a jog west into Kensington Market – never used to be fashionable, even just to visit. Way back, it was just plain, ethnic, good value – inexpensive stores, factories that sold wholesale to you if you had connections, and eateries that gave you your 2¢ worth, usually plain.

And so it remains. Each new wave of immigrants – Jewish, Chinese, Portuguese, East and West Indian, South American – added its own flavour to the mix, but Spadina-Kensington's basic bill of fare is still "bargains galore." Here you'll find gourmet cheeses at gourmand prices, fresh (not fresh-frozen) ocean fish, fine European kitchenware at half the price in the ritzy kitchen stores in the Yorkville area, yards of remnants piled high in bins for cheap Halloween costumes and quilts, designer clothes minus the labels, and jazzy night spots.

Take several hours to explore the ins and outs of Toronto's Second Avenue, the garment district. Park your car at the convenient and reasonable lot, west off Spadina between St. Andrew and Baldwin streets, or get off the College streetcar at Spadina and head south. Begin on the east side. Warning: avoid this area like the plague on Saturdays when it is clogged with suburbanites (and their large cars) on a treasure hunt.

The east side of Spadina is a cheerfully unkempt collection of textile shops, cut-rate garment stores, and wholesale jobbers. Our first great buy leading south is at...

Evex Importers and Distributors (977-1776), 369 Spadina Avenue. Shelves crammed with top-quality luggage and handbags at low, low prices; and it's a drop-off centre for expert repairs too.

B. Silverstein and Son (977-1831), 327 Spadina. A huge wholesale dry-goods store, and a great place to stock up on clothing for the whole family at prices that are positively nostalgic. **Silverstein**'s offers brand names at low prices. You'll do especially well with socks, underwear, and towels.

Slack's (977-3619), 323 Spadina. This children's clothing shop is run by the friendly Shlagbaum family, and we think it's the best in the city. They're basically a children's-wear wholesaler, importing and distributing to Toronto's big department stores. But they'll welcome you into their newly enlarged store where you'll find row upon row of better-quality infant and children's wear, great styles, and brand names such as Health Tex and Jordache, all at terrific prices.

Mes Enfants Ltd. (596-8227), 215 Spadina. This infants'- and children's-wear shop is not a bargain basement, but you'll get good value for your money here. They stock gorgeous merchandise – top Canadian labels and imported French and Italian lines – with prices a little lower than the same goods would fetch at ritzy stores. Unlike many of the stores on Spadina, they will take Visa or a personal cheque. Watch for their specials and sales.

Another Warning: You are now entering the real garment district. Proceed with caution, with one hand firmly on your wallet. No, you probably won't get your pocket picked, but you will definitely see so many bargains that you'll succumb. Again and again. From here south to Adelaide, you'll find the biggest concentration of factories and clothing outlets in the city. Watch out!

The Jeanery (593-0699), 163 Spadina, just south of Queen. This trendy casuals shop for the whole family has eight branches in the Toronto area. It specializes in designer jeans, jackets, and tops at prices lower than those of the big department stores. You can also buy wholesale here.

Next door is **Peter's Place** (593-0047), 161 Spadina. Specializing in quality women's evening wear, coats, sportswear, and dresses all at wholesale prices.

Fashion Party (593-2737), 49 Spadina Avenue (right down at Front Street; if you start tripping over the train tracks and fall into Lake Ontario, you've gone too far). This cleaned-up warehouse is a fun place to shop for great value in women's clothing and accessories. Designer labels and prices may be slashed, but the top-quality clothing is perfect. Most clothes here are at least 30 per cent less than their rich, still-labelled cousins at Creeds and Holt Renfrew. Unless *you* tell your friends where you bought it, they'll never know. In one room all the clothing is priced at 80 per cent off. They really do hold fashion parties in private homes, so the in-store stock is constantly changing.

Head back up Spadina, this time on the west side, for more bargains.

Stop first at **Rosebuds & Rascals** (598-4941), 49 Spadina. A high-style, trendy children's fashion discount house, with sizes from infants to 14. Run by fashion writer Audrey Gostlin, this store has a quick eye for the latest in innovative design. It's a must for the parent who wants to dress a prince on a pauper's budget. *We* certainly don't mind buying last season's fashions at a fraction of the retail price. Do you?

Just Kids, Inc. (363-5818), 138 Spadina. This wholesale store is always crammed with parents hunting through the racks of high-fashion and designer children's wear at 25 to 50 per cent off the retail prices. With such fabulous children's wear stores on Spadina, you've got to be crazy to buy retail.

Black Whisker Fashions II Imports (368-0668), 204 Spadina. A good shop for dressier women's clothing "au gout de Paris," as its sign reads. You have to hunt through a lot of ordinary merchandise, but a discerning buyer can definitely walk out with something unusually good. Don't let its rather dingy basement location turn you off the real bargains to be found.

Just up the street you can't miss the garish **China Court Mall** (366-2593), 208 Spadina. It's a rather seedy yet picturesque Chinese-style complex of specialty shops, complete with a covered Chinese bridge, which is perfect for the Chinese New Year dragon dance. It's fun to browse through the exotic, aroma-filled stores: a grocery selling Chinese frozen fast foods, bakery, candy shop, restaurant, kitchenware, gift shop, books and magazines, a Chinese hairdresser, even a Temple of Knowledge. You'll find almost everything Chinese you ever wanted to buy.

Paul Magder Furs (363-6077), 202 Spadina. New and used furs at reasonable prices.

Freda's Imports Inc. (593-0304), 300A Spadina just above Dundas. Here we come to one of our favourite women's clothing stores in the city. Freda Tordanous has been designing dapper uniforms for such institutions as the Ministry of Tourism, The McMichael Gallery in Kleinburg, Thomas Cooke, Ontario Place, and Budget Rent-a-Car for more than a decade. Recently, she has also returned to her first love, designing exquisite couturier clothes.

As you enter her beautiful little shop, you feel the bargain-basement atmosphere of Spadina Avenue slip away. Freda travels to Europe several times a year to personally select her fabrics. Here, in her Spadina shop, she fashions them into stunning garments at unbeatable prices. Freda's has been the haunt of our city's best-dressed bargain lovers for years.

Next, you run into **Switzers' Deli-City** (596-6900), 322 Spadina and **United Bakers Dairy Restaurant** (593-0697), 338 Spadina. These two Jewish havens of mouth-watering European delicacies are great places to recuperate from all your bargain shopping. And these places are bargains, too. It's Switzer's for meat, United Bakers for dairy, depending on your mood, religious persuasion, and philosophy regarding carnivores.

On our way north again, heading for the edge of the Spadina shopping district at College, we pass – and visit:

The Plaiter Place (593-9734), 384 Spadina. A treasure trove of all sorts of wicker furniture, baskets, and gifts.

Fortune Housewares (593-6999), 388 Spadina, is our favourite kitchenware shop in the city. They carry top-quality European pots, bakeware, woodenware, utensils, knives, and gadgets at very reasonable prices. The staff is extremely knowledgeable and more than helpful. There's a good selection of cookbooks, too, for those who wish to do more with the pots than hang them on the wall.

We now enter a strip of top-notch Chinese restaurants on both sides of Spadina; each serves delicious food at low prices. Our favourite remains **Szechuan Chungking** (593-0101), 428-430 Spadina, famed for its spicy chicken, if not for its spicy washrooms.

For a change of taste, try **Moishe's Tel Aviv Restaurant** (921-1917), 440 Spadina. This is a landmark on the Spadina strip, offering some of Toronto's best Jewish and Israeli food – great beet borscht and home-made soups, kreplach, blintzes, hummous, tahina, and falafel.

Gwartzman's Art Supplies (922-5429), 448 Spadina. For years, hungry artists and students have patronized this well-stocked store for its low, low prices.

And finally, almost at College Street, we reach the **El Mocambo Tavern** (961-2558), 464 Spadina, which (in spite of its appearance) is one of the major entertainment centres of Toronto. (See **Don't Knock the Rock**, pp. 218-221.)

Crest Grill (922-4715), 466½ Spadina, is a first-rate greasy spoon, with great people watching as well as cheap, homemade food. Frequented by local artists, and gamblers, this dive (complete with pinball machines), is authentic Spadina Avenue.

There you have it, the Spadina/Spadeena walk. To paraphrase the old New York rye bread commercial, You Don't Have to Be Jewish/West Indian/Portuguese/Chinese/Vietnamese/Spanish/Artistic/a Student/Hungry/Naked/to Love Spadina. Personally, we're rather glad that Mr. Baldwin lost his view of Lake Ontario.

TO MARKET, TO MARKET – KENSINGTON, THAT IS:
"SORRY, WE'RE OUT OF PIGEONS, TRY NEXT DOOR"

A delightful side tour off Spadina Avenue is the **Kensington Market**. After a morning on the hot (or snow-covered) pavement of Spadina Avenue, exploring the few square blocks that make up **Kensington** is a refreshing change. Here you'll find bargains too – but the edible kind.

All your senses will be titillated by this steamy, smelly, raucous, colourful European-style old marketplace. Come and explore, especially during warmer weather when the shops show their goods on the streets: Russian rye breads, barrels of dill pickles, fresh fish on ice, mountains of cheese, bushels of ripe fruit, and crates of chickens and rabbits. This is one area of Toronto where bargaining is socially acceptable.

Kensington market sprang up just after the turn of the century, when Russian, Polish, and Jewish inhabitants set up stalls in front of their houses. Since then, **Kensington Market** (named after the area's major street) has become a United Nations of stores. Unlike that organization, however, these people get along with each other. Some Jewish and Eastern European stores remain side-by-side with Portuguese, Caribbean, Latin American, and East Indian stores, with Vietnamese, Japanese, and Chinese stores sprinkled around the edges.

So enjoy. Enjoy the colour, the bustle and the mixture of smells, tastes, and languages as you eat and buy your way through **Kensington Market**. Most shops are open every day, except Sunday, from 6:00 a.m. on.

We begin walking west along Baldwin Street and step into **XOX Postcards** (596-8200), 140 Baldwin. This tiny shop is floor-to-ceiling with every imaginable postcard from the arty to the ridiculous. Get all nostalgic as you look over, and can buy, postcards that once took a nickel to buy, a penny to mail, and less than a month to arrive.

Then grab a mouth-tingling patty or roti at the **Kensington Patty Palace** (596-6667), at 172 Baldwin. It can't possibly be better in the Bahamas. Then cross the road to the south side, to **Lottman's Bakery** (593-0245), 18 Baldwin. Here you'll find all kinds of European and Jewish breads, pastries. Pick up some bagels and rolls to accompany some of the luscious cheese available around the corner. This is a great old-time bakery, putting out goodies far better than mamma used to make.

Turn left and walk south on Kensington Avenue, where you'll find a trio of creameries making beautiful music. The first you'll encounter is **The Global Cheese Shop** (593-9251), 76 Kensington, the cheapest and noisiest cheese store in town – mountains of cheeses and equally high, if less nutritious, levels of blaring music. You can taste everything before you buy, so go with empty stomach and full wallet.

You might pass it up and enter the quieter, cleaner and friendlier **Kaplan's Creamery** (593-9273), 74 Kensington. Their farm-fresh slabs of butter are delicious, and they carry some of the best cottage cheese in the city.

Daiter's Kensington Creamery (593-9281), 64 Kensington. The original, although they now have several branches uptown. All their dairy products are fresh and tasty, their yoghurt and creamed cottage cheese are superb, and they also carry a full range of deli take-out, including smoked fish, salads, and groceries.

Continuing south on Kensington Avenue, you pass a series of fruit and vegetable stores, crammed with the freshest of local produce and imported West Indian specialties. Further along, you'll find a few interesting shops sparked by the recent artsy renaissance in **Kensington Market**. They are tucked away among shady trees and freshly painted vintage houses.

Okamé (593-8879), 46 Kensington. A beautiful little gift shop specializing in Japanese antiques, folk art, and traditional crafts that predate the silicon chip and transistor. One of their specialties is authentic Samurai swords.

Courage My Love (979-1992), 14 Kensington. One of the area's busiest stores. Its long, crowded room bulges with recycled clothes from Victorian to New Wave, jewellery, buttons, and drawers full of paraphernalia from the bright lipsticks of the 50s to garter-belts and bow-ties.

Tiger's Coconut Grove (593-8872), 12 Kensington. A delicious Jamaican snack bar, which serves one of the best and most refreshing pineapple-coconut colada drinks in the city.

Kensington Silver Studio (596-8869), 2 Kensington. Attractive, hand-made jewellery, worth a look.

You're at the foot of the market at Dundas Street now, so grab a cheap and delicious *dim sum* bun at **Arc Court** (593-9235) on the corner and head back up to Baldwin Street. Continue further west, away from Spadina and deep into the market, to explore the copious fresh fish stores, poultry stores with their wares clucking from their cages on the street (it drives the animal protection people crazy), and bin upon bin of dried beans, seeds, fruits, and candies in front of the quasi-health-food stores.

We always buy the freshest of eggs at **Imperial Poultry and Egg Market** (593-9296), 191 Baldwin. They sell both product and producer. The freshest of fish is found at **Vieira Fish Market** (593-9255), 185 Baldwin. Kids love to watch the live fish swim about in the tank. Then try to explain away dinner.

Our favourite dried fruit and nut store is the **Casa Acoreana** (593-9717) at the corner of Baldwin and Augusta. "Come in and go with all the nuts!" their window sign invites. Take them up on it.

Stop for a hot bowl of delicious home-made soup at **Louie's Coffee Shop** (593-9294), 197½ Baldwin. You'll pick up local lore from the colourful proprietor Joseph Oksenhendler and fill your belly with scrumptious Jewish delicacies such as blintzes, knishes, potato latkes, and gefilte fish. Garish wall murals of the market hang over your head and almost into your soup. Louie even sells frozen yoghurt these days.

Around the corner, south on Augusta, you'll come across one of the best health-food bakeries in the city: **Kensington Natural Bakery** (598-0564), 193 Augusta. The breads and pastries are made from organic, stone-ground, whole-grain flours, baked fresh daily on the premises. They distribute their goods throughout the city in health-food shops, but here you get their delicious products fresh out of the oven. We're especially partial to their farmer's rye bread.

Heading north up Augusta, you enter Little Portugal with-out even crossing the Atlantic: shop after shop of Portuguese bakeries, fish stores, fruit stores, restaurants, and bargain dry-goods and clothing stores specializing in lace and crochet-work.

Try a yummy Portuguese bun, crisp on the outside and soft on the inside, at the **Iberica Bakery** (593-9321), 209 Augusta. And find any Portuguese foodstuff you may want at **Melos Food Centre** (596-8344), 151 Augusta.

And there are two very good Portuguese restaurants on Augusta: **Lisbon Plate** (593-9700), 184 Augusta. Two can eat well for about $20, and their business lunches still run under $5.

Octavio Restaurant and Tavern (924-6364), 277½ Augusta. Upstairs but worth the climb. As with most Portu-guese places, it is strong on seafood, and some claim that it has the best cod in the city.

By the way, lovers of religious architecture will want to visit the two lovely old synagogues in the market area: **Anshei Minsk**, at 10 St. Andrew's Street (which runs paral-lel to Baldwin, between that street and Dundas, running west from Spadina). Just a few short blocks away is the **Kiever Synagogue** at the corner of Denison Square and Bellevue Avenue, running south from College and closer to Bathurst.

Finally, you can rest your weary bones and stomach at a lovely little park, "Bellevue Square," at the corner of Deni-son and Augusta: shady trees, benches, a wading pool, and playground. You've earned it, after spending all that time in Toronto's United Nations – without starting a single war – we hope.

MIRVISH VILLAGE: THE ONE-BLOCK WALK (ALIAS THE SUNDAY LIFESAVER)

In the beginning was the Weird. And the Weird was **Honest Ed's**.

Some claim that Ed Mirvish invented the concept of the discount house; in fact, his mother did. Either way **Honest Ed's** is a sight to behold, if not buy in. "Ed's Wacky World," proclaims one side of the building. "Honest Ed's No Midwife-...But the Bargains He Delivers Are Real Babies!"

For thirty-five years, people have been flocking to the huge, barn-like building at the southwest corner of Bathurst and Bloor, often standing in line for hours to purchase the specials advertised in the previous day's newspaper: "Door Crasher Sale! Five Pounds of White Flour, 79¢!"

Enough of Ed's. There are more sedate pleasures around the corner; but all because Mirvish had a problem. You see he owned nearly all the houses on the first block of Markham Street, and was going to tear them down to make a parking space for the store. But zoning by-laws wouldn't let him. Our entrepreneur had to think up an alternative. And what a remarkable alternative it is.

Markham Street is now a unique shopping, dining, and artistic world with brightly painted bathtubs full of flowers and gaslight lamps lining the sidewalks. It has officially been declared a tourist attraction, meaning that the stores may legally be open on Sunday. A brief walk, south on Markham's west side and then north on its east side, is a worthwhile Sunday stroll.

Ed's Ice Cream Parlour boasts lots of flavours and good quality cold stuff, as well as hot stuff such as capuccino. It is filled with the knick-knacks that characterize Mirvish's giant restaurants down on King Street: Tiffany lamps and pictures galore. Park the kids there if they are old enough, while you continue on down to **Journey's End Antiques**, a huge establishment, followed by **The Plantation** (more antiques), and **Antiques-Gifts-Betty Engel**. For details on antique stores in the Village, see **The Oldest Walk in the World**, pp. 146-150. Then run back for the kids. **The Children's Book Store** is one of the world's largest bookstores for kids and a magnificent place to browse, buy, or collapse. Folksingers, artists, and writers for children often make personal appearances and sing, show off, or read from their work, usually on Sundays.

Then comes **Studio Jewellers**, with **Gallery Gabor** in the basement; **Doris Robertson Antiques**, and **The Canadian Centre of Photography and Film**. The CCP has major shows of world-class photography and it's well worth a visit.

Then you come to the most popular store in the village, **Memory Lane**. "Welcome to Yesterday" says the sign, and that is precisely what it does. Vintage movie posters, old comic books, and piles of magazines from the good old days make this place irresistible.

Stroll the full block to Lennox Street, where the residential homes begin. Before you turn north and go up the east side of Markham, note the wonderful house at the corner of Markham and Lennox. The hexagonal corner tower, the fine leaded-glass butterfly window to one side of its front door, and the stunning oval window on the other. It is old Toronto architecture at its most attractive.

On the east side of Markham is **King Fook Chinese Restaurant**, which can satisfy the nibblers, followed by **La Mode De Vija**. Well-known Canadian and American designer clothes are discounted year round and by as much as 70 per cent during its regular sales.

Then comes the **Mecene Gallery**, **The Green Iguana Glassworks**, **Carlo & Adelina's Place**, one of Toronto's most admired Italian restaurants.

The Wool Mill Shop is next up the street, followed by **Paris-Brest**, a French restaurant, and **Atticus Books**. **David Mirvish Books**, and **David Mirvish Books on Art** come next. For many people, they *are* Markham Street.

Mirvish's bookstores (yes, yes, David is Honest Ed's son) sell high quality at attractive, and sometimes bargain, rates. And the *Sunday New York Times* is cheaper than it is in New York.

Markham Village is not San Francisco's Pier 39 or Baltimore's Inner Harbor. But it *is* open on Sunday – a rare feat for any neighbourhood in Toronto, even in the 1980s. And considering the village is only one block long, even the weariest feet will go.

How to Get There:

Take a Bathurst bus or streetcar to Bloor, or take the Bloor subway to Bathurst. Then walk one block west to Markham Street. You'll recognize **Honest Ed's**, I can assure you. You can drive to the corner of Bathurst and Bloor, but then what? Parking is almost non-existent. You can risk parking on Bathurst Street or on Bloor, but after an hour you'll probably get a ticket, and after 4:00 p.m. on a weekday, your car will be towed away and held for ransom.

NORTH YONGE STREET: THE CALL OF THE NORTH

Just as New York City is filled with Manhattanites who refuse to believe that there is life after 92nd Street, there are thousands of Torontonians who claim with great pride that their noses bleed from the altitude north of Bloor.

They are denying themselves plenty. For anyone who wishes to escape the hustle of downtown Toronto, Yonge Street from Eglinton north makes for a refreshing afternoon stroll.

The area has changed over the years, as more and more

young families with cosmopolitan tastes have moved. Now, this tree-lined boulevard offers up some real treasures; dozens of stores and restaurants invite browsing, nibbling, and buying.

Friends who live in the area tell us that they never go downtown anymore, because these few short blocks are their own village: a police and postal station, movie houses, drug and hardware stores, elegant clothing shops, gourmet groceries, Chinese fruit stores – and best of all, some exceptional food and gift shops.

So stuff your credit cards into your wallet, and your kid in the stroller, and head up to Yonge and Eglinton. Just take the Yonge Street subway to Eglinton, or drive to the major intersection and park.

The **Yonge-Eglinton Centre** sits tall and proud at the northwest corner of those streets. In it are fine bookstores, a medium-sized Eaton's department store, dozens of specialty shops, and a world of ethnic and fast food on the subway level. It is worth a walk through, if nothing else.

Then come up for air and walk up the west side of Yonge Street. The first block you come to is Orchard View Blvd. Just a half-block in, on the north side, is the Northern District Library, one of the best public libraries in the city. It has a marvellous selection of books, a superb children's section, and it loans *free* thousands of 16mm films – even videotapes! Right below the library is a most pleasant restaurant, **Café Bibliothèque** (489-3215).

Desserts Desserts (485-1725), 2352 Yonge Street. Superior, superior. This has got to be the hottest dessert place in town. Five hundred varieties of cakes, pies, cheesecakes, and pastries are freshly baked on the premises. In summer, there's a charming outdoor patio. The place is licenced for drinks and also serves soups, salads, quiches that a real man could love, and omelettes.

Loh's Old Fashioned Homemade Ice Cream (487-1219), 2368A Yonge Street, lower level. One of the city's best ice-cream shops. The confection is made daily in full view in the store window, and you can taste the freshness and purity of the all-natural ingredients. From a delicate vanilla to the most exotic tropical flavours, this is ice cream nirvana! If you are not yet in a diabetic coma, move on to ... **Sloane's** (481-3230), 2442 Yonge Street. A moderately expensive ($50 for two for dinner), sophisticated *nouvelle cuisine* restaurant. If you're not hungry for a real meal yet, remember this nugget for the future.

Chocolate Squirrel (486-0512), 2460 Yonge Street. A great-smelling shop with reasonable and attractive edibles to take home as gifts. This first of four shops carries the finest of imported chocolates and candies gift-wrapped in glass or boxes, sure to please the chocolate addict.

Sperlings' Simply Splendid Food (482-8696), 2558 Yonge Street. An elegant restaurant where you can enjoy *nouvelle cuisine* and agree with their name. It's always crowded, but all their delicious cheeses, pâtés, soups, salads, and meats are available to take out for a picnic in one of the nearby parks.

The Little Pie Shoppe (485-6393), 2568 Yonge Street. Dieters beware. This is the lair of the best butter tarts in the city.

Upper Yonge Junction Trains and Hobbies (488-7141), 2582 Yonge Street. Pretend you're doing it for the kids. Lose yourself in the world of model railroads and wooden ships. The very helpful staff can show you all the accessories the model buff ever needs. Just bring along your dreams of adventure.

Rood's Pastry Shop (488-5813), 2620 Yonge Street. One of the country's great pastry shops in the tradition of elegant European baking. The cases are full of gorgeous concoctions with such fanciful names as Hazelnut Progress and Meringue Legs. They specialize in creating gorgeous custom-designed cakes for all celebrations, ranging from towering wedding cakes to hilarious and delicious incarnations of Big Bird and Oscar the Grouch.

Vittorio's Osteria (483-3694), 2637 Yonge Street. Across the road and heading back south toward Eglinton lies one of the city's best Italian restaurants. In Italy, an "osteria" is an unpretentious neighbourhood eatery, but the line-ups attest to the extraordinary quality of the food at **Vittorio's**. The menu is limited to ensure that everything will be given the proper attention. The pasta is a dream and the veal is so buttery you can cut it with a fork, if you would dare to be so presumptuous. About $50 for two, including wine.

Pastissima (482-4175), 2633 Yonge Street. Right next door to Vittorio's is this splendid pasta shop and specialty Italian food store. They have superb recipes printed up, so take home a bunch of their freshly-made-in-view pasta and try your own hand at Italian cooking.

Mullen & Cie (481-8889), 2615 Yonge Street. Rivaling Sperling's, this shop prepares elegant foods for take-out. Choose from among their hors d'oeuvres, soups, perfect pâtés and terrines, quiches, entrées, sensational salads, and desserts. You can't go wrong. Pick a beautiful day, walk in and buy yourself a glorious picnic to enjoy *al fresco*. It's expensive, but unlike many expensive things, it is well worth it.

Down to Earth Crafts (487-4252), 2597 Yonge Street. Now we hit a stretch of treasure-filled Canadiana craft shops. This is the first of them, filled with lovely Canadian crafts, clothing, hand-knits, fabrics, and notions.

El Cid (483-8185), 2579 Yonge Street. One of the city's better Spanish restaurants, the air is fragrant with parsley, garlic and olive oil, and the food is beautifully prepared. Sample such classic dishes as garlic soup, paella, and flan. About $35 for two.

Ontario Craftsmen (487-9327), 2533 Yonge Street. This long-established craft shop is a great place for foreign visitors. Here you'll find some beautifully hand-crafted wares to take home with you. All artifacts are made right here in Ontario. There's an excellent selection of Indian and Inuit crafts, ceramics, wall hangings, and jewellery.

Articraft Shoppe (487-8537), 2527 Yonge Street. Our favourite gift shop in this area. The owner, **Céline Wade**, has gathered together the handiwork of the finest artists from all over Canada and has put together beautiful one-man shows. You may find her stock is too good to give away, and end up indulging in gifts for yourself.

The Poke-About (489-3711), 2493 Yonge Street. A browser's paradise, crammed with inexpensive gift items: glass, brass and chinaware, place mats, stationery, puzzles, toys and stuffed animals, soaps and candles, paper party goods, and much more. There's something for everyone.

Oliver's (Bakery, 485-1051; Deli, 485-1066; Bistro, 485-1041), 2433 Yonge Street. A charming three-in-one food emporium that offers you eat-in or take-out baked goods and delicacies. Their home-made pasta, salads, pâtés, entrées, and pastries are delicious. Their cheddar cheese bread is legendary, and their croissants are among the best in town. If you don't walk out of Oliver's carrying a load of breads, you are either on a very strict diet or a glutton for punishment.

La Grenouille (481-3093), 2387 Yonge Street. Rest your weary feet! You've come to the end of our north Yonge Street walk, almost back where we began. If you still have room after all the tippling and tasting, this is a great place for dinner. It's a superb French seafood restaurant with reasonable prices. Frogs legs, as the name of the restaurant implies, is the specialty of the house. About $40 for two.

Enough.

THE OLDEST WALK IN THE WORLD: LOOKING FOR THE LATEST IN ANTIQUES

The *New Yorker* ran a cartoon that said it all: an old house sits on the end of a street. A large sign in front reads, "We Buy Junk and Sell Antiques."

Well, you can find lots of both in Toronto. It's impossible to keep up-to-date on Toronto's antique dealers: in 1982, the Toronto Antique Dealers Association listed more than two hundred dealers. But many of these may no longer be open by the time you read this book

You see, antique dealing is an unstable business, dependent on the vagaries of the economy more than most. Many dealers work in antiques only as long as they're enjoying themselves; many are retired or refugees from big business.

So what we've done is list accessible shops that have consistently offered quality antiques and interesting collectibles.

Markham Street (alias **Markham Village** or **Mirvish Village**), one block west of Bathurst running south from Bloor, is an antique hunter's paradise.

Journey's End (536-2226), 612 Markham Street. Overflowing with furniture, silver, glass, china, jewellery, paintings, and decorative items.

Doris Robertson Antiques (531-8064), 600 Markham Street. Antiques run the gamut from pine to art nouveau.

Upper Canada Antiques (536-8667), 588 Markham Street. Specializing in early Canadian furniture, they will also repair, restore, and refinish Grandma's rocking chair.

Plantation Antiques (533-6466), 608 Markham Street. Delightful antique collectibles from the old country, the United States, and Canada.

Some of Toronto's finest antique shops are on Bloor, on Avenue Road just north of Bloor, and farther up the street on the Davenport curve. It's all within walking distance of Bloor Street, which is easy to reach by either the University or the Bloor subway line.

Gold Shoppe (923-5565), 86 Bloor Street West at Bellair. Antique jewellery, diamonds, estate silver, china, and glass. The gold in its name tells only part of the story.

Ronald Windebank Antiques (962-2862), 21 Avenue Road in the Four Seasons Hotel. Specialists in pre-1870 furniture, porcelain, and all types of early brass and copper for kitchen and fireplace.

Stanley Wagman & Son Antiques (964-1047), 33 Avenue Road. Fine porcelain and silver, and furniture to put the porcelain and silver upon.

Carol Solway Antiques (922-0702), 88 Yorkville Avenue. Exquisite china and many items of furniture, also specializing in glass.

Michel Taschereau Antiques (923-3020), 194 Davenport Road. Canadian pine furniture and even more English and French furniture and porcelain.

Bergdon Galleries, Ltd. (924-3865), 180 Davenport Road. Almost next door to Taschereau and well worth checking out for sculpture, furniture, clocks, and more.

Navarro Gallery (921-0031), 33 Hazelton Avenue. Art deco and art nouveau.

Glen Manor Galleries (961-2286), 102 Avenue Road. Fine china, antique furniture, and art glass.

O'Neil Antiques (968-2806), 104 Avenue Road. Fine American and Canadian antiques, furniture, and accessories of the eighteenth and nineteenth centuries. No, you didn't have to be there.

On Queen Street, just west of University (easy to reach by the University subway line or the Queen streetcar), there is a strip of antique-and-collectible shops, loaded with junk and occasional hidden treasures. (See **Queen (Street) for a Day**, pp. 122-127 for specific recommendations.)

The Queen East-Jarvis-King area is another gold mine. The Queen streetcar or Yonge subway line will take you there.

Nitty-Gritty Antiques and Collectibles (364-1393), 111 Jarvis Street. Be sure to check out their very good selection of Canadiana furniture upstairs.

The Door Store (863-1590), 118 Sherbourne. Talk about truth in advertising! This shop has a large selection of doors and windows, most of them true antiques.

Brian Mitchell Antiques (361-0350), 187 Queen Street E. Fine English antiques and porcelain.

Antique Aid (368-9565), 187A Queen Street E. Fine antique and estate jewellery, porcelain, china, and silver.

Cathcart Antiques (368-4228), 246 Queen Street E. A good selection of collectibles.

Fine antique stores run up and down Yonge Street and its side streets, especially between Bloor and Summerhill. If you love antiques, you'll want to explore Yonge Street.

The Paisley Shop (923-5830), 889 Yonge Street at Davenport, about a kilometre (half a mile) north of Bloor. One of Toronto's longest-established antique stores; it has some of the best period pieces in the city.

Prince of Serendip (925-3760), 1073 Yonge Street. Odd

fixtures, iron and brass beds, and unusual decorator items, specializing in large Victorian light fixtures.

Now continue north to the CPR railway tracks. Just north of it is Birch Avenue, which runs west off Yonge. (If you are coming down Yonge, Birch is six blocks south of St. Clair.) Here you will find a cluster of antique stores.

White Swan Antiques (960-1417), 8 Birch Avenue. Antique nautical items, silver, and jewellery.

The Wildlife Gallery (922-5153), 18 Birch Avenue, **The Map Room**, and **The Marine Gallery**, are all housed in Exploration House, and carry some fascinating stock: antique maps, landscape and marine paintings, animals in art, scientific instruments, and antiques on nature themes from as far back as the sixteenth century, when Will Shakespeare was still knee-high to a pewter dish.

Fifty-One Antiques (968-2416), 20 Birch Avenue. No relation to Heinz 57. It covers three floors and specializes in seventeenth- to nineteenth-century English and continental furniture, paintings, and accessories.

And now back to Yonge Street, still heading north.

Perkins Antiques (925-0973), 1198 Yonge Street. Perhaps the best Canadiana antique store in town, with an excellent stock of furniture, ceramics, prints, and old English pewter.

Jack Morris Antiques (925-5541), 1212 Yonge Street. Decorative accessories, fine reproductions, and eighteenth- and nineteenth-century English and French furniture.

David Robinson Antiques (921-4858), 1236 Yonge Street. Specializes in antique lighting, fine reproductions, antique textiles, and antique clothing.

Wolfson Antiques (485-1047), 2003 Yonge Street a few short blocks south of Eglinton. Oriental objets d'art, Georgian silver, porcelain lamps, paintings, and fine antique furniture.

Maxine Treleaven Antiques (489-5855), 2523 Yonge Street. One km (half a mile) north of Eglinton, but well worth the trek. It's a lovely antique shop specializing in treen – beautifully finished woodenware – and nice, small pine and cherry Canadiana pieces. And you don't need to use silver polish on treen.

Heading back on Yonge just south of the train tracks is MacPherson Avenue, which runs west from Yonge. Here you'll find:

Sawtooth Borders Inc. (961-8187; 487-4728), 5 MacPherson Avenue. A little shop specializing in antique quilts. Its friendly owner, Gloria Rosenberg, will tell you anything you want to know about that art form. Her customers come from far afield for her expertise.

If you wander down to the foot of Yonge on your way to buy some goodies at the St. Lawrence Market, there's one more excellent shop to visit. **Town of York Antiques** (367-9627), 106 Front Street E. has fine Canadiana and folk art.

And down by the riverside:

Harbourfront Antique Market (363-9622), 222 Queen's Quay West. For a few hours of fun, don't miss Canada's best antique flea market held each Sunday. It has the atmosphere of a friendly village as more than two hundred (count 'em!) antique dealers spread out their wares on the grassy lawns by the lake each summer. In the winter, they move indoors. It's a wonderful place to bargain-hunt for antique clothes, furniture, folk art, quilts, old bottles, and comics. It's also a great chance to meet the rural Ontario dealers, many of whom you might wish to visit on their own territory. And part of the fun is picking through the junk. (You always wanted that February 9, 1958 issue of *Life* magazine, didn't you?)

There are several worthwhile shops uptown in the Eglinton-Mt. Pleasant Road-Bayview area. Here are a few:

Bernardi Antiques (483-6471), 707 Mt. Pleasant Road. Well worth peeking into.

Florentine Antiques (488-2762), 703 Mt. Pleasant Road. Fine eighteenth- and nineteenth-century furniture and antiques. There are many excellent small pieces for apartments.

Lorenz Antiques (487-2066), 701 Mt. Pleasant Road. Eighteenth- and nineteenth-century furniture, silver, china, pottery, and crystal.

Wellington House Militaria (489-4885), 615 Mt. Pleasant. Specializes in military medals, badges, posters, and militaria of all nations. Maybe you can get a purple heart without being wounded.

Vintage Radio and Gramophones (481-6708), 1661 Bayview Avenue. As its name implies, this shop specializes in old radios, wind-up gramophones, and telephones. The next time a friend brags about his latest stereo equipment, show him the oldest mono around.

Where the Auction Is

Sotheby Parke-Bernet (Canada) (596-0300), 156 Front Street W. After Christie's, the most prestigious and longest-lasting auction house in the world. Next to Prince Charles and Lady Di, the 1964 marriage between New York's Parke-Bernet and Sotheby's of London may be the most joyous union of our era. The items are Canadian only. The two auctions a year in each area – Inuit (Eskimo) and Indian art, and Canadian art – are very special occasions. You'll see books, maps, prints, paintings, sculpture, and much, much more. This is the Rolls Royce of auction houses, but you can frequently knock down excellent goodies at Honda Civic or even 1956 Dodge prices.

Waddington McLean (362-1678), 189 Queen Street East. The firm goes back to 1850, even if some of its highly uneven merchandise does not. Probably the largest auction house in Toronto, it has regular sales every Wednesday and Saturday mornings, with items ranging from junk to junk to real finds. What am I bid on the latter?

D. & J. Ritchie (364-1864), 429 Richmond Street East. Known for fine art, antiques, and furnishings, auctioned and appraised.

Robert Deveau Galleries (364-6271), 299 Queen Street E. Auctioneers and appraisers of antiques, fine art, and Oriental rugs.

Gallery Sixty-Eight Auctions (421-7614), 3 Southvale Drive, east of Bayview and south of Eglinton. Well and widely loved because they can be counted on to carry top-name works of art. Customers, including famous ones, come up from the United States for the auctions. And you can be put on their mailing list incognito, without even having to prove you're famous.

Art galleries, both commercial and public, advertise regularly in the Saturday *Globe and Mail* and *Toronto Star*. Be sure to check the *Globe*'s art page every Saturday for the dates and places and offerings of the various auction houses. It's in the entertainment section, and there is no better place in the city to discover what's coming up on the block. Indeed, it should be your head if you miss Sotheby's rare auctions or one of Gallery Sixty-Eight's remarkable evenings. But remember, try not to wave to a friend across the auction room – you may find yourself the less-than-proud owner of a Victorian fourteen-piece tea service, which you had always managed to do without.

TORONTO'S BOOKSTORES:
WHERE THE BEST-READ PEOPLE
BROWSE

Maybe Toronto's Marshall McLuhan was right – maybe we *have* moved into a post-printed-word age. Yes, kids don't read as much as they used to; yes, Canadians, like our unfrozen neighbours to the south, watch TV more than twenty-five hours a week and read less than an hour or two.

Still, try sniffing a VTR. Or running your hands lovingly over the microchips of an Atari. It can't be done.

Books, on the other hand, are warm to the touch and pleasing to the eye. And if they are getting just a bit expensive, you can always wait for the paperback, when it will cost nearly as much as the hardcover.

Toronto is rich in bookstores. They sell new books, used books, best sellers, and remainders (those books that either didn't sell very well, or did, but went into paper before the hardcovers sold out). There are national and local chains and then there are the specialty book shops – only antiquarian or travel books, or how-to, or sci-fi, or....

This is only a selected list, of course, but it is a start. Readers, unite. You have nothing to lose but your ignorance, your pre-conceptions, and breathing room in your den.

The National League

Coles – The Book People. Bookselling in the finest supermarket tradition. It is the largest bookstore chain in Canada, and one of the largest in the world. You'll not only find the latest and not-so-latest best sellers, but art supplies, stationery, and bin after bin of remainders. There are more than 150 **Coles** outlets across the country, so you'll probably trip over a few in Toronto, even when you're not looking for them. There's a **Coles** at 299 Yonge Street (977-4549); in the Eaton Centre (979-9348), and in many shopping malls.

Classic Bookshops. Less frenetic, more traditional than Coles, and with higher quality books, this is the finest of the big chains. Their largest store is at 285 Yonge Street, just below Dundas (977-1912). Some other locations are: 131 Bloor Street W. in the Colonnade (924-8668); the Royal Bank Plaza opposite Union Station (865-0090), the finest business-book selection in the city; five outlets at the Toronto International Airport, and one in most shopping malls in and around Toronto. Many are strong in photography, fiction, poetry, psychology, and computers. Lots of remainders as well. Clean, well-lit places, all.

W. H. Smith. The legitimate child of the venerable English chain, which has over a dozen stores in Toronto. Good, solid, middle-of-the-road selection as well as the latest periodicals. Bright, breezy, and handy. Locations include the Eaton Centre (979-9376); Hudson's Bay Centre at Bloor and Yonge (967-7177); 1500 Yonge near St. Clair (923-4608); First Canadian Place at King and Bay (862-7933), and the Toronto Dominion Centre just across the way (362-5967).

Local Pleasures

The World's Biggest Bookstore (977-7009), 20 Edward Street, just west of Yonge and one block north of Dundas. It is actually a child of **Coles**, but it definitely deserves its own listing. Its name does not lie. More than a million books are literally piled on seventeen miles of shelves on two floors. It reeks of supermarket (although it was actually born a bowling alley), and it is a bit intimidating, as I suppose any place the size of two football fields would be. Remainders by the tens of thousands, garish black-and-white signs screeching out the section headings; but lots and lots of bargains. It is the CN Tower of bookstores.

The Book Cellar, pun intended. Lovely, loving local stores. The fine choice of classical records and superb selection of political and intellectual journals make them favourites with many. At 142 Yorkville (925-9955) and 1560 Yonge near St. Clair (967-5577). The background music and the wide aisles welcome you to the world of fine books.

Bob Miller Book Room (922-3557), at 180 Bloor Street West just west of Avenue Road. Downstairs on the lower concourse of an office building, it is well worth the extra steps. The clientele is primarily from the University of Toronto, and you'll find the best literature selection in the city here. The staff has been with Bob for years, and so have his thousands of grateful customers.

The Albert Britnell Book Shop (924-3321), 765 Yonge Street. Just above Bloor and, fittingly, just down from the Metro library. It is a Toronto legend, now run by its third generation of the Britnell family. Many of the staff have stayed with the Britnell's for more than a quarter-century. You will find care (and a search service) that are rare anywhere. Marvellous ambience, great browsing.

SCM Bookroom (979-9624), 333 Bloor Street West, between University and Spadina. One of the major stops for U. of T. students, religious scholars, and laymen. Begun over a quarter-century ago by the Student Christian Movement, it is a non-profit collective, offering ten per cent discounts on many books, and devoting its entire basement to theological topics.

Book City (961-4496), at 501 Bloor Street West near Bathurst. Strong on good, remaindered books, with a fine choice of magazines. Usually open late into the night, with a knowledgeable staff and great browsing.

Specialty Bookstores – New and Not Quite

The Children's Book Store (535-7011), 604 Markham

Street, just west of Bathurst and south of Bloor in Mirvish Village. This is a magical place. Besides its beauty and wondrous size, it has magnificent pop-up books (many on a table for kids and adults to destroy before buying one that works), fiction, picture books, and collections on everything from where babies come from to dinosaurs to being a kid caught up in a divorce. There are frequent readings by internationally known children's authors. Owners Judy and Hy Sarick have created the largest, best-stocked bookstore of its kind on this kid-obsessed globe. There is no condescension here, only knowledgeable staff who understand and love children and the literature they long for.

The Children's Book Store also has the best selection of records for children you will find anywhere. Many of them are Canadian: Sharon, Lois, and Bram; Raffi; Jerry Brodey; Bob Schneider; Ken and Chris Whitely. No one who buys records with any of those names on the cover will ever, ever be sorry.

Lindsay's Books for Children (968-2174), 110 Bloor Street West near Avenue Road. In the lower level of one of the handsomest new structures in the city, this is a good bookstore for children. It's strong on science, history, sports, music, and hobbies, from ballet to stamps.

Longhouse Books (921-9995), 630 Yonge Street, a few blocks south of Bloor, is unique and remarkable. It stocks only Canadian titles – over twenty-thousand back titles and new publications on every subject. The respect and love for Canadian writers and writing is palpable, and if you can't find that obscure, small-press collection of Canadian poems here, it doesn't exist.

David Mirvish Books on Art (531-9975), Markham Street. Just across the street from **The Children's Book Store**. If your kids are civilized, leave them reading Judy Blume while you sneak across the street and plough through the piles of top-quality remainders and often wildly discounted, new best sellers. Magnificent art books, catalogues from art galleries and museums around the world, cookbooks, Judaica, Canadiana, world literature, and film. Beautifully lit, well laid out, and begging you to browse.

Edwards Books & Art now has three locations: 356 Queen Street West near Spadina (593-0126); 421 Bloor Street East at Sherbourne (961-2428); and 2301 Yonge Street, just above Eglinton (487-5431). Much like David Mirvish's fine store, this chain advertises huge discounts on best sellers and remainders each Saturday in *The Globe and Mail*. Gems are often to be found in their many out-of-print books.

Can-Do Bookstore (977-2351), 311 Queen Street West, is the only one of its kind in Canada, and stocks more than 17,000 titles for the mad, obsessed do-it-yourselfer. How to cook, fix up your bathroom, play the drums, sail a yacht, start a business – and, if that doesn't work out, how to go bankrupt. Crafts, hunting, fishing – you name it.

This Ain't the Rosedale Library (368-1538), 110 Queen Street East, a few blocks east of Yonge. They have the largest selection of baseball books in Canada. Not a mass-market store, but strong on rock and jazz books, poetry, and small-press Canadiana. And how can you resist a place that answers its phone, "This ain't the Rosedale library!"

Toronto Women's Bookstore (922-8744), 85 Harbord Street near Spadina. Strongly feminist in orientation and the best place to discover the latest works on women's political and legal issues, divorce, childbirth and abortion, the woman's body, and non-sexist books for children. Macho men may feel uncomfortable, but at least the store will raise their eyebrows, if not their consciousness.

Bakka Science Fiction Book Shoppe (596-8161), 282 Queen Street West. The largest science-fiction and fantasy bookstore in the country. Rare books and posters as well.

Theatrebooks (922-7175), 659 Yonge Street below Bloor. An astounding collection of plays from around the world, and large sections on make-up, sound, lighting, production, costume design, film, dance, opera, and acting technique. To buy or not to buy, that is the only question.

Cobblestone Books (366-4867), 92 Queen Street East. The largest and most distinguished selection of remaindered books in the city. Let's face it: isn't it nicer to have *Garp* in hardcover for $2.98 than in paperback for $3.25?

Librairie Champlain (364-4345), 107 Church Street. The best French-language bookstore in the country, over 125,000 books, many for children.

Even More Specialized Bookstores
Open Air Books & Maps (363-0719), 10 Adelaide Street East. In the lower level of an office building, it is the oldest travel bookstore in Canada. More than ten thousand Fodor, Frommer, Baedeker and Michelin guides, oodles of atlases and road maps, and specialized travel books. Lots of nature and food books as well, and lots of surprises.

Gulliver's Travel Book Shop (537-7700), 609 Bloor Street West. Just down the block from Mirvish Village, it is a fine bookstore worthy of its name.

Hortulus Books (960-1775), 101 Scollard Street. More than you ever wanted to know about landscape architecture, flowers and plants, agriculture and gardening. Most of their stock is out of print titles and you're not likely to find them anywhere else.

Science Den (924-8895), 50 Cumberland Street. Add science to your den. **Sleuth of Baker Street** (483-3111), 1543 Bayview Avenue below Eglinton, will not be mysterious to anyone interested in its wares. **Ballenford Architectural Books** (960-0055), 98 Scollard Street. The largest selection of titles on architecture in the country. **Nautical Mind** (869-3431), fittingly found down near the lake at 245 Queen's Quay West. All there is to know about sailing, ships, and sea.

Used, Rare, and Antiquarian Books: For People Who Don't Watch TV

Queen Street, running west from University to Spadina, is a treasure trove of used-book stores. Here are a few:

Gail Wilson – Bookseller (598-2024), 198 Queen Street West. A good selection of paperback and hardcover books, strong on fashion, folklore, technology, agriculture, plus a general stock covering most subjects.

Village Book Store (598-4097), 239 Queen Street West. Specializes in illustrated books and out-of-print Canadian art books, as well as books on antiques and book collecting.

About Books (593-0792), 280 Queen Street West. Strong on modern literature and first and special editions.

Arthur Wharton Books (593-0582), 308 Queen Street West. Specializes in science fiction, history of science and technology, railway books, and general fiction.

Abelard Books (366-0021), 519 Queen Street West. A strong emphasis on literature, classics, religion, philosophy, music, and film.

Here are some others:

Old Favourites Bookshop (977-2944), 250 Adelaide Street West, just east of Spadina. More than a quarter-million used books, magazines, and journals. Books are piled everywhere, but carefully catalogued and fairly priced.

David Mason (922-1712), 638 Church Street below Bloor. Overflowing with the finest rare and out-of-print books. Collectors from around the world come to pay homage to Toronto's finest bookstore of its kind. Anyone who is looking for pre-1900 literature or anything of an antiquarian nature can do no better than make this pilgrimage.

Atticus Books (922-6045), 698 Spadina Avenue, and (533-7540), 589 Markham St. Between them, more than 35,000 used books on academic subjects, as well as antiquarian books.

Alphabet Bookshop (924-4926), 656 Spadina Avenue. Well stocked with modern literary works and first editions. Lots of paperback fiction and Canadian studies.

Acadia Bookstore (364-7638), 232 Queen Street East. Specializes in rare books, and has a good selection of Canadiana.

Fifth Kingdom Bookshop (929-5649), 77 Harbord Street. Should satisfy any warlock with its mystical and metaphysical books, astrology, current consciousness, health, and healing.

Most Every Newspaper in the World, so You Can See What's Happening Back Home

Lichtman's News & Books can be found at 595 Bay at Dundas in the Atrium (591-1617); at 34 Adelaide Street West near Yonge (368-7390); at 1430 Yonge Street just below St. Clair (922-7271); and in the Bayview Village Shopping Centre at Bayview and Sheppard (221-5216). Here is where you'll find not only best sellers but magazines, and the widest selection of newspapers from around the world, often only a day old.

THE CULTURE VULTURE

Back in the 1950s C.P. Snow described "the Two Cultures" of Art and Science – and warned that we would be in Big Trouble until the two started a warm, lasting dialogue.

Well, C.P., we're doing our best. In this chapter, you will not only find Art (the Art Gallery of Ontario; theatres and concert halls; orchestras, operas, and ballets), but Science as well (a planetarium, an observatory, and the amazing Royal Ontario Museum, where Evolution rubs shoulders with Greek vases – art and science together in a mixed metaphor).

Alas, culture is almost a dirty word. Visiting a museum is often like eating your vegetables, not fun, but good for you. Yet Toronto is so rich in museums of all kinds, many both sympathetic and even encouraging to kids, that we do not hesitate in recommending the following – and sensible shoes.

THE ROYAL ONTARIO MUSEUM: MEET YOU AT THE DINOSAUR

"ROM wasn't built in a day," the fund-raising signs declared. Give to the **Royal Ontario Museum**, they cried. We need your help!

Boy, did they. Although The Canada Council once called the ROM "Canada's single greatest cultural asset," it certainly wasn't treated that way. When it opened in 1912, the sinking of the *Titanic* the same day pushed it off the front page, and it's been a bit like that ever since. By the 1970s, the Museum facility was becoming senile: the building at the corner of Avenue Road and Bloor Street had no climate control, and thousands of artefacts were in danger of turning to dust – except when it rained: then very tasteful buckets would appear at strategic spots on the top floor, just in case.

There was no space for the more than six million items. From a four-hundred-piece collection of New Guinea masks, drums, and bone daggers, to a settee and chairs from the court of Louis XIV (much coveted by the Louvre), to ancient Chinese tomb figures – the ROM simply had no place to show them all.

They do now. Or rather, they are doing it now. After closing down for eighteen months, the **Royal Ontario Museum** finally reopened its first galleries in late 1982.

HENRY
MOORE

Regular phases will continue to open until the 1990s at a total cost of over $60 million. When completed, the ROM will be the second largest museum in North America, next only to New York's Metropolitan Museum of Art.

The Royal Ontario Museum is unique in that it has science and art and archaeology all under one roof. Yes, it will still have every kid's favourite – the dinosaurs. And it will have such creative displays as the **Gallery of Evolution**, which will depict the development of life on earth and show a short film on how Darwin got his bright idea on his voyage to the Galapagos Islands.

How do we love the ROM? Let us count the ways: A mineral collection that is one of the best in the world. More than one million insect specimens. Giant Ming tomb sculptures from seventeenth-century China. **The Discovery Room**, a fascinating hands-on learning experience for children (and adults) over six. There are now atriums, seats to collapse in every now and then, a pleasant restaurant, access for wheelchairs, and some inspired ways to eliminate "museum fatigue." (That's when the visitor feels as if he's been pummelled to numbness by information. And don't say you've never felt it.)

One of their answers was **Mankind Discovering**, at the entrance of the ROM – a gallery about the museum itself designed to catch your interest, whet your curiosity, and help you choose what you want to see, with a minimum of sensory overload. No, ROM was not built in a day, and it will be another decade before all the new phases are completed. But we're willing to wait. In the meantime, any time is the time to visit the ROM.

How to Get There:
Take the Bloor subway to Bay; exit at Cumberland and walk one block south. Better yet, take the University subway to the Museum stop. There is very little parking in the area, so beware of private transport. Phone 978-3692 for further information. The museum is open seven days a week; senior citizens get in free every Tuesday.

CANADIAN CONTENT: THE CANADIANA GALLERIES

The **Canadiana Galleries** are part of the **Royal Ontario Museum**. Here is where you can see early Canadian furnishings, glassware, and silver, and six settings of furniture in displays typical of eighteenth- and nineteenth-century homes of Quebec, the Maritimes, and Upper Canada.

How to Get There:
The Canadiana Galleries are located in the Sigmund Samuel building at 14 Queen's Park Crescent West, just west of the Parliament buildings. Take the University line subway to the Queen's Park stop; get off at the northwest corner, and it's just about a five-minute walk. If you drive, there is some expensive parking in the hospital lot just south and east of University and College. Call 978-3692 for further information. The hours are Mon.-Sat., 10:00 a.m.-5:00 p.m.; Sun., 1:00-5:00 p.m.

THE ART GALLERY OF ONTARIO: MOORE THAT MEETS THE EYE

The best part of the **Art Gallery of Ontario** is not even inside the building. It's Henry Moore's sculpture "Two Forms," which Moore-haters, Moore-lovers, and especially kids, find irresistible. Everyone longs to climb in and around and out of it, but only the kids dare. It's an inspired, painless way to introduce kids to art.

From its extremely modest beginnings in 1900, the AGO has recently moved into the big league, in terms of exhibits and support. Its membership numbers about thirty thousand, which is the highest per capita in North America. And recent international exhibits featuring King Tut, Vincent Van Gogh, Turner, Judy Chicago, and William Blake have strengthened the gallery's image and raised its profile.

The **Art Gallery of Ontario** is housed in a new, gleaming white building, built on the smaller, dingier, old one, and occupies an entire city block of Dundas Street, two blocks west of University and just east of the heart of Chinatown. It is pleasantly laid out and doesn't give off those dreadful "Do Not Touch" vibrations that so many museums and galleries do. (Indeed, there is a "Hands On" room on the lower level for children, open on Sundays, summers, and holidays. There they are invited to play with different textures, sculpt, paint, make slides, and creatively muck about, while one parent gets a chance to escape and get some culture.)

The Henry Moore Sculpture Centre on the second floor has the largest public collection in the world, thanks to the British sculptor's generous donation of millions of dollars' worth of sculptures, casts, drawings, prints, and other materials spanning over half a century of his prolific career. Moore's close and warm relationship with the AGO goes back to when the city fathers refused to put up public funds to purchase his Archer (now firmly ensconced in front of the

New City Hall). The people decided to fight City Hall, raised the money privately, winning the affection – and plasters – of Moore ever since.

Also on the second floor is the **Samuel and Ayala Zacks Wing** with its fine collection of twentieth-century sculpture. **The Canadian Wing** features works from its three-thousand-item collection including major works by such Canadian painters as Emily Carr, Cornelius Krieghoff, David Milne, Homer Watson, and a broad selection from the Group of Seven.

While the AGO is not the Met or the Museum of Modern Art, it does possess major works by Tintoretto, Rubens, Rembrandt, Hals, Van Dyck, Hogarth, Reynolds, Augustus John, Picasso, De Kooning, Rothko, Noland, Oldenburg, and many others.

Apart from the art, the AGO has a fine continental and fully licenced restaurant, and one of the best fine-art bookstores in Canada. And visit the gorgeous historic house, **The Grange**, directly behind the art gallery; see **Great Buildings** (page 61) for further information on this delightful place.

How to Get There:
Take the University line subway to the St. Patrick station, then go three blocks west by foot or streetcar to McCaul Street. The hours are: Tues., Fri., Sat., and Sun.: 11:00 a.m.-5:30 p.m.; Tues. and Wed.: 11:00 a.m.-9:00 p.m. Closed Monday. Admission is free to everyone on Thursday evenings from 5:30-9:00 p.m. Phone 977-0414 for information. There is no parking for visitors, alas. Find a meter on the streets in the area or park in the garages behind the Mt. Sinai Hospital or in the Village by the Grange complex, on McCaul.

ART FOR ART'S SAKE: TORONTO'S FINEST AND MOST INTERESTING GALLERIES

Toronto is a highly cosmopolitan art centre, second only to New York City. More than three hundred commercial art galleries are listed in the yellow pages, offering every kind of art for viewing and sale from Picasso to Warhol, from classic to Inuit and Indian, from representational to my-five-year-old-can-do-better-than-that.

The following galleries are our personal favourites, listed by locale, so you can aesthetically leap from gallery to gallery with the ease of Mona Lisa's smile, which is not on sale in Toronto. The most exciting galleries in the city are those exhibiting modern works, and our selection reflects this bias. We've also left out some fine galleries that are somewhat off the beaten track, but once you've made it through these, you'll be enough of a connoisseur to track down the rest.

Most galleries are closed Mondays and open Tuesday to Saturdays, 10:00 a.m.-5:00 p.m. Call first to double check.

Many interesting galleries are located in the Bloor-Yonge-Yorkville-Hazelton-Scollard-Prince Arthur area, so head there first:

Gallery Moos (922-0627), 136 Yorkville Avenue. In 1959, German-born Walter Moos came to fill an important need: a gallery for contemporary art in Toronto. Moos is one of the deans of art in our city, and a great promoter of Canadian art. He is a very discerning, knowledgeable, reliable dealer, whose second-floor gallery has Picassos, Chagalls, Miro's, and Dufys, as well as the works of such internationally admired Canadian artists as Gershon Iskowitz, Ken Danby, Sorel Etrog, and Jean-Paul Riopelle.

Galerie Dresdnère (923-4662), 12 Hazelton Avenue. Created in 1960 by an ex-Montrealer who, like Walter Moos, saw an increasing interest in art in Toronto. Having owned a gallery in Montreal Simon Dresdnère can present the best art from that great city. Galerie Dresdnère can be counted on to show a fine selection of Canadian abstract and conceptual paintings, as well as graphics and wall hangings.

The **Pagurian Corporation Limited** (968-0255), 13 Hazelton Avenue, is a three-storey house overflowing with remarkable Canadian art, ranging from paintings by Krieghoff and prints of Kurelek to early Canadian maps and antique harpoons. A fascinating place to browse or buy, and to broaden one's views.

Nancy Poole's Studio (964-9050), 16 Hazelton Avenue. The gallery represents, among others, a vital school of art from the London, Ontario area, two hours west of Toronto. Her annual folk art show is superb, and she handles one of Canada's recently discovered major talents, the Indian woodcarver, Joe Jacobs.

The Glass Art Gallery (968-1823), 21 Hazelton Avenue. This is the only gallery of its kind in Canada, and it's a very exciting showroom of avant-garde work. You'll see stained glass, blown glass, laminated and crystal sculpture, and you'll be stunned by their beauty.

Mira Godard Gallery (964-8197), 22 Hazelton Avenue is the place to encounter major Canadian artists such as Alex Colville, Kenneth Lochhead, David Milne, Jean-Paul Lemieux,

Charles Gagnon, and Christopher Pratt. You'll also find exhibitions of the work of such important international artists as Max Bill and Barbara Hepworth. Another former Montrealer who has graced our city and made it an artistically richer place to be, Ms. Godard's gallery is as beautiful as the art she displays.

Waddington & Shiell Galleries (925-2461), 33 Hazelton Avenue. The galleries are beautifully designed, typical of Toronto at its renovating, revitalizing best: an historic building made attractively viable for works from Noland to Matisse, with Inuit art as well, and many contemporary Canadian painters.

Sable-Castelli Gallery Ltd. (961-0011), 33 Hazelton Avenue. In the same building as Waddington, it is one of the most exciting galleries in the city, specializing in top Toronto artists and fine Americans as well. Through his association with the renowned New York art dealer Leo Castelli, Jared Sable has been able to honour his walls with the works of such figures as James Rosenquist, Claes Oldenburg, Jasper Johns, Frank Stella, and Andy "famous-for-more-than-fifteen-minutes" Warhol.

Gallery Quan (968-7822), 112 Scollard Street. A fairly new gallery, but it has already begun to make wonderful artful waves, thanks to Eva Quan. There are two galleries here: one is an experimental space called the **Street Gallery**, where they feature photography, video and performance art, xerography, installations, and works by new artists. In the upper, main gallery, they have a stable that includes William Ronald, David Partridge, David Blackwood, Kosso Eloul, as well as newer artists such as Christopher Broadhurst, Robert Kost, and the exceedingly popular Brian Marshall-Schieder.

Marianne Friedland Gallery (961-4900), 122 Scollard Street, is run by a refined, highly knowledgeable specialist in late-nineteenth-century prints and graphics. She also displays major works of African art, as well as such twentieth-century masters as Avery, Calder, Dubuffet, Hofmann, and Miró. This is one of the finest places in Toronto to stop, look, and ask. You'll always get an answer.

Gallery One (929-3103), 121 Scollard Street. Renowned for its excellent colour-field painters from the United States and Canada, such as Larry Poons, Jules Olitski, and Douglas Haynes. They also carry contemporary Canadian photography, landscape, and Inuit art.

Bigué-Osler Galleries (968-2970), 160 Davenport Road. Just up the street from Scollard, this is a warm, welcoming gallery, specializing in comfortable, rural landscapes from Quebec. Here, you'll find modern Montreal paintings that are still recognizable, yet vibrant and expressionistic.

Carmen Lamanna Gallery (922-0410), 840 Yonge Street. The most avant-garde dealer in the city, Carman Lamanna has an unerring eye for new talent. He specializes in conceptual art, much of which is not visually appealing, but is intellectually challenging. Some of his featured artists are David Rabinowitch, Colette Whiten, and Ian Carr-Harris. It is not surprising that many of Lamanna's clients are curators of public and commercial galleries around the world.

Isaacs Gallery (923-7301), 832 Yonge Street. Avrom Isaacs was the guiding force of the Toronto art scene in the 1950s, and continues to be one of our most respected dealers. He was one of the first to show abstract and expressionist art, and gave tremendous support to non-objective art when Canadians did not yet dare to buy it. Many of those he's shown have since become well known: William Kurelek, Robert Markle, Michael Snow, Mark Prent, Gordon Rayner, Joyce Wieland, Greg Curnoe, and Dennis Burton.

Roberts Gallery (924-8731), 641 Yonge Street. It is the oldest gallery in the city, and sells more traditional Canadian art. For everyone who knows that the Group of Seven is not a rock band, this is an excellent place to visit.

The Innuit Gallery of Eskimo Art (921-9985), 9 Prince Arthur Avenue. Just a block north of Bloor and west off Avenue Road, this is the finest gallery of its kind. From Frobisher Bay to Baker Lake, Resolute Bay, and Fort Chimo, the finest of Eskimo art can be found right here, way down south in Toronto. Prints, drawings, sculpture, wall hangings, and antiquities are all beautifully displayed.

Albert White Gallery (923-8804), 25 Prince Arthur Avenue. The place to go in Toronto to buy the work of famous British artist Henry Moore. But Calder, Lichtenstein, and Picasso have also been viewed here. Mr. White also has great interest in Pre-Columbian and African art. The gallery is nothing if not eclectic.

Kaspar Gallery (968-2536), 27 Prince Arthur Avenue. More traditional than most, the gallery shows Group of Seven painters, as well as very representational work from nineteenth- and twentieth-century Canadian artists.

Graphics: Someday Your Prints Will Come

There are many print shops in Toronto, but we recommend two that offer modern and affordable, top-quality graphics.

Gallery Pascal (977-4021), 334 Dundas Street W., right

across from the Art Gallery of Ontario. This was the first gallery in Canada to specialize in contemporary Canadian original prints. The special nature of the place grew out of Doris Pascal's fervent belief that art should be affordable, not only for the rich.

Marci Lipman Graphics (922-7061), 231 Avenue Road, two blocks north of Davenport. Hundreds of prints and posters to choose from; wonderful, colourful, and pleasure-full prints by Canadian and American artists, some for as little as $25.

Off the Beaten Track, But Well Worth The Trip

Jane Corkin Gallery (979-1980), 144 Front Street West, sixth floor. A very special place, out to prove – and it has proven it – that photography is a major art form. From Robert Bourdeau to André Kertész to Richard Avedon, this is one of the most thrilling galleries in town.

Klonaridis Inc. (979-1090), 144 Front Street West, sixth floor. Run by Alkis Klonaridis, a young dealer of discerning taste, the gallery displays local talent and imports some of the newest and best from New York and elsewhere south of the border. This place is a must for those interested in new, exciting art.

Bau-Xi Gallery (977-0600), 340 Dundas Street West, opposite the Art Gallery of Ontario. Founded by an artist and dealer from Vancouver, Paul Wong, the gallery provides a window on contemporary Canadian west-coast art, much of which is easily affordable.

Wynick-Tuck Gallery (364-8716), 80 Spadina Ave., 4th floor. They represent Canadian contemporary artists whose work expresses a wide range of untrendy, often imagistic concerns. Most of their artists over the years have become well established, which attests to the importance of this gallery.

Olga Korper (363-5268), 80 Spadina Ave., 4th floor. Korper is one of the most accessible and knowledgeable dealers in Toronto. She's a trail-blazer who has discovered important artists, including Patrick Tribert, Agnes Ivan, Anat Brink, and Helen Sebelius. This is a fine place for beginning collectors to visit.

Yarlow-Salzman Gallery (598-4644), 185 Richmond Street West. One of the best collections of vintage and modern photography in Toronto: Brassaï, Walker Evans, Eugene Atget. Drawings, prints, paintings, and sculpture by people like Saul Steinberg (of *New Yorker* fame) and Jasper Johns have also been displayed.

THE MCMICHAEL CANADIAN COLLECTION: MUSÉE DE BEAUX-ARTS, EH?

The popularity of the **McMichael Gallery** in Kleinburg, just north of Toronto, is illustrated by the predicament of the local businesses when the gallery closed its doors for renovations in late 1981 and did not reopen until almost a year later: the excellent, nearby **Doctor's House and Livery Restaurant** saw sales drop by fifty per cent. The rest of the village estimated they lost more than $2 million during that fateful year.

The reasons why the McMichael attracts nearly 300,000 visitors annually are many: the charm of Kleinburg; the natural sanctuary on the crest of the Humber River valley where the gallery stands; the building itself, constructed from native stone and hand-hewn timbers; and, most important, the remarkable art of the **Group of Seven** painters and some of their contemporaries.

The Group of Seven were a gathering of talented young men who began to look to the Canadian landscape for inspiration back in the early decades of this century. This might not seem revolutionary to us today, but at a time when nineteenth-century British styles were still holding the colonies in an artistic stranglehold, it was a great leap forward.

Tom Thomson, one of this country's most exciting artists, worked in a studio cottage that has been relocated on the grounds of the gallery. Although not one of the Seven, Thomson "opened the doors of the wilderness" to his artist friends, **Frank Carmichael, J.E.H. MacDonald, Frederick Varley, A.Y. Jackson, Arthur Lismer, Lawren Harris**, and **Frank Johnston**. These men, like Thomson, captured the passion and fury of the raw and powerful Canadian landscape.

Many of the more than eight hundred works of art on display at the McMichael will thrill and inspire you, especially those of **Thomson** and **Emily Carr**. You'll also enjoy the works of **David Milne, Clarence Gagnon, J.W. Morrice**, and bold Inuit carvings.

An added plus is the brief, pleasant ride up from Toronto and the gorgeous country setting, where you can picnic, wander about, and enjoy a taste of the country that so inspired these painters. Many people stop off at the McMichael Gallery on their way to commune with nature. Therefore, weekdays (other than Monday, when it's closed) are the best time to visit the gallery and avoid the crowds.

How to Get There:
Take Highway 401 to Highway 400. Go north on 400 to the second interchange, Major Mackenzie Drive. Follow the McMichael signs to the village of Kleinburg. Phone 893-1123 for further information.

THE MCLAUGHLIN PLANETARIUM: STAR LIGHT, STAR BRIGHT

Did you know that our sun is about five billion years old? (It has only about another five or six billion years to go, so you'd better live it up.) Did you know that some stars are as hot as 20,000 degrees while our sun is only 6,000 degrees on its surface? Did you know that if our sun were to be divided into one million equal parts, every one of those little suns would still be bigger than earth?

If you didn't know those things, you'd better scamper on down to the McLaughlin Planetarium.

Planetariums are an acquired taste, like wine, golf, and Terminal Two at the Toronto International Airport. But what makes them irresistible is the fact that you can see hundreds of comets, galaxies, nebulae, and stars without incurring frost-bite, just leaning back in plush, comfortable chairs.

Nearly half a million people have enjoyed Toronto's planetarium since it opened in 1968. It's the largest of its kind in Canada, and in terms of size and facilities, one of the better ones on this globe. The only stipulation that **Robert Samuel McLaughlin** made when he gave $2 million from his earnings as the head of General Motors to the city of Toronto, was that it be the best. And if it is not the best in the world, it is certainly close.

The stars in a planetarium show are not real, of course; they are images of light beamed from a 1500-watt lamp at each end of a massive projector. Only about half of those stars are projected at any one time, which still beats what your naked eye can pick up in a real sky under ideal conditions. Nine thousand stars as well as such favourites as Mercury, Venus, Mars, Jupiter, Saturn, the moon, and the sun are created for you by 150 lenses. Hundreds of projectors hidden around the base of the dome 23 metres (75 feet) high serve to create such thrilling special effects as spacecrafts, black holes, and (gulp!) alien landscapes.

The planetarium shows, all produced by the planetarium staff, take three to four months to create, which means there are up to four new shows a year at the McLaughlin. You might see comets falling, the movements of the planets around the sun, star clusters, meteor showers, and oodles of galaxies that make you feel even smaller than your older brother can. There have been shows on the Star of Bethlehem, astrology, space travel, and much more. Check the advertisements in the Toronto papers for times.

Also in the **McLaughlin Planetarium** is **Laserium** which is especially popular with teenagers and quite remarkable. Two krypton lasers are placed in the centre of the planetarium so 360 spectators can ogle the kaleidoscope of patterns and colours created by projecting a laser beam through scanners, filters, and prisms onto the huge dome. It's all brought to you by the laser beam, which transmits phone messages, cuts out tumours, zaps TV and radio broadcasts, and, with the help of the boys down in Washington and the Kremlin, allows for warfare in outer space. How nice to see a scientific discovery used not only for peaceful purposes but for entertainment, too.

All the crazy colours and patterns and circles and squares and slashes and splotches are accompanied by loud music – rock, waltzes, Vivaldi, the Beatles, and synthesizer – assisted by one of the finest audio systems in the city. The laser-for-fun was created in California by a cinematographer, who put on the first show of its kind in 1973. Since then **Laserium** has been seen in one version or another by more than four million people around the world.

Toronto's **Laserium** is the only one in Canada, and the shows tend to be crowded. It's family entertainment, but children under six are not permitted. Anyone under fifteen must be accompanied by an adult.

Senior citizens may see the planetarium show free each Tuesday.

The **Planetarium** number is 978-8550; for information on **Laserium** shows, call 598-1866.

How to Get There:

The **McLaughlin Planetarium** is located just south of the **Royal Ontario Museum**. Take the University line to the Museum stop. If you drive, there is a parking lot just north of Bloor on Avenue Road and lots just east of Avenue Road along Bloor. But they are expensive.

THE DUNLAP OBSERVATORY: AN ALL-STAR CAST

The existence of the **David Dunlap Observatory** is thanks to a newspaper article. In 1926, the wealthy and recently widowed **Jessie Donaldo Dunlap** read an article in a local magazine bemoaning Toronto's lack of an astronomical research centre. Mrs Dunlap decided to build a memorial to her late husband that would fill this need and also acknowledge his lifelong fascination with astronomy. A site on Yonge Street about fifteen miles north of the University of Toronto was chosen, and the dome was erected on the highest point of land. Constructed in 1935, the Dunlap remains to this day the largest astronomical observatory in Canada.

Children and adults alike will be fascinated by the photos of sunspots, nebulae, and galaxies; but the big thrill comes when you are led outdoors to the domed observatory. The entire upper structure of the dome enclosing the seventy-four-inch reflecting telescope can be rotated and opens to the sky. You climb a ladder and peek through the twenty-five ton telescope at the planet, star, or moon that is "playing" that night.

Remember, visitors are admitted only in large groups on Saturday night from mid-April to early October. (But no tours take place on long weekends.) But individuals or small groups who call for reservations can join the next tour that has the space.

To arrange a visit, call 884-2112 to request the time you want. Admission is free and children accompanying adults are welcome. It can get extremely chilly on that hill and under the unheated dome, even in midsummer. Dress warmly for your close encounter.

How to Get There:

Drive north on Yonge Street to Highway 7 and continue north for three kilometres (two miles). You'll see the large white dome on your right. Drive just past it and turn right on Hillsview Drive.

THE MARINE MUSEUM OF UPPER CANADA:
SEND IN THE MARINES

Near the eastern entrance of the Canadian National Exhibition grounds and open year-round is an interesting little museum that is a lot more fun than it sounds. Their brochure claims that the Marine Museum "is devoted to the waterways of Central Canada and the Great Lakes-St. Lawrence System, with emphasis on the development of shipping." Sounds like pulling teeth.

But give it a visit. It's actually housed in the last remaining building of the historic Stanley barracks, built way back in 1841, and the history of shipping, from Indian canoes to massive twentieth-century tankers, is fascinating and informative.

Viewing an early trading post, relics from sunken ships and ancient diving gear is irresistible. So is the 27-ton steam engine taken from a Great Lakes ship. And how about the tug *Ned Hanlan*, named after the famous athlete and oarsman whose family gave its name to one of the Toronto Islands? It's a 24-metre (80-foot) steam tug that served the islands for three decades before being dragged along and across Lakeshore Boulevard to its eternal resting place. In the summer, a tour of the old dry-berthed tug is included in the price of admission. Come on over, landlubbers; you don't even need deck shoes.

How to Get There:
Take the Bathurst streetcar (Number 511) down into Exhibition Place, or walk through the Princes' Gate and on to the parking lot. If you drive, come west on Lakeshore Boulevard, through the gate at Exhibition Place, and then west to the parking lot. During the run of the CNE, leave the car anywhere and take public transportation. Phone the Toronto Historical Board (595-1567) for information. If you're hungry, try the **Ship Inn**, a licensed restaurant within the **Marine Museum**, open for lunch, Monday-Friday, year-round.

LITTLE MUSEUMS AND GALLERIES: PUTTING THE "AMUSE" BACK IN MUSEUMS

Museums need not be overwhelming and intimidating. Check out some of these charming little museums that take the "Where do I begin?" out of gallery-going.

Metro Police Museum (967-2688), 590 Jarvis Street near Bloor. You'll find old uniforms and lots of good info on how police catch criminals today. There are displays of some of the murders and crimes in this safest of all cities. Or so we thought. There is one catch: tours are conducted only for groups of twenty or more, by appointment. And the minimum age is fourteen. We don't want to give little Johnny any ideas, now, do we?

The **Redpath Sugar Museum** (366-3561), 95 Queen's Quay East down by the waterfront. We know, we know. Sugar is dangerous, deadly, bad for the heart, and delicious to boot. But our dentist asked us to include this item.

But there's more to sugar than cavities. The six display areas of the **Sugar Museum** are bursting with facts, not all of them pleasant. Sugar harvesting's connection with the slave trade is shown through pictures and documents. Vintage sugar tools are everywhere – beet toppers and sugar-loaf breakers. And a twenty-minute film, *Raising Cane*, is a lot of fun to watch. The curator of the museum is always there to answer questions from "What is sugar?" to "Is it true that Nathan Pritikin has a contract out on my life?" to the latest refining processes.

The **Redpath Sugar Museum** is open Monday-Friday from 10:00 a.m.–noon and 1:00 p.m.–3:30 p.m. You can park in the lot at the west gate and check in with the guard. He can be found just east of the Toronto Hilton Harbour Castle by the lake.

The **Puppet Centre** (222-9029), 171 Avondale Avenue, two blocks south of Sheppard running east from Yonge. The only major puppet centre in Canada is housed in a former public school, which was closed down in 1980 when someone realized that Canadians had stopped having babies.

More than four hundred puppets from all over our globe are exhibited, showing the four major types: hand, marionette, rod, and shadow. (Bet ya didn't know that!) You'll see rod-and-hand puppets from the USSR, ornate Chinese hand puppets, Punch and Judy puppets from France, Italian paladins (wooden knights), and lots more. You might feel nostalgic when you see Howard the Turtle from the old TV show *Razzle Dazzle*, and the original Fitzgerald Fieldmouse from the *Maggie Muggins* show, both on the CBC in its early years.

If you phone ahead, you might be able to put together a formal tour, which is very worthwhile. The museum is open weekly, but we won't promise there are no strings attached.

The **Beth Tzedec Museum** (781-5658), in Beth Tzedec Congregation, 1700 Bathurst Street, a few blocks south of Eglinton. What began as a branch of the much-admired Jewish Museum of New York City, now contains some of the finest artefacts by and about Jews outside Jerusalem and Manhattan: ancient glass, pottery, coins, Hanukkah menoras (candelabras), mediaeval spice boxes (to usher out the Sabbath), illuminated marriage contracts, and much more.

It's a stunning little museum inside the synagogue building, and echoes thousands of years of culture.

The **Museum of the History of Medicine** (922-0564), in the Academy of Medicine, Toronto, 288 Bloor Street West, traces the science back to the Indian medicine man, when it was an art. It looks at the history of pediatrics and the study of disease in ancient humankind. Here you will see an appendix removed a century ago; a phrenology bust that purportedly showed how your personality was determined by the bumps on your head (if you were mugged, you probably became even more interesting); a chloroform mask, and many other highlights from the days preceding socialized medicine. Admission is free, and the people there are always happy to answer your questions. We promise it won't hurt.

The Toronto Sculpture Garden, 115 King Street East, is an open area that has been welcoming picnickers since the fall of 1981, and more formal feeders since the fall of 1982 when an onsite restaurant opened. The outdoor sculpture garden is walled in on three sides, which undercuts the open-air feeling. But the concept is wonderful: to take art to the people – out of the museums and into the streets, almost. Only a few short blocks from Yonge and Front streets, the **Toronto Sculpture Garden** is within easy walking distance for thousands of Torontonians and visitors. If the weather is decent, it's worth a walk around. The admission is free, of course; the gates to the garden are open all day.

Out Of Town But Not Too Far

The **Canadian Automotive Museum** (1-576-1222), 99 Simcoe Street S., Oshawa, about 48 kilometres (30 miles) east of Toronto. More than five dozen motor-driven machines of different varieties covering two floors – almost bumper to bumper. You'll see a Ford tank truck from 1918, the world's only 1903 Redpath, Colonel Sam McLaughlin's McLaughlin-Buick, and more recent beauties.

Display of Dolls (1-727-9729), 157 Yonge Street N., Aurora, due north of Toronto along Yonge Street. This is a very personal little museum. Mrs. Ritchie has more than eight hundred dolls on display from her collection of two thousand. She will repair dolls and make wigs and dresses for yours. Bring your doll for identification or repair. But be prepared to leave it there for a while. It takes time to fix it right!

Museum of Time (1-705-458-9221), #5 Sideroad, east of Cookstown in Innisfil Township, about 56 kilometres (35 miles) north of Toronto along the 400 Highway. Here you can view about one thousand watches and clocks, with a father-and-son team giving ninety-minute tours of their stunning collection. Call ahead to make sure they are home. And for heaven's sake, be on time.

Ontario Electric Railway Historical Association (1-519-856-9802), on the east side of the Guelph line (exit 38 along the 401), about 14 kilometres (9 miles) north of 401, less than an hour west of Toronto. This place might make a pleasant stop to or from the African Lion Safari, should you be in the mood to see forty-two old streetcars, of which fourteen actually move and slide along. There are two car barns and a station dating back to 1912, and you can jump aboard an old trolley and ride on two loops over thirty-eight acres. And don't miss the **Trolley Extravaganza**, on the last Sundays of June and September, when they run all fourteen cars all day! The low admission is good for *all* rides.

Canadian Warplane Heritage Foundation (1-679-4141), at the Hamilton Civic Airport, just west of Hamilton off Highway 2. Here you lovers of the wild blue can see displays of aviation memorabilia and a number of aircraft used by Canadians before, during, and after the Second World War and the Korean War. More than twenty of these beauties are actually still airworthy, and another twenty are being restored to fly at airshows. They *will* get off the ground, Orville. There are picnic grounds, and sightseeing rides are offered by three flying schools in the vicinity.

Ontario Agricultural Museum (1-878-8151), about five kilometres west of Milton, Ontario, which is 56 kilometres (35 miles) west of Toronto. A lovely place for people who just can't get enough of Black Creek Pioneer Village and the Riverdale Farm. There is a crossroads community, two farmsteads from the nineteenth century, lots of sheep, poultry, goats, and horses, and oodles of farm machines, all spread out over eighty acres. You can buy small lunches, but you may wish to bring your own picnic.

THE METROPOLITAN TORONTO LIBRARIES: WORDS, WORDS, WORDS – AND A LOT OF BOOKS, TOO

We know, we know. Your city has libraries, too. But Toronto really does have some remarkable libraries, with some remarkable architecture and remarkable services. And here are some remarks about them:

The **Metropolitan Toronto Library** is probably the handiest library in existence, being just one block north of Yonge and Bloor in the very heart of the city. And it is a welcoming place. Physically stunning, it has none of that foreboding "Abandon stupidity, all ye who enter here" quality of many major libraries. The street level is really a storefront, inviting you in with a newspaper-reading room, an orientation area, a display gallery, and even an area where snackers may snack and smokers may cough.

Arranged around an interior atrium, which is open to all five floors (zooming up ten storeys), it gives a glorious sense of open space, miles of windows and skylights and lots of hanging plants. The library structure was designed by one of Canada's most admired architects, **Raymond Moriyama**, who also did the science centre. You really should visit. This isn't just a library; it's an experience. Here are a few facts that might make that experience more memorable.

A fascinating fabric sculpture,"Lyra", designed by artist **Aiko Suzuki**, overhangs the pool and waterfall in the foyer. The concept was to create a transition from the hustle and bustle of Yonge Street to the quiet atmosphere of a library. The sculpture took eight months to complete, and the library is delighted to report that Suzuki walked more than 400 km (250 miles) back and forth in her studio to create it.

Glass-enclosed elevators rise swiftly and silently up the side of the atrium, and you can admire the beautiful banners that hang from the ceiling, poetically and visually announcing all the collections. Each banner has a fitting, often profound illustration; the one for science and technology has a drawing from Goethe's *Theory of the Evolution of Plants*.

And for those of you who like statistics, the book capacity is 1,220,750 volumes, spread out on 45 km (28 miles) of shelves. Browsers will be ecstatic to learn that fully one-third of these books are on open shelves, which can provide hours, indeed decades, of unexpected pleasures and surprises. And in one of the audio carrels, you can slide on headphones and listen to any one of ten thousand record albums. A musical world of your own just a few feet from the busiest corner in Toronto.

The **Arthur Conan Doyle Room** houses the finest public collection of "Holmesiana" anywhere. There are records, films, photos, books, manuscripts, letters, even cartoon books starring Sesame Street's Sherlock Hemlock. For detective story aficionados, this is the place.

What other city has a library that is a tourist attraction and information centre and hideaway as well?

How to Get There:

The library is at 789 Yonge Street. Just take the Bloor subway to Yonge or the Yonge line to Bloor, and walk up one block. The main phone number is 928-5150, and the switchboard can give you the number to the various departments or connect you. Look up Public Libraries in the telephone directory to reach them directly.

The **Spaced-Out Library** houses the largest public collection of science fiction material in the world, thanks to the kind donation of thousands of items by the world-renowned sci-fi author, anthologist, and critic Judith Merril.

Lovers of science fiction will find this branch of the Toronto public libraries a treasure trove: more than twenty thousand novels, short stories, plays, poetry, tapes, and magazines. Sci-Fi may be found in Russian, Japanese, German, French, Danish, and Italian. There are more than seven thousand different magazines, including occult ones dating back to the 1940s, and a complete collection of *Galaxy*. There are books by Jules Verne, illustrated books by Magritte, Dali, and Escher, Buck Rogers comic strips from before the Second World War, papers on the Loch Ness monster, and much, much more. This place is truly spaced out, and a joy.

How to Get There:

The Spaced-Out Library is located at 40 St. George Street just above College on the second floor of **Boys and Girls House**. Take the College streetcar from the Yonge or University line subways west to St. George. It's closed on Wednesdays, and in August when we assume the staff blasts off. Phone 593-5351 for information.

The **Osborne** and **Smith Collections** at **Boys and Girls House** are world-renowned collections of kids' books. Dr. Edgar Osborne, a British librarian, presented his private collection of about two thousand children's books to the Toronto Public Library in 1949, trusting the colony of Canada to do well by it. They have indeed, building the collection to more than twelve thousand volumes.

The earliest book is a fairy tale printed in 1476; there are letters written and illustrated by **Beatrix Potter** of Peter Rabbit fame; and you can see the earliest Canadian picture book, *An Illustrated Comic Alphabet*, drawn in 1859. Stand in awe of the book recommended for good, Puritan children: James Janeway's *Token for Children: being an exact account of the conversion, holy and exemplary lives and joyful deaths of several young children*. It literally scared the hell out of them.

Little Goody Two-Shoes is an actual children's book, and you'll thank heaven for Dr. Seuss when you read such didactic rhymes as this one about a brother and sister who ate some wild berries:

But long they had not been at home
Before poor Jane and little Tom
Were taken sick and ill, to bed
And since, I've heard, they both are dead.

That'll teach 'em!

The Osborne Collection has books from 1476 to 1910, and the **Lillian H. Smith Collection**, set up to celebrate the fiftieth anniversary of children's libraries in Toronto, covers 1911 to the present. As with the **Spaced-Out library**, the books here do not circulate, but you'll find more than enough to keep you interested, if not shaken.

How to Get There:

The collections are in the **Boys and Girls House**, 40 St. George at College, the same building as the **Spaced-Out Library**. Phone 593-5350 for information.

Films and Video Cassettes Available

Like all major cities, Toronto has little local libraries sprinkled throughout the city and its suburbs. But it does have one superb service that must be publicized: it lends 16 mm films and sometimes video cassettes at no cost. The films are lent for twenty-four hours, and easy-to-use sound projectors may be rented for a service charge, should you need one. There are over fourteen thousand films – one of the largest film collections in North America.

And what films! Dozens and dozens of full-length classics, from *Citizen Kane* to *The Battleship Potemkin* to *The Night of the Living Dead*. Hundreds of classic cartoons. A historical collection of shorts and documentaries, many from the National Film Board – the list goes on. Here are the libraries that lend 16 mm films (all have catalogues of their holdings for your perusal).

North-Central Toronto:

Toronto Public Library, Northern District branch (484-8250), 40 Orchard View Blvd. near Yonge and Eglinton.

North York Film Library (222-9011), 5145 Yonge Street.

York Public Library (781-5208), Main Library, 1745 Eglinton Avenue West near Dufferin.

East End:

East York Public Library (425-8222), S. Walter Stewart Building, Memorial Park and Durant Avenue near Coxwell.

Scarborough Public Library, Albert Campbell District Library (698-1191), 496 Birchmount Road near Danforth.

West End:

Three branches of the Etobicoke Public Library:

Albion Library (741-7734), 1515 Albion Road near Highway 427.

Richview Library (248-5681), 1806 Islington Avenue above Eglinton Avenue West.

New Toronto Library (252-7254), 110 11th Street near the Lakeshore and Royal York Road.

All these films are available to adults who live, work, or study in Metropolitan Toronto.

LIVE AND IN PERSON

O'Keefe Centre (766-3271), at Front and Yonge Streets. Home of the Canadian Opera Company and the National Ballet of Canada. It is also home to visiting comedians, pre-Broadway musicals, Neil Simon comedies, road shows from Britain and the United States, Anne Murray, and almost anyone who can fill it. We've seen the film *Napoleon* there, and even Janis Joplin.

When the O'Keefe Centre was built, its 3,167 seats made it the largest concert hall on the continent. The acoustics leave much to be desired, and its cavernous nature makes almost anything but the most lavish opera or musical seem dwarfed; but you'll certainly feel like you are going to a cultural event. Even if it *was* Janis Joplin.

The O'Keefe is owned by the city now, and it generously offers half-price seats for students and senior citizens for many of its shows. It's hardly a beautiful structure, and it will forever look as though it was built in 1960 for $12 million (it was). But it is one of Toronto's major theatres, and with the explosion of culture here, it has been, and is, most welcome.

Just across the street from the O'Keefe Centre is another major theatre, helping to make Front Street a tiny mini-Broadway. The **St. Lawrence Centre for the Arts** (366-7723) was opened in February 1970, and it immediately showed itself to be sensitive to the concerns of the community it was to serve: its first public use was a forum in the **Town Hall**, its smaller stage, on the most controversial issue of the day – the possible building of the Spadina Expressway. Hundreds had to be turned away.

But more than theatre is offered at 27 Front Street East: **Music at the Centre** has become the largest and one of the most popular programs of its kind in Canada. Over the years, in the **Town Hall**, violinists of the quality of **Nathan Milstein**, pianists of the renown of **Alfred Brendel** and **Anton Kuerti**, ensembles of the calibre of the **Amadeus** and **Orford** quartets and the **Beaux Arts Trio** have shown off their talent.

Centre Stage Company also has a public affairs program, **Forum**, which takes place up to two dozen times a year in the **St. Lawrence Centre Town Hall**, at no cost.

In the early 1980s, the **St. Lawrence Centre Theatre**

was renovated. It reopened in March 1983, and the new effects – expanded lobby facilities, more seats and better acoustics – should add to the major role the Centre's two halls play in our city's cultural life. Amen.

How to Get There:

The St. Lawrence Centre is located on Front Street at the corner of Scott, just a block east of Yonge. There is parking on the Esplanade, but taking the subway to Union station or King is easiest. Phone 366-7723 for further information. The daily newspapers announce current and upcoming events.

The **Royal Alexandra Theatre** (593-4211) is literally a jewel. You can find it at 260 King Street West, just west of University and across the street from the new Roy Thomson Hall. Built back in 1907, the "Royal Alex" was the place to be seen in Toronto.

With very good reason. The plush red seats, the gold brocade, the baroque swirls and curlicues, the box seats to the left and right of the stage, the two balconies from which you can easily get a nosebleed – all this makes theatre going a refined experience.

Not surprisingly, all this magnificence was about to be torn down in the 1960s, but was rescued by none other than Honest **Ed Mirvish** of discount store and Mirvish Village fame. He not only restored the theatre to its former glory, but he even made it a profitable venture, which is more than any *government* could have done.

In 1982 Mirvish bought another theatre (but don't try walking to it) – the famous **Old Vic** in London, England. He beat out several London interests, in a stunning victory for Canadian Imperialism.

If you wish to see plays that reflect Toronto or Canadian culture, you'll have to go to the smaller, alternative places listed below. But the Royal Alex gets the big road shows, the British musicals, the Broadway dramas, and rarely, a local production. Ah well, it's still a beautiful, beautiful theatre.

Alternative Theatres

Tarragon Theatre (531-1827), 30 Bridgman Avenue. One block east of Bathurst and north of Dupont is an unpleasant area of railroad tracks and old factories. But don't judge by appearances. It's also the natural habitat for indigenous Canadian theatre. Almost anything worthwhile in our drama first saw the light of day here.

Theatre Passe Muraille (363-8988), 16 Ryerson Avenue. Another unfashionable part of town: one block east of Bathurst, north from Queen Street West. This has long been the home of collaborative theatre, much of it very successful, very Canadian, very good. Certainly one of the best, most innovative little theatres in Canada.

Toronto Free Theatre (368-2856), 26 Berkeley Street. One block west of Parliament and just south of Front Street. Although the admission is no longer free, it remains free-wheeling and fascinating, and has seen most of Canada's finest performers and playwrights showing their wares.

Toronto Workshop Productions (925-8640), 12 Alexander Street. The most accessible location of the alternatives – two blocks north of Carlton, just east of Yonge. Over the years, it has done very important, highly creative Canadian work.

Bathurst Street Theatre (535-0591), 736 Bathurst Street. This one-time church has converted to theatre space – but the gods remain. It's very handy, just one block south of Bloor and Bathurst (around the corner from Honest Ed's and Mirvish Village). The premises are used by dance groups and some of the better theatre groups in the city. The pews aren't very comfortable, but at least they don't stop in the middle and pass the hat.

Bayview Playhouse (481-6191), 1605 Bayview Avenue, three blocks south of Eglinton. A pleasant, comfortable theatre used by a number of local companies and road shows.

Theatre Plus is a company that has provided reliable, occasionally fine, productions of world drama mainly during the summers at the **St. Lawrence Centre** (366-7723), on Front, east of Yonge.

The Village Gate Toronto (927-9010), 410 Sherbourne Street, between Carlton and Jarvis Streets. This is the most recent addition to Toronto's entertainment/theatre scene. A Canadian branch of the world-famous New York club, it began its northern incarnation in March of 1983 with proven material: *One Mo' Time!*, the largest-grossing off-Broadway show in history. Very wisely, the owners have included a dining area and a cabaret on the premises, so Name Artists will be appearing late at night following the major musical shows. Local jazz and comedy personalities also perform late into the night, in their cabaret lounge.

Adelaide Court Theatre (363-1031), 57 Adelaide Street East, just east of Yonge, one block above King. Once the city hall for the Town of York, the building has been lovingly restored into two theatres. It is used by a number of various theatrical troups, including **Le Theatre Du P'Tit Bonheur** (363-4977). A real live French-speaking theatre troupe, which can be counted on to perform the latest and best plays from *la belle province*. Parlez-vous français?

Alumnae Theatre uses a beautiful converted **Firehall** (364-4170), at 70 Berkeley Street, just a block up from Front Street, west of Parliament. Over the years, this has been a trustworthy place to see interesting, occasionally experimental plays.

Hart House Theatre (978-8668), is smack in the middle of the University of Toronto campus, just off Queen's Park Crescent W. Amateur, student, and occasionally professional productions here have given Torontonians the chance to see daring, often highly controversial (and uncommercial) plays, usually at low prices. It's the main theatre space of the university.

Second City is in the **Old Firehall Theatre** (363-1111), 110 Lombard Street. This is where most of the geniuses of SCTV cut their teeth, and its revues tend to be the most reliable comedy in town.

Skylight Theatre runs only in the summer. More's the pity. Founded in 1980 by young Toronto directors, it obtains grants from Metro Toronto, the city of North York, and the Ontario Arts Council – which means it's free for you and me. In its first three seasons, **Skylight** (named because it uses an open-air stage in a North York park) presented productions of *The Little Prince*, *Frankenstein*, and *The Three Musketeers*, which were more satisfying than almost everything we've seen at Stratford and Shaw over the years. Excellent performing, stunning visuals, superb direction – **Skylight Theatre** is already a Toronto highlight.

There are two catches. One: It could rain. And two: you'll probably be so impressed with the production you'll want to donate a bit to support them. You could do worse.

How to Get There:

Skylight performs in **Earl Bales Park** (781-4846); take the Bathurst Street bus to about a mile north of the 401 and enter at Bainbridge, a few blocks south of Sheppard Avenue West. If you drive, go along the 401, then north on Bathurst.

Young People's Theatre Centre (363-5131), 165 Front Street E. near Sherbourne, eight blocks east of Yonge. When it opened back in 1977, the theatre printed thousands of buttons reading "I'm a Young People." They drove English teachers crazy, but it was worth it.

At last, after years of hard work and prayer, Toronto finally has the only theatre centre in the country devoted solely to children. But unlike purveyors of much of traditional kid's fare, this place does not condescend or compromise its dramatic integrity. There have been musicals, kid classics, puppet shows, concerts, and such broader-than-just-for-the-prepubescent shows as *Twelfth Night*, *Romeo and Juliet*, and *The Diary of Anne Frank*. Housed in the 1883 stables of the TTC, it is a warmhearted place to visit and support. Upstairs, above the main stage, is the **Nathan Cohen Studio**, named after Canada's greatest theatre critic, who supported children's theatre for years. Down in the lower level are hideaways where kids can run about and grab a nosh.

How to Get There:

Take the Yonge subway to King Street, the King streetcar east to Sherbourne and walk south one block. There is a new, very large and very cheap municipal parking lot which can be entered along the Esplanade near Yonge. It's worth walking from.

There are other small theatres and cabarets in Toronto; they are listed in the daily newspapers and magazines. And there are two out-of-town theatres that are very much part of the Toronto, as well as the Canadian, cultural scene.

Out-of-Town Theatre Festivals

The Stratford Shakespeare Festival was mocked by the brilliant Canadian theatre critic Nathan Cohen as "Canada's most untouchable sacred cow." In some ways he was right. Since its much-heralded opening in 1953 (with imported stars **Alec Guinness** and **Irene Worth**, imported director **Sir Tyrone Guthrie** and imported costume designers, etc. from Mother England), the festival became a kind of theatrical black hole, sucking up performers and interest from the then-just-borning theatre scene in Toronto.

Over the years, there have been some stunning shows, and just as many overblown, overpraised, overdesigned ones. But it *does* perform all the plays of Shakespeare and many other world dramas as well – if rarely anything Canadian. It's almost a ritual to go up to Stratford; it's a lovely two-hour drive along 401 west, then up Highway 8 to Stratford. And with the innovative work done in the smaller theatres, the **Avon** and the **Third Stage**, Stratford remains a major part of our theatrical scene and self-image.

The season usually runs from May through October; phone 363-4471 in Toronto for pamphlets, prices, and maps.

The Shaw Festival in Niagara-on-the-Lake has grown from its modest beginnings in 1962 to be a worthy challenger to Stratford for Toronto dollars and support. Like Stratford, the Shaw can be fearfully uneven. Since it traditionally limited itself to the plays of George Bernard Shaw and his contemporaries, it rarely had the chance to do anything else, until recently. (Besides, Shaw lived to ninety-four and wrote some stinkers!)

Still, the drive down the Queen Elizabeth Way, swinging around Lake Ontario to the beautiful, historic town of Niagara-on-the-Lake is a wonderful ninety minutes – especially if you go in August and September and treat yourself to the fresh peaches, cherries, and grapes at roadside stands. And the magnificent 830-seat theatre, floating in an exquisite four-acre park, is very special. The original playhouse, a court house some 130 years old, still retains its quaint charm. And, when a play at the Shaw Festival is well done, it can be a knockout.

The Shaw runs between May and October; you can call 361-1544 for a schedule. And even if you hate theatre or can't get a ticket, you will not be sorry to spend a day in Niagara-on-the-Lake. See our notes on The Prince of Wales Hotel in our **Out With The Inn Crowd** section, page 241, for some reasons why.

ROY THOMSON HALL:
THE NEW SASSY, GLASSY, CLASSY HALL

Roy Thomson Hall's brief life (it opened in September 1982) has been a swirl of controversies. First, they had to compromise on the design. World-renowned Vancouver architect Arthur Erickson's original plan was a daring one, with a glass exterior faceted like diamonds, catching the light at various angles. But it was too expensive, so they made him alter it.

And then, the name. It was to be called the New Massey Hall, since it was replacing the much-loved original Massey Hall, which had served this city since 1894. But then the family of the newspaper magnate (who knew nothing about music, but plenty about big bucks) Lord Thomson of Fleet, came up with the largest private donation ($4.5 million) and won for themselves an eternal commemoration of their paterfamilias. "Philistine!" cried outraged Torontonians, but no one else topped that donation, so the name stuck. It has, however, been popularly abbreviated to R.T. or Arty Hall; so there may be some justice after all.

Now that it's open, the beauty of its design and the sensitivity of its acoustics have silenced most of the critics. The spectacular glass-curtained outside wall gleams in the sunlight (although not as spectacularly as the architect would have wanted), and the inside looks like a jewel: 2,812 seats seem to float in a subtle play of monochromatic tones: greys and silver and chrome and concrete.

Behind the stage is a massive 5,207-pipe organ, built by a craftsman from London, Ontario. It has an electronic memory that allows the organist to program and recall combinations with the push of a button.

Is **Roy Thomson Hall** a success? Well, you judge. But we'll give you a hint. At her first recital there, **Leontyne Price** sang eight encores – just for the sound of it.

One thing we guarantee: going to a concert in Roy Thomson Hall is a visual experience as well as an aural one. It is the new home for the Toronto Symphony and the Toronto Mendelssohn Choir, one of the world's finest large choral groups. You'll also be able to catch solo vocal series, chamber music, piano, violin, and organ recitals, orchestras from around the world, and even such popular entertainers as, yes, Anne Murray. Prices will range from about $5, up to $20 and more for individual concerts and performances, so save up your cash. Rush seats are sold the day of a performance, beginning two hours before show time.

How to Get There:

Roy Thomson Hall is located at 60 Simcoe Street at the corner of King Street West, just a block west of University. Parking is available underground, and in many lots in the immediate vicinity, but a subway down University to St. Andrew will get you there just as quickly and much cheaper. Phone 593-4828 for information. Regular advertisements appear in the Toronto newspapers.

MASSEY HALL: TORONTO'S CARNEGIE

Looking at it now, it's hard to believe that a city of the size, wealth, and class of Toronto (oops, getting a bit self-aggrandizing, there) could tolerate such a cramped dingy place as its main concert hall. Then again, for the hundreds of thousands who have experienced its near-perfect acoustics and its handsome, U-shaped tiers sloping down towards the stage, **Massey Hall** has been a happy place to go.

Since the 1890s, Massey Hall has been home to the Toronto Symphony, and a friendly place to catch Gordon Lightfoot's yearly concerts, world-famous solo artists, string quartets, the occasional rock group, Pete Seeger, and The Chieftains. The nearly 2,800 seats are not terribly comfortable and a small number are blocked by the various pillars that hold up the structure; but it continues to offer great acoustics and a venerable place to hear the greats, near-greats, and ingrates of the music world.

How to Get There:

Massey Hall is at 178 Victoria Street at Shuter, just a block north of Queen and east of Yonge. Take the Yonge subway to Queen, and exit at Shuter. Phone 363-7301 for information, and check the daily papers for concerts throughout the year.

YET ANOTHER CONCERT HALL

The **Edward Johnson Building** has within it **Walter Hall** and the **MacMillan Theatre**, which are run by the University of Toronto's faculty of music. For people who wish to see and hear some of the more esoteric artists of the present, and the hopefuls of the future, this is a good place to check out. During the academic year, this is the place to find solo recitals (on a magnificent organ), serious jazz trios, experimental works, baroque chamber works, the U. of T. Orchestra, Concert Band and Wind Symphony, and faculty artists. It is also home to the Opera School (one of the finest of its kind anywhere), which stages several operas a year. But you have to be quick. They sell out every performance.

How to Get There:

The Edward Johnson Building is squished behind the McLaughlin Planetarium, which in turn is right next door to the Royal Ontario Museum. Take the University subway to Museum and exit on the west side. Phone 978-3744 for information about concerts, many of them free or almost free. You may also wish to pick up a free copy of the University of Toronto newspaper, **The Varsity**, which will often list concerts. The rag can be picked up at various places around the U. of T. campus, including outdoor boxes along College Street west of University on the north side.

THE TORONTO SYMPHONY:
THEY'RE PLAYING OUR TONE POEM

Now into its sixties, the Toronto Symphony is not about to retire. Since 1922 it has been making some rather beautiful music. And with conductors of the quality of Karel Ancerl, Seiji Ozawa, Walter Susskind, Sir Ernest MacMillan, and Andrew Davis, it has achieved world acclaim. The TS has performed around the world in the capitals of Europe, the Orient, and the United States. When it's at home it presents about three concerts weekly from September to June and a mini-season at Ontario Place each summer.

Attracting such performers as Itzhak Perlman, Pinchas Zuckerman, Yehudi Menuhin, and Isaac Stern, the TS is a major cultural force in our city, with a growing international reputation that does it – and Toronto – credit.

How to Get There:

The Toronto Symphony performs at Roy Thomson Hall, 60 Simcoe Street. There is lots of parking in the area, and the hall can be easily reached by the University subway. Exit at St. Andrew. You can purchase tickets at the Roy Thomson Hall Toronto Symphony Box Office, and subscriptions at its Ticket Centre, 146 Front Street W., Suite 460. With a VISA, Master Card, or Eaton's account, you may phone 598-3375 and charge it. Or call Teletron, 766-3271.

THE NATIONAL BALLET OF CANADA: FEET, DO YOUR STUFF

The Bolshoi is two centuries old; the **National Ballet of Canada** can trace itself all the way back to November 12, 1951, when it made its official debut on the cramped stage of the old Eaton Auditorium on College Street.

Baby has come a long way. In little more than three decades, the company has done some extraordinary things and reaped some revered awards. **Martine van Hamel** won first prize in the junior women's division in Varna in 1966; **Karen Kain** and **Frank Augustyn** were 1973 prize-winners in Moscow; and in 1981 only the USSR won more awards at the Fourth Moscow International Ballet Competition: National Ballet dancers **Kevin Pugh** and **Owen Montague**, among others, wowed the Russians like Napoleon did.

From such classics as **Coppelia**, **Giselle**, **Swan Lake**, and **Nutcracker** (the latter a perennial favourite in December, as you might well imagine), to more daring, contemporary ballets, the National Ballet can be counted on to perform well, and often very well. Such greats as Rudolf Nureyev, Peter Schaufuss, and Mikhail Baryshnikov have often danced with and/or choreographed for the company, which has enhanced its international stature. And its new artistic director is the great Erik Bruhn.

How to Get There:

The National Ballet performs at the O'Keefe Centre, at the southeast corner of Front Street and Yonge, in November, February and May, and every summer at Ontario Place. The National Ballet office number is 362-1041.

THE TORONTO DANCE THEATRE:
ON YOUR TOES

The **Toronto Dance Theatre** is the oldest contemporary dance company in the city. Since its beginning in the 1960s, the TDT has created more than eighty works, over a third of them using original scores commissioned from Canadian composers. It tours Canada, hitting the West and the East in alternate years, and has played major festivals in Europe, the United States, and Britain.

After a decade of success, the Toronto Dance Theatre purchased a beautiful, renovated church, St. Enoch's, built in 1891, and a neighbouring hall built in 1921. This is the home of its school and some forty full-time students a year.

Toronto Dance Theatre has its roots in the Martha Graham tradition, but has created a style of choreography and dance that is identifiably its own.

How to Get There:

The Toronto Dance Theatre performs at 80 Winchester Street in Cabbagetown. It is one block north of Carlton Street east of Parliament and can be reached by car or the Carlton streetcar. Phone 967-1365 for times, prices, and information.

THE CANADIAN OPERA COMPANY:
THE COC D'OR

For more than twenty-five years, the **Canadian Opera Company** has been presenting quality work at the O'Keefe Centre. From the most popular operas, such as *Carmen, Die Fledermaus*, and *Madama Butterfly* usually performed in the original language, to more modern or rare works, such as *Jenufa* or *The Coronation of Poppea*, the COC has proven trustworthy and often daring.

Nearly every season (which tend to be, like Gaul, divided into three parts: fall, winter, and spring) there is at least one première and two or more new productions of major works from the operatic repertoire.

Like all important companies, the COC often hosts world-class performers – Joan Sutherland, Grace Bumbry, Martina Arroyo, Gwyneth Jones, Jon Vickers, Maureen Forrester, Louis Quilico, Tatiana Troyanos, Marilyn Horne, Johanna Meier – the list is endless. Tickets need not be ferociously expensive, and there are senior citizen and student discounts available. The COC box office is down near Harbourfront (where the company performs mini-operas in a tent during the summer), 417 Queen's Quay West. It is possible to subscribe by phone: call 363-8231.

How to Get There:
The **Canadian Opera Company** performs in the O'Keefe Centre, at Yonge and Front Streets. Take the subway south to Union Station and walk one block east. Its phone number is 363-6633.

MOVIE HOUSES IN TORONTO: E.T., CALL THE BOX OFFICE

Toronto is movie city. Other people in other cities work, marry, make love, and die. In Toronto, they go to the movies. Admittedly, some of the classier people go to films, and the most impressive ones go to the cinema. But go, they do. An average of 250,000 people in Metro go to the movies every week.

And what choices we have! In one three-block radius, there are forty movie houses: **Cineplex** in Eaton Centre has twenty-one tiny cinemas, and across the street is the six-screen **Imperial**, just down from the ten-theatre **Carlton Cinemas** as well as a few other, old-fashioned, one-screen places. You remember *those*.

The Sound of Music ran for years in Toronto, whatever that says about our taste. Then again, *La Cage aux Folles* also ran for more than two years, which says something else about our taste, doesn't it?

There's a flip side to all of this: Toronto is subject to the strange machination of a provincial–in more ways than one–censor board (we kid you not–and you thought this was the 1980s). It has saved our citizens from the decadence of *The Tin Drum* and all of *Pretty Baby.* The chairperson of the censor board has even gone on record as saying that she objected to (but could not save us from) the breakdown of family values in that little shocker, *Breaking Away.* So don't expect to find your friendly neighbourhood porno movie in *this* city.

Now you can read, so we needn't list for you the multitude of movie houses across the city; they advertise daily in the major newspapers and in the listings of the city magazines.

Instead, here is a list of where you'll find low-priced films, classic films, foreign films, and even junky films, but in a charming atmosphere and/or at discount prices.

Ontario Film Theatre (429-0454), in the **Ontario Science Centre**, 770 Don Mills Road. A provincially funded film house, which has been much admired and visited since its opening back in 1969. Showing current, foreign, art films, and retrospectives, it has an excellent sound system, an enormous screen, comfortable seats, and no sticky floors, since eating, drinking, and smoking are banned.

The Film Theatre shows movies for senior citizens on Wednesdays for free. Other times there is a family rate of $4, which is a wonderful deal if you believe kids are cheaper by the dozen. Phone for a tape of film times; listings are in *The Globe and Mail* Saturday edition, and in the *Star*'s Thursday entertainment section. If you can live for two hours without popcorn, this is the best movie house in the city.

Revue Repertory (531-9959), 400 Roncesvalles Avenue. Located just a few blocks south of the Dundas West subway stop on the Bloor line, it's in the west end and worth the travel. Since 1972 they have been showing good double bills, and half are foreign films. For $3 (half that for children and seniors), this is a reliable, responsible, important part of Toronto culture.

The **Kingsway** (236-1411), 3030 Bloor Street West. Out in the far west end at Royal York Road. It's one of a recent mini-chain of low-cost, double-bill, second-run theatres; the other theatres in this chain are listed next. You pay $1.99 for each movie but only 99¢ per movie if you become an annual member for $5 – get it? Since the double bills are often top quality films, this 620-seat theatre is one of the best deals in town. As is:

Bloor Cinema (532-6677), at 506 Bloor Street West just a few feet east of Bathurst. The same deal as the Kingsway (above) and changes its double bills daily. As does:

The **Fox** (691-7330), out in the Beaches, at 2236 Queen Street E., east of Woodbine. Another steal. There are 340 seats here, in an old-style movie house that will flood anyone over forty with nostalgia.

Brighton (537-9767), 127 Roncesvalles Avenue. Take the Bloor subway west to the Dundas West stop, then the King 504 car south past Queen. Although it's owned by the same two whiz kids as the three theatres above, you have to pay $3 for the double bill here (seniors and kids, $1.50), but you get a dollar off with that crazy membership card used at the Kingsway/Bloor/Fox theatres. 550 cheap, cheap seats for all you big spenders out there.

The **Willow** (221-4878) is at 5269 Yonge Street, about 3 km (1½ miles) north of Highway 401. It has excellent double bills featuring recent films – two movies for $2.75, with seniors and kids less than half of that. With 1,000 seats and the best popcorn in town, according to some critics, this is a nice change from places like...

Cineplex (593-4535) in the **Eaton Centre** complex at Yonge and Dundas. What other film house made the *Guinness Book of World Records* for twenty-one (count 'em!) mini-screens and mini-theatres ranging from 57 to 200 seats. Prices are the same as most first-run movie houses, but where else can you get the choice of classic retrospectives, new stuff, kiddie films, Hollywood reruns, and lots more? Many complain about the small screens and the rear-screen projection, which, they claim, is harder on the eyes than standard front-screen projection. But it is a sight to see: computerized box office, advance purchase, and lots more futuristic fun.

Carlton Cinemas (296-3456), 20 Carlton, near College and Yonge. Subtitled a "festival of fine films," that is what it is: ten mini-cinemas, part of the expanding, Toronto-based **Cineplex** chain, showing art, foreign, and oldie films. You'll pay full price, but it's nice to know that there is one (of ten) places where you can be guaranteed a chance to see that art film you missed last year. Unlike **Cineplex**, the films are front-projected.

Roxy (461-2401), 1215 Danforth Avenue at the Greenwood stop on Bloor subway line. Kid-schlock and lots of fun. The *Rocky Horror Picture Show* has been running here every Saturday night for nearly a decade. If you haven't seen it, don't; it gives the phrase "cult film" a bad name. You can see excellent double bills for $2.50, and if you walk out after seeing only one, you get 50¢ back! If you want to see what the kids are coming to, as well as a film or two, then this is the place to go. Seniors and juniors, only $1.00.

Nostalgia Theatre is upstairs above the **Kingsway** and shows classic comedies, musicals, dramas, and westerns.

Mount Pleasant (489-8484), 675 Mt. Pleasant Road below Eglinton has 375 seats and some of the best, close-to-first-run double bills in town at reasonable prices. And just a few blocks away and owned by the same company is:

Crest (488-0044), 551 Mt. Pleasant Road. For many years one of the few professional theatres for live plays in the city, it has now reverted (forverted) to films. Rumour has it that it might go "live" again.

Art Gallery of Ontario (977-0414), 317 Dundas Street West, two blocks west of University. Often has excellent film series on such topics as opera on film and women directors.

York University (667-2100), on Keele Street north of Finch, and the **University of Toronto** (978-2011), near College and University. Each has film societies, film series, and

189

special showings of classics, often at bargain-basement prices. Either phone each university or pick up their newspapers *The Excalibur* (York) and *The Varsity* (U. of T.) for details.

Should you be of ethnic persuasion, there are many film houses that show the best and worst of the mother country. A few examples:

The **Japanese Cultural Centre** (441-2345), 123 Wynford Drive. Often shows free or low-priced Japanese fare, with English sub-titles. But no sushi.

Italian Theatres: There are many, from the huge and comfortable **St. Clair Theatre** (652-1414), 1156 St. Clair Avenue West, to the smaller **San Carlino Theatre** (243-0818), 1296 Weston Road. Both, unfortunately, tend to show grade B Italian films or popular American stuff dubbed into Italian.

Chinese Theatres: If you speak the language and like weepy romances and kung fu fooeys, then check out the **Golden Harvest Theatre** (977-2463), 285 Spadina Avenue, the **China Cinema** (463-7175), 735 Queen Street East, the **Pagoda Theatre** (596-8553), 526 Dundas Street West, **Chang's Theatre** (960-0589), 290 College Street, and the **Shaw Theatre** (921-3726), 362 College Street.

Greek Theatres: If it is Greek to you, try the **Titanis Theatre** (465-0040), 147 Danforth Avenue, and the **Rex Danforth** (461-1101), 635 Danforth.

Indian Theatres: Would that their movies were as spicy and hot as their curry; but no such luck. Ah, well. Indian movies are shown at the **Palace Theatre** (466-7226), 664 Danforth Avenue, The **Lansdowne Theatre** (535-1700), 683 Lansdowne Avenue, and the **Naaz** (469-0001), 1430 Gerrard Street E.

Cinesphere at **Ontario Place** shows 35 mm, 70 mm, and even bigger films, usually classics and Disneys, during the winter, and twenty-minute "mammoths" from May to September.

THE BEST SEATS IN THE HOUSE

Okay. You've made it down to the theatre, or the hall, or the night club or the stadium. Now where on earth should you sit? Occasionally, the most expensive seats are not always the best, as we have been crushed to discover.

Here then is a very select list of the very best seats in the house.

Thomson Hall. They claim that every seat in this stunning new theatre is good, but *we* know, *don't* we? And you know, now, as well: rows H and J in the orchestra are the best ones to grab here (and the grabbing will cost you $25 and up for each one, we warn you). Head for the left-hand side of the orchestra floor (the even-numbered seats) and all seats designated L upstairs. But as long as you're getting the best row, get the best numbers as well: 1 to 11 on the odd side, and 2 to 10 on the even side. Tell 'em we sent you.

St. Lawrence Centre Town Hall. It's rather narrow, so the best seats are rows D-J, seats 9-20. Keyboard side seats are between 1-8 close to the stage, and up to 12 and 13 up at row J.

Massey Hall. Smack in the centre between rows G and M are the most desired by the cognazzi, or whatever you call them. Best seats are in the first balcony 32-50.

The **O'Keefe Centre.** Of the nearly 3,200 bright red seats, the ones to get are A 47 and A 48, the widest seats in the house, in the centre of the theatre, with an aisle in front to stretch your legs in. Alas, they are also the special ones, reserved for the Queen, Big Shots, and Not You.

So you can be pretty safe if you buy seats immediately to the left or right of them to get about the best in the house. Of course, should She be in town, you'd better know where the Falkland Islands are and to whom they belong.

In the **St. Lawrence Centre Main Stage**, where only theatre is presented, the best seats in the house are rows E-N, seats 1-10, fanning out to 12-26.

Royal Alexandra Theatre. Row L in the middle is probably best. Then again, the front row in the first balcony is best for musicals, if you want to see everything that is happening. Then again, if it's a drama and you want to hear Nora slam the door, any one of the first few rows in the centre will do, past the guaranteed whiplash of rows A and B. Come to think of it, if you have more than $40 to spend on two tickets, you *should* demand the best, right? Around seat 18 is the centre of the hall in the first few rows.

Imperial Room of the **Royal York Hotel:** You can't lose if you sit on the lower level, although the first row of tables on the upper level is also fine, if you don't want Peggy Lee shattering your wine glass.

Maple Leaf Gardens. These depend on what you're there for. If it's a rock concert, you'll get the best sound in the lower reds of section 50. (Sitting directly in front of the stage is good, too, especially if you want to end up like Beethoven. And we don't mean famous.)

For tennis, sit at one end of the stadium or the other, so your neck doesn't fall off from following the ball.

Hockey? Check out the red section, higher up, where you'll get the best overall view of the entire game being played. Of course, since those seats have been someone else's season's tickets since early in this century, it's kind of a tease to mention them, isn't it?

CNE Stadium. For baseball, the box for Hot Shots is located in section 23, rows 1, 2 and, 3. It's on the third base line to the right of the dugout. And if the special people are put there, why shouldn't you be nearby? If you want to catch foul balls, hang around sections 19, 21, or 23, behind home plate.

For football or special events, it is informative to know that the Queen and her entourage get placed in row 24, section 42, on the north side of the stadium. What the Queen and her entourage are doing spending their precious time lolling about at football games, we have no idea.

DISCOUNT CULTURE AND SPORTS: HEY, BIG SPENDER

Everyone likes a bargain. In fact, we have some off-shore drilling permits we can sell you real cheap. But that's another story. The point here is that Toronto does not have half-price ticket places, like Manhattan does. What Toronto does have, however, are a number of deals on tickets to various events, some of which are not advertised very well. Here are a few.

The **Toronto Symphony** (598-3375). There are traditionally fifty to one hundred rush seats for most performances, which are in the $6 range. They go on sale exactly two hours before the performance begins so a quick visit to Roy Thomson Hall might settle your evening plans very quickly and reasonably.

There are student and senior citizen discounts as well, but only on subscriptions for Toronto Symphony events. Check these out, should you fit into either category. If you are a geriatric doctoral student, you might even get in free who knows?

The **Canadian Opera Company:** About six dozen rush seats go on sale at 11:00 a.m. on the day of each performance at the O'Keefe Centre. They usually run around $5, which beats the $10 to $40 regular cost. And student and senior rushes go for $4, a half-hour before each performance begins.

Individual Theatre Discounts: Many of the theatres in town, both professional and amateur, road show and local, offer discounts on single ticket sales. The cost varies from one production to the next. Check out the **Tarragon**, and many others of the so-called alternative theatres. They usually have PWYC (Pay What You Can) Sunday matinees, where – if you have no money or no conscience – you can get away with moving a few measly bucks toward the ticket seller.

For example, the **Royal Alexandra**, which rarely has discounts, will sometimes offer one on a show that has a long run. And there are other theatres, such as the **Passe Muraille**, which offer fifty per cent off before opening night, in a sardonic attempt to beat the critics. You take your chances, but you might save up to $10 per ticket.

Should you see something in town that interests you, call them up – and not only to find out if tickets are available, but if they are available at a discount. As many airlines have discovered, better a plane full of people paying half fare than an empty plane.

Toronto Argonaut Football (595-9600): Argo tickets have gone for as little as 99¢ at A & P Supermarkets, if you buy $5 worth of groceries. Other grocery stores have similar deals on sports events, as well as on the Canadian National Exhibition.

Toronto Blue Jays Baseball (595-0077): There are over a dozen discount days each season when savings of $1 can be had on most seats. Since the team rarely seems to win, some wags have suggested that the team pay the fans to come.

TV Tapings: Yes, indeed, Toronto has a number of television shows that are taped before live audiences. They might not offer the excitement of seeing Ed McMahon in person in L.A., but if seeing Ed McMahon in person is your idea of an exciting time, this book isn't for you.

CFTO, which is the Toronto station of the private CTV network, has many programs that you may sit in on and might even enjoy: *Definition*, *Stars on Ice*, *Thrill of a Lifetime*, *Headline Hunters*, *Ronnie Prophet*, and more. The CFTO studios are located most conveniently: simply drive east along the 401 to McCowan Road. (It is on the way to the Metro Zoo, and the two visits could be combined.) Get off on McCowan, turn north, and make a left onto Channel 9 Court. You can see the large studios from the highway. Call CFTO (299-2000) and find out what shows are being taped, when, and in which studio. Kids who have never seen a TV show being produced, with all the mistakes, stops and starts, might find this a very thrilling afternoon or evening. Tickets are always free.

The **CBC**, or **Canadian Broadcasting Corporation**, offers free passes to tapings of a number of shows, including *The Tommy Hunter Show*, which offers country music, and *Front Page Challenge*, a game show which is more than a quarter-century old now and as much of an institution in this country as Niagara Falls and Liberal Prime Ministers.

In fact, the CBC also gives out free tickets to tapings of radio shows, which might bring on waves of nostalgia to anyone who remembers when radio was *it* in the 30s and 40s. Some of these shows include comedy troupes who are really very good, such as *The Frantics*.

Phone the CBC (925-3311), and ask for when and where you can watch, or even be involved in, a taping. Since the *CBC* facilities are scattered across Toronto like so many dandelions (and some critics think the weed image is apt), we can't tell you exactly where the taping will be. But in many cases it is done at a studio on Yonge Street, about halfway between Bloor and St. Clair.

Halfback Discounts. A few times a year, the Ontario government allows people to take their losing Wintario tickets (that's our provincial lottery, or at least one of them) and use them as 50¢ discounts for many theatres in town. You can use up to four loser-tickets per admission, for a total saving of $2. So if you're a gambler and in Toronto long enough to play Wintario and lose, save your bummers and you might be able to use them – even to buy books.

EAT, DRINK, AND BE WEARY:

EATERIES, SLEEPERIES (IN TOWN AND OUT), AND TORONTO FOR KIDS

Each section in this chapter has its own mini-intro; so all we want to mention here is that while we *have* tried to be exhaustive in listing sites, buildings, events, parks, neighbourhoods, shopping areas, and cultural highlights, we have *not* attempted to be exhaustive here.

A complete listing of better restaurants in this richly restauranted city would run hundreds of pages. So would any solid line-up of nightclubs, hotels, pubs, and so on. But all the places listed here *have* been visited – some as recently as days before this book went to press – and we've tried to be as fair and as informative as possible. And for the sake of those of you who have been blessed/cursed/overwhelmed by the joys of parenthood, we've gathered together the most kid-oriented places to visit and dine in. Toronto is *not* a place where you will regret bringing Junior along. Nor will Junior. Otherwise, we'd have labelled this chapter "Eat, Drink and Be Wary." But we didn't, did we?

TORONTO'S RESTAURANTS: A HIGHLY (SOME MIGHT CALL IT LOWLY) PERSONAL LIST

Toronto has become, in a remarkably short period of time, a very fine restaurant town. Less than two decades ago, the choice was between some greasy spoons, boring but decent WASP establishments, one or two good Chinese establishments and perhaps a French restaurant, and hidden delis.

There's been an explosion, and it's all to the good. Now, in a book like this one, dedicated to recommending sites, parks, walks, neighbourhoods, and so much else, we cannot even pretend to be definitive. Heck, we can't find the space for more than a handful of our many favourites. Here is our own very personal list of the best, the cheapest, and the finest. We hope it serves a purpose as well as the following serve a dinner. Prices include wine, when possible.

We recommend – strongly – that you pick up *The Toronto Restaurant Guide*, which contains over three hundred reviews of our city's finest and favourite (they are not always the same). It also has complete information on restaurant wine lists and where to find the finest cellars.

The Very Best

Oh, this is tough. We have to give our votes to...

Scaramouche (961-8011), One Benvenuto Place, a few blocks south of St. Clair, just west of Avenue Road. The room is elegant, the palms and hyacinths not overbearing, the lighting low, the food rarely less than perfect. The marinated salmon, the pâté of chicken liver, the noisette of lamb, the chocolate mousse cake...Everything tastes as good as it looks, and it looks like a work of art. A new *prix fixe* menu runs $35 and changes weekly.

It's not cheap; dinner for two will easily run $100. But you will remember the food (and the view of downtown Toronto - the restaurant is built into a hotel that stands on the top of the Avenue Road hill) long after you pay off Visa.

Napoleon (929-5938), 79 Grenville Street just west of University and north of College. When the owner/chef inquires if you are pleased and listens carefully to the answer, you can be sure you will be treated and fed well. The pheasant in black currant sauce, rack of lamb, steak au poivre, and much-acclaimed veal with pears and mushrooms are spoken of with reverence. This is a special place; you'll wait a long time to get a reservation, and with good reason. Easily $80 for two.

Fenton's (961-8485), 2 Gloucester Street, a few blocks below Bloor and just east of Yonge. It's physically beautiful and the food matches. Très nouvelle cuisine, and très delicious: try the sea-bass salad, the sweet fish terrines, the chunks of veal with mango chutney and kumquats, daringly cooked in spicy curry. Open seven days, Fenton's will cost about $25 for two for lunch, over $50 for dinner (downstairs is about 40 per cent cheaper). Decor can never make up for food; but this place has excellence in both.

Lhardy's (967-1818), 634 Church Street, one block east of Yonge and two blocks south of Bloor. For nearly a decade, it has been one of Toronto's best *nouvelle cuisine* restaurants; it's in a charming house not far from the heart of Toronto's shopping district. The calf's sweetbreads in a green peppercorn sauce, the lobster in wine, the quenelles of duck - this is truly one of Toronto's finest. You'll pay $60-70 for two and not regret it for a moment.

Favourite Chinese

Is there any other cuisine that never dries out chicken or

overcooks vegetables? There are more than a hundred Chinese establishments in this city, and we've eaten in dozens of them and almost never had a bad meal. But two stand out:

Pink Pearl (977-3388), 142 Dundas Street West, between Bay and University. Reservations are needed, or you are in for a mouth-watering wait. Unlike most of the formica-tabled Chinese eateries, the decor here is excellent. And the service. And need we add: the stuffed crab claws, the scallops with garlic and snow peas, the green pepper filled with shrimps served in black bean sauce. Licenced to serve liquor, which many Chinese places are not. About $50 for two.

Szechuan Chungking (593-0101), 428-430 Spadina Avenue, just south of College. A superb yet inexpensive treasure. The food is Szechuan in origin, which means that many of the dishes are spiced with red chili to raise the roof of your mouth and your culinary consciousness. Chicken with peanuts, mustard and chicken soup, broccoli with garlic sauce – this place has a fire sale every day of the week. It has beer and wine, and should run you only about $20 for two, possibly less.

Japanese Joys

Nikko Garden Restaurant (977-2164), 460 Dundas Street West, just east of Spadina. Sitting proudly amid the bustle of Chinatown, it has been warmly welcome there for more than two decades. Not only are its standard sukiyaki and tempura dishes first rate, but the squid with soybean paste dressing and buckwheat noodles in broth are much beloved. Licenced, it should run you between $40 and $50.

Sasaya (487-3508), 257 Eglinton Avenue West, near Avenue Road. A ways up north, but its taste is firmly in the East. A sushi bar is the ideal way to discover the wonders of raw fish, and the tempura, beef, salmon, or chicken teriyaki are all excellent. About $35 for two.

Furusato (967-0180), 401 Bloor Street East, near the Don Valley Parkway. Graceful and elegant, with its lovely prints and folding fans. The shabu-shabu, which is beef and vegetables simmering in broth, and the chawan mushi (chicken, shrimp, and vegies in an egg custard) are a must. It's more expensive than most Japanese restaurants: dinner for two could hit $50, but it's worth it.

Greek Glory

Aristedes (921-6325), at 80 Scollard Street, just north of Bloor and west of Bay. It only opened its doors in 1981 but it promptly rose to the top of what is a superb selection of Greek restaurants in Toronto. (See our **Greek Toronto** walk, pp. 118-120 for more.) The fish soup and avgolemono (the amazing combination of chicken, egg, and lemon) are superb and so is the tzatziki – spiced yoghurt served with warm pita. Dinner for two will set you back about $35.50. Its worth every single penny.

Fabulous Fish

Quenelles (967-6131), 636 Church Street, one block east of Yonge and south of Bloor. Shares the building, kitchen, and marvellous talent with food with Lhardy's. Less formal and less expensive than its older brother next door **Quenelles'** genius lies in the ocean and stream. From lobster and hollandaise sauce to oyster Lorraine, from salmon to trout to Dover sole, you'll not taste fresher or better cooked fish in the city. Add *al dente* vegetables, crisp salads, and deft service, and you might feel like floating away. Around $50 for two.

Joso's (925-1903), 202 Davenport Road at Avenue Road. The favourite of many fish-lovers in Toronto. This place is strong on octopus, clams, and squid as well as the fresh fish of the day. Joso makes fish sing almost as well as he himself did a dozen years ago, when he was part of a folk-singing duo. A reasonable $45 for two.

French Fantasies

Les Copains (869-0898), 48 Wellington Street East. Opened in the late 1970s, it rapidly became one of the top French eateries in Toronto. It is a lovely mixture of old and new cuisines: remarkable fish soup, one of the best house dressings in the city on Boston lettuce, fine hors d'oeuvres, and main courses from Dover sole to breast of duck. Creative, careful, light yet saucy. About $60.

Le Pigalle (593-0698), 315 King Street West. Living proof that French food need not be expensive. Perhaps it helps to be off the beaten path, out on King Street edging towards Spadina and away from the Royal Alex and the city centre. The onion soup is among the best, the pâté excellent, and the quiches delicious enough for a real man to enjoy. Standard, high-quality French fare at extraordinarily fair prices. Around $35.

Very Vegie

The Parrot (593-0899), at 325 Queen Street West, a few blocks west of University. Gives the lie to the too-often-true truism that vegetarian food has to be boring and tasteless. The menu changes up to twice a month, hopping from cuisine to cuisine around the world: the Middle East to Spain to North Africa to France to Mexico. Since it serves fish and seafood, it might not be considered strictly vegetarian, but it is strictly top-notch. About $35. Open Tues. lunch to Sunday brunch. We recommend brunch, at about $15 for two.

Cheap and Cheerful

Bumpkin's (922-8655), 21 Gloucester Street, just below Bloor and east of Yonge. A prime location with unfashionably low prices. The food is not magical, nor profoundly creative, but always fresh, good quality, and well done (or rare, if that's what you requested). The huge crowds suggest they are doing something right. And where else in the city can you have solid French fare for under $25?

Mars (921-6332), 432 College Street, just east of Bathurst. A classic greasy spoon, but with spotless silverware. Formica tables, cramped seating, and always, good, solid fare. Old-fashioned cabbage soup, fine cheese blintzes, great liver smothered in onions – this is a place my late father would have felt at home in, and everyone else, it seems, still does. Superb rice pudding and remarkable bran, corn meal, and blueberry muffins help you forget that your credit cards are worthless here. This is an old-fashioned place, remember? Under $15 – cash.

United Bakers Dairy Restaurant (593-0697), 338 Spadina Avenue, just north of Dundas. It is strictly dairy (there's even a very good vegetarian chopped liver), run by the third generation of the same family. Magnificent boiled or baked white fish. Perfect pickled pike. (Say it fast ten times.) Formica tables and simply magnificent Russian-Polish-Jewish cooking. In what other restaurant can you order soup and have it placed steaming before you in less than 20 seconds? And when you taste the soups – or anything else, for that matter – you'll know why this place has thrived for more than seventy years, and why the Jews have lasted for more than four thousand. Under $15 for two.

Excellent Eglinton

Sabatino's (783-5829), 1144 Eglinton Avenue West, just three blocks west of Bathurst. There *is* life north of Bloor. Life, and excellent cooking. Perfect pastas and vivacious veal make wonderful main courses; appetizers like zucchini stuffed with breadcrumbs, and tomatoes and shrimps in a white wine, garlic, and cream sauce should leave your taste buds dancing. A more than fair $60.

La Fringale (487-3636), 339 Eglinton Avenue West, just west of Avenue Road. The mussels in white wine, the thick cream of cauliflower soup, the superb poached breast of chicken in a Henry IV sauce, the roast quail – not adventurous, but ever so good. Easily $35-55 for two, which should well satisfy your fringale (a sudden hunger pang *en français*).

Incredible Italian

Pronto Ristorante (486-1111), at 692 Mt. Pleasant Road, just south of Eglinton. Physically beautiful, it seems to do no wrong: Fine antipasto, delicious pasta dishes, delicate veal, chicken, and seafood. It recently doubled in size, yet it's still hard to get in. With good reason, even at $55 for two.

Carlo & Adelina's Place (532-5929), 591 Markham Street, just south of Bloor and one block west of Bathurst, is as warm and welcoming as its name. The pasta and the sauces are home-made, and you can't lose with the cannelloni and the tortellini. At $45 for two, it's like eating in the home of an Italian friend, who happens to cook very, very well.

Mastro's Restaurant (636-8194), 890 Wilson near the 401 and Dufferin, is handy to the airport and major highway hotels and is one of the best Italian places around. For less than $16, the daily four-course dinners are a real find: a great seafood salad, superb sauces, and home-made pastas. Great vegies, too. It's not downtown, but it tastes like downtown: downtown Rome. About $45.

Ristorante Boccaccio (789-5555), 901 Lawrence Avenue West, just west of Dufferin. Located in an Italian community centre, it looks and tastes far more impressive than that sounds. The pastas are not only home-made, but daring and different; the rigatoni and spaghetti carrettiera are especially noteworthy. Come to think of it, the ravioli was a knock-out too. This is a very special place to eat; it makes you glad the Italians won the World Cup in Soccer. About $35-$50.

Tremendous Trattoria

Since the second world war, Toronto has been blessed with close to a half-million Italians, who have added immeasurable vibrancy and joy to this city. Not to mention dozens of heavenly restaurants of their ethnic persuasion, which we will mention, if only in passing.

In a word: within a few short blocks of Dufferin and St. Clair, there are many inexpensive trattoria-type places that will save you a flight to Italy. You can hardly miss with any of these Italian restaurants, but we'll toss off two of our favourites, to give you a start:

Venezia (654-8648), 1338 Lansdowne is renowned for its pasta, particularly the fettucine verde capriccio, and the tortellini. And the veal dishes are living proof that the animal did not die in vain. Lower in price than some of the Italian places listed above, which are far classier and trendier, you will bless us for telling you about this one.

Il Focolare (656-8510), 1351 St. Clair Avenue West is also beloved for its pastas. Like Venezia – and other fantastic trattorias in this immediate area – you'll probably pay no more than $30 for two, while your tastebuds dance.

Perfect Pizza

Vesuvio's Pizzeria (763-4191), 3010 Dundas Street West. It was Toronto's first, and therefore, its oldest, take-out pizzeria, and we nod to tradition and respect our elders. Besides, it has won so many taste contests that we have to list it here. While many swear by **Mama's** (alias **Monte Carlo Restaurant**) (781-4656), at 1028 Eglinton West, or **Bitondo's** (533-4104), 11 Clinton Street, even their fans have to admit that Vesuvio's uses some of the finest ingredients and has the best-textured dough in the business. A large pizza will run you about $8-10 or eight thousand calories, whichever comes first.

Camarra's Pizzeria and Restaurant (789-3221), 2899 Dufferin Street, below Lawrence Avenue W. is our new favourite. Since 1958, this place has been turning out remarkable pizzas (and we are mortified that it took us into the 1980s to discover it). They deliver to a giant area – Royal York Road to Avenue Road, and from Sheppard Avenue to Dupont – and when you taste their fried crust and perfect toppings, you may start speaking Italian, out of joy. A large pizza, 15" in diameter and divided into 12 slices will run you about $6.50, with 85¢ added for each topping. Fabulous pizza.

Delicious Deli

Switzer's (596-6900), 322 Spadina Avenue, just above Dundas. One of Toronto's original delicatessens, full of Spadina Avenue hustle and bustle. The air is pungent with corned beef, dill pickles, and fresh rye bread, and you can't go wrong with any of the fine sandwiches, potato salad, cole slaw, and some of the best french fries around. This is classic, New York-style, fast service, eat-and-get-out deli, and it's wonderful. About $15 for two.

Yitz's (487-4506), 346 Eglinton Avenue W. at the corner of Avenue Road. Less noisy and vulgar than Switzer's, it serves good quality deli, as well as liver, steak, and lots of other kosher-style goodies. Note we say kosher-style – don't bring any rabbis in here, but do bring in anyone who loves good Jewish deli. About $20, with drinks, under $15 without.

Shopsy's (365-3333), 33 Yonge Street. One of the great landmarks of Jewish eating in Toronto, **Shopsy's** has moved to a new location near the O'Keefe and St. Lawrence Centres – handy for a quick bite before or after the show.

Moe Pancer's Delicatessen (633-1230), 4130 Bathurst Street north of the 401. Proclaimed, by real aficionados, to have the best pastrami in Toronto. And isn't it worth going up almost to Sheppard Avenue to eat the best pastrami in Toronto? Yes? So, go. About $10-15.

Indescribable Indian

Shala-mar (425-3663), 427 Donlands Avenue, and **Lalazar** (421-1770), 429 Donlands are right next door to each other, and they are right up there on the list of Indo-Pakistani food fanciers, who are more than willing to head out to the east end, just above Greektown. From samosas to pakoras to lamb korma to creamy raita, you cannot lose. And the way both of these fine restaurants are nightly crowded with East Indians certainly suggests that they have got their curries in the right place. Around $25 for two, probably less.

Happy Hungarian

Country Style (537-1745), at 450 Bloor Street W. just east of Bathurst. Just what its name implies: good, solid, reliable, country-style Hungarian food. With specials every day, ranging from veal stew to goulash soup to chicken paprikash, this place is as delicious as it is reasonable. You won't get liquor here, but you'll be too full to drink anyway. About $15 for two.

The Korona (961-1824), at 493 Bloor Street W. Another Hungarian special place with top-notch veal paprikash, glorious green peppers stuffed with beef, great bean soup...You won't be any thinner, but neither will your wallet. About $10 for two; no liquor available.

This is Hungarian row, and there are equally good places up and down the street, should the above two be overcrowded, as they usually are. Check out the **Tarogato** (536-7566), 553 Bloor Street W., or the **Continental** (531-5872), 521 Bloor Street West, just down the block.

Marvellous Middle-Eastern

The Jerusalem (783-6494), at 955 Eglinton Avenue W., two blocks west of Bathurst. The restaurant is run by Christian Arabs right in the heart of a Jewish area and the neighbours keep it busy. Which is more hopeful than anything we've seen at the United Nations recently. For a dozen years, this place has provided some of the finest falafel, pita, tahini, tabbouleh, and shish kebab west of Eden. There's even a take-out just a few doors down, so the happiness can continue at home. About $30 for two can bring your own special peace to the mid-East.

Cedars of Lebanon (482-3799), 2005 Avenue Road, a few

blocks south of the 401, has rapidly become one of Toronto's most trustworthy Middle-Eastern eateries. With the same superb food as made at the Jerusalem, you will quickly learn the difference between houmos and tahini, and between shish taouk and shish kafta. The Bible says that one should "grow like a cedar in Lebanon"; this place should do the same. Also about $30 for two.

Ravishing Russian

The Barmalay (651-5415), 994 St. Clair Avenue W., east of Dufferin. Actually Russian-Jewish, and their food is delicious. The Russian salad, borscht, blintzes, pelmenies (perogies)– this is one of the most pleasurable restaurants in our fair city. And the delightful antics and charm of former-actor and owner, Gregory Bruskin, will only add to the nonstop satisfaction. Steppe this way, please! About $30 for two.

Best Burgers

Markelangelo's (363-3035), 55 Colborne Street, just east of Yonge and south of King in the heart of downtown. A rather presumptuous name, but they have been faithful to it. Filled with the art work of **Robert Markle**, it is strong on hamburgers and darned good at it. Yes, you can get excellent and creative chicken, and fine salads, but it is the six-ounce hamburgers that have brought rave reviews. You'll spend less than $20 and spend a pleasant hour in stunning surroundings. Who says you have to stand to eat good hamburgers?

Best Brunch

Most of Toronto's finer restaurants are opening for Sunday brunch, so phone and verify. But of the many we've tried, here are our personal favourites, next to **The Parrot**.

The Prince Hotel (**Le Continental**) (444-2511), 900 York Mills Road, west of the Don Valley Parkway and south of the 401. Expensive, gorgeously displayed, and guaranteed to fill you until you are ready to burst. What do you do? Start flooding your plate with the piles of fresh fruit? Or go right to the caviar, lobster, smoked salmon, crepes, coq au vin or ravioli? But what if you don't leave room for the dozens of desserts, from cheesecake to mocha cake to chocolate mousse to strawberry flan? Easily $40 for two. But look at it this way: you won't want to eat until the following Tuesday afternoon, so you've really saved some money.

Yevshan Zillia (596-6626), 525 King Street West near Bathurst provides a marvellous chance to have a truly different Sunday meal: patychky (meat on a stick), varenyky (perogies), holubtsi (cabbage rolls), chicken in sour cream sauce,

buriaky (beet salad), and sauerkraut. A charming and low-priced way to spend a Sunday afternoon. About $20 for two.

NIGHTLIFE:
WHO WAS THAT MAN/WOMAN/CHILD/ DOG/FANTASY I THINK I SAW YOU WITH LAST NIGHT?

Runway 23 (244-1711), in the Skyline Hotel, 655 Dixon Road. The best spot on the airport strip to watch airplanes take off and land at Toronto International. The decor is plants, glass, and bucket chairs. The cocktail hour gets business people; young working people come later. There's no food, but hors d'oeuvres are free 5:00-8:00 p.m. Music is live, middle of the road, from 9:00-1:00 a.m. There's a sit-down bar, and lots more room to sit down – the place holds 350. Dancing, as well.

The Lighthouse (869-1600), in the Harbour Castle, 1 Harbour Square, at the foot of Bay Street by the lake. An upper-middle-class clientele of tourists, but not just hotel guests. The rotating restaurant has a glorious view of the city and the Toronto Islands; it takes an hour to go 'round once. Be warned: Leave your purse on the window ledge, and ten minutes later, it will be gone – not stolen, just back around the circle. But this is Toronto, so you have a good chance of getting it back. The decor is brown and rust and plantsville. Every month there is a different theme buffet. But it's the view you came for, remember?

Stop 33 (924-9221), in the Sutton Place Hotel, 955 Bay Street at Wellesley. Three-and-a-half million bucks were spent to create the atmosphere here, and it looks it; it's elegant and boasts a beautiful view. There's a dance floor, Andy Warhols on the walls, a long bar with stools and sofas. This is something of a tourist spot. No cover charge, except Saturday night, with dress casual but no jeans. Who would dare wear jeans, no matter who designed them, in a place like this?

The Aquarius Lounge (967-5225), 55 Bloor Street West at Bay, in the Manulife Centre. On the fifty-first floor, it is the highest piano lounge in the city. The busy time in the summer is Thursday-Saturday after 8:30 p.m., but there is a high turnover so the wait is never too long. In the winter, when all Torontonians hibernate, the lines begin as early as 8:00 p.m. This is not a place to meet people, and it is not trendy in the way that most bars in the Yorkville area are. But its romantic atmosphere makes this a marvellous place for a date, relaxing and comfortable.

There is no cover or dancing, and the dress code (no jeans) is not usually enforced. But the incredible view goes on all the time.

Park Plaza Roof Lounge (924-5471), in the Park Plaza Hotel at the northwest corner of Bloor and Avenue Road. Once described by novelist Mordecai Richler as "the only civilized place in Toronto." Compliments like that we could do without. But it is very special; the decor is plush, older European-style, with chandelier, marble tables, and waiters serving in red jackets. A hang-out for the upper-middle-class, professionals, business people, literary folk. Lunch is served, each day, and drinks are moderately priced.

Top of Toronto (362-5411), in the CN Tower, 301 Front Street West. The world's highest free-standing bar and a simply astonishing view. Or maybe it's only spectacular; we don't recall.

The Fifty-Fourth (366-6576), on guess-which-floor of the Toronto-Dominion Tower at Bay and Wellington. Dancing, dining and lots of sights to see.

Magic Carpet Room (675-1500), on the sixteenth floor of the Constellation Hotel, 900 Dixon Road. Subdued music and a good view of the airport at night.

Love is a Many Singles Thing

Contrary to popular opinion, there are many people in Toronto who are not married, with 1.7 children (the .7 are the punk rockers). There are, indeed, tens of thousands of never-marrieds, separated, divorced, widowed, widowered, in-betweens, on-the-rebounds and just-plain-lookings who need places to go.

As in most capitalistic societies, needs tend to be filled for anyone with three bucks for a beer. Alas, like socialist societies there is frequent queueing, although in singles' bars, line-ups and crowds are part of the raison d'être.

Some of these places are more sophisticated or more seedy than others, but they tend to have certain things in common: loud music, usually provided by a DJ (God forbid people should be able to hear each other), ages running the gamut of 23-35, much practising of "impression management," great crowds (even on weeknights), trendy, attractive decor, a lot of "beautiful people," a "tense" rather than "nice" feeling felt by those who find these things superficial, and, alas alacka-day, more men than women. No one ever said life was fair.

The following is a highly personal list. And with singles' bars, isn't being highly personal the whole idea?

Rooney's (924-2923), 1365 Yonge Street at Rosehill, two

blocks south of St. Clair. There's no cover, but there is an occasional enforced minimum Thursday-Saturday evenings, the busiest periods.

The clientele at Rooney's is your affluent, older, sophisticated crowd, ranging from 25-45. About seventy per cent are regulars, and it's apparently a good pick-up place.

It's dimly lit, with pink, muted lights, and a long, sit-down bar. There's a medium-sized dance floor and lots of round, smoked-glass tables for four with large, plush tub chairs. A wine carpet (so it won't show?) and mirrored pillars complete the picture. A DJ plays disco stuff. There's a piano, but one senses it's there only to give the atmosphere some class.

Drinks are expensive and the French cuisine in the dining room is fairly steep as well, but as good as others in town.

Scotland Yard (364-6572), 56 The Esplanade, just east of Yonge and south of Front Street. The decor echoes its name. It's a popular singles' spot where it's fairly easy to meet people. The clientele, aged about 25-35, is attractive and tends to be professional. There are line-ups on weekends; it's Toronto's watering hole on Sunday nights.

No jeans are allowed, but then there's no cover charge either. There's dancing to a DJ playing popular rock, disco, and punk, moderately priced drinks and many, many people. If you hate crowds, avoid Scotland Yard at all costs – on weekends, anyway.

Brandy's has two locations: 58 The Esplanade, in the Yonge-Front area (364-6671), and in the Yonge-Eglinton Centre (489-5303). These have been called "the popular singles bars of the broad masses." Both are packed summer and winter, but rarely are there line-ups on weeknights.

The Esplanade location has the older, professional crowd, more cliquey than the northern branch; more tense, uppity. Yonge-Eglinton is a good-looking crowd, a bit younger, with a surprisingly equal male-female ratio and so many Lacoste shirts that you think you're lost in the Florida Everglades.

The service is excellent, and regulars are known by the staff and catered to with back-door privileges and more generous drinks. Loud. Dancing. Do you come here often? Haven't I seen you someplace before? This is no place for a quiet rendezvous. Decor at both locations is attractive and the atmosphere is classy yet decidedly not snobby.

Friday's (485-1222), 204 Eglinton Avenue E. near Mt. Pleasant Road. Vulture city. A hot singles' bar, loud and very, very crowded. There is a tense "whom shall I go home with tonight?" atmosphere. The clientele is often polyester, both in clothes and people. Burned-out beach boys go here to die. More males than females. The decor is, in fact, most pleasing – multi-levels, Casablanca fans, oodles of ferns. Every person of the female persuasion should expect to be approached an average of once a minute.

And here are some honourable mentions.
Misty's (677-9900), in the Airport Hilton, 5875 Airport Road. A huge, comfortable room with phony Tiffany lamps galore. Wednesday nights are solid gold, blasting out the hits of the 50s and 60s; Thursday nights are country and western. On any given evening, the parking lot is overflowing with Camaros and John Travolta clones. Expect line-ups on weekends.

Muddy's (364-8266), 74 The Esplanade. Often more guys than gals, and part of the Front-Yonge grouping of singles' bars.

Post Script: When writing about Toronto's singles' scene, it is necessary to mention the new meeting place: the super-market. No kidding. This is becoming *the* place, as people take to shopping for their groceries (and emotional needs) at night. May we therefore present:

The Kitchen Table (961-9991), 1560 Yonge just above St. Clair. Not only a most elegantly decorated supermarket, which you pay for, but its layout is such that they must have had this ulterior motive in mind. The place is filled with discreet little corners and private aisles, and it's not too hard to spark up meaningful conversation over artichokes or green beans, near the carrots or celery. Open til midnight, seven nights a week. Lettuce be friends?

Yorkville Trendy

There are many different places that fall under (and over) this category, but they all have one common element: the crowd who bops from one place to another. We call them the Yorkville Trendies. Usually they have good taste, but bring their own special designer brand of superficiality and preten-tiousness to any nightclub atmosphere. This is, quite often, most interesting to observe.

There are two types of people in this group: the haves and the have-nots-who-will-not-admit-it. There are many afflu-ent, successful business, entertainment, and literary people who hang out in Yorkville and environs. They hang out there, to be fair, because they like it and because they have good taste. The other bunch – the Pretenders, if you will – like to look like the first group, and could do a lot worse. They bury themselves in status symbols (you could read famous names on the backs of jeans all night), and they go to see and be seen. They go to Yorkville because The Haves go there, and it's still slightly cheaper than zapping off to New York.

There are many cafés, restaurants, and interesting night spots in Yorkville – too numerous to mention – which can best be discovered by a stroll in the area.

Drake's (968-6777), 136 Yorkville Avenue. Called a "New York style nightclub" by its management, and a piano bar by us. The clientele are upper class, professional. A lot of industrialists, real-estate giants, crooks, models – you name it. Peter Allen heads right here when he plays in Toronto, and many of the city's top celebrities can be seen.

Interestingly, the place is busiest on weeknights; that's when the regulars come. On weekends, when the elite head off to their cottages or Manhattan, the suburban crowd moves in. Things don't pick up until nearly 11:00 p.m.

The service is excellent; the decor is, well, trendy – lots of mirrors, black tile, white tablecloths covered with candles and flowers.

The genius behind **Drake's** is Paul Drake, who played the Windsor Arms for more than a decade. He's not your average piano player; he's a full-fledged entertainer, playing tunes that lean toward middle-of-the-road and jazz. People still talk about Drake's eight-week marriage to the Princess of Belgium, but it's his brilliance at the keyboard that is really worth talking about, and has lasted a lot longer. **Drake's** is an affordable place to rub shoulders and credit cards with the rich.

October's (961-7704), 7 Bellair Street, running north from Bloor west of Bay. What one might call a nostalgic nightclub. It opened in the summer of 1982 and was popular from Day One as a hang-out for the sophisticated older crowd.

The crowd varies: on weeknights there are more singles; on weekends, more moms and pops and older folk come to hear big-band music of the 40s. There is just as much picking up done at this stand-up bar as at any other, but there is less tension due to distractions – the fancy decor and orchestra.

October's is a stunner: a massive open space – there's room for 426 in its lounge, two dining sections, and three bars – and the chandeliers, stained glass, and dim lighting add to the atmosphere. No jeans or T-shirts are allowed. There is a large dance floor, where you can move to James Regan and the **October's** orchestra. Even at midnight on a Thursday night, people pour in; **October's** is a twelve-month-a-year success story.

Bellair Café (964-2222), 100 Cumberland. Considered *the* meeting place. In the summer, the outdoor patios and the lounge are the first to fill with Yorkville Trendies. The crowd is mixed, age-wise; but generally older folk are in the posh dining room, the kids in the lounge. This is a moneyed crowd: sophisticated, well-behaved, lots of businessmen. It's owned by the genii who run **Rhodes**, **Bemelman's**, **Toby's**, and the **Jarvis House**, and the decor is très classy. If you wear grey, you might vanish into the ultra-modern surroundings, complete with Canadian art and marble tables. There's no dress code, but the management is known to be "selective" at the door. The clientele, which runs from 30-55, goes upstairs to the lounge to hear live piano music before 9:00 p.m. After 9:00, it's good, live jazz. There's no dancing, but then there's no cover charge either.

Bemelman's (960-0306), 83 Bloor Street W. Hereby awarded a Yorkville Trendy Spot Honourable Mention. True, it's not on Yorkville, or even Cumberland, for that matter, but it is nearby on Bloor Street W., which is close enough. The Trendies love it. A restaurant and bar, with both gay and straight clientele, ranging in age from 25-55. At lunch, it's mostly business people. Upscale would be the word here; it is busiest Wednesday-Saturday, but even when it's not busy, it's busy. Lots of chandeliers, brass rails, ferns, marble counter tops, a stand-up bar lined with stools. The service is very good, with friendly and efficient bartenders who've been there since the beginning. It's noisy on weekends, what with the crowds and the taped background music, mostly mellow stuff from the 40s and 50s.

Gable's Restaurant and Disco (968-1429), 115 Yorkville Avenue. Fittingly done up in Early Clark and Late Gable: lots of memorabilia of the late movie star as well as wrought-iron chairs and white tablecloths.

The management claims the disco and stool bar is for couples and singles, while the decor of the dining area (steaks and salads, about $30 for 2) is intimate – that's French for "dim lighting." On busy weekend nights, the patio and disco are crowded with Yorkville Trendies; yet, peering through the bistro windows off Yorkville, you wouldn't know a disco is back there.

About one-third of the crowd are regulars, and there are lots of tourists; the disco age range is 25-35. Frankly, Scarlett, there are thousands every week who give a damn, especially on Thursday, Friday, and Saturday nights.

Hemingway's (968-2828), 142 Cumberland Street. Unique, but not because of its pretentious name. The crowd (seventy per cent are regulars) is middle to upper class, professional, and not very pretentious at all. They are good looking (though not intimidatingly so), and the atmosphere is sort of homey and less tense than other Yorkville places.

The stand-up bar has a nice and easy atmosphere (and it's not a singles' bar, stresses the management). The food is fine, but **Hemingway's** is better known for its bar atmosphere and clientele.

The decor here is not Yorkville glitzy but more literary, with a green interior, comfortable high-back chairs, mirrors, and artsy posters on the walls, and real, live books lining one wall.

There's entertainment all through the week, mainly middle of the road stuff on piano, with jazz on Sundays. There's no cover, and dress is very casual, just as Ernest would have wanted.

P.W.D. Dinkel's (923-9689), 88 Yorkville Avenue. A classic hot spot that attracts the Yorkville Trendy crowd who come to meet and mingle. The age range is 25-35, and regulars make up about three-quarters of the crowd. It has a 50-50 male/female ratio, which is just like God and Noah wanted; and the two stand-up bars are where the action is, with dozens of men hanging out and looking out.

A black-and-white-tiled dance floor is where trendies perform for their audience; above and around are the usual mirrored rotating ball and flashing disco lights. The music is a variety of disco (if that's not a contradiction in terms), and middle-of-the road sounds. Weekends are busy, and leave your jeans (designer or otherwise) in the closet. John Travolta, come home.

The ABCs of R and B

If you don't know what *R & B* stands for, you'll learn soon enough after visiting the top place for it in Toronto.

Club Bluenote (921-1109), 128 Pears Avenue, just north of Davenport and west of Avenue Road. *The* rhythm and blues spot in the city. Yes, there are other places which play R & B along with jazz. But this place is truly dedicated to "blue-eyed soul," a first in Toronto. It is with this distinction that we list it on its own.

The **Bluenote** is unique, known for its off-the-cuff atmosphere. Many world musicians and singers frequent it when in Toronto, and it's not unusual for these folks to get up and do their stuff. **David Clayton Thomas** (once of Blood, Sweat, and Tears), **Patsy Gallant**, **Martha Reeves**, and **Dinah Christie** have all entertained the faithful. As of the fall of 1982, **Club Bluenote** began a Sunday night jam, where many of Toronto's top musicians are encouraged to drop by and play. The house band, **George Oliver and Gangbuster**, plays three sets a night, with the middle one featuring guest singers of the 1960s.

The Club has a cosy decor, with Tiffany lamps and lots of browns. It's popular with singles and couples.

Eat for $20 and dance for free.

Nightlife: Audience Participation

The "me" generation. The "we" generation. The "Hey, you!" generation. Perhaps all three. One thing is for certain: there are times when most of us wish to become involved. When you are hit with that most basic need, try one of these.

Diamond Lil's (244-1711), on the ground floor of the Skyline Hotel, 655 Dixon Road. It's a saloon, not a salon, that is supposed to remind you of the gold-rush days of the Klondike. So what you get are walls made of the finest barnboard, low-level lighting, and an upstairs balcony where you almost expect Clint Eastwood to rush in shooting, if that's your cup of brew. The nightly entertainment is provided by **Diamond Lil**, who is accompanied by a six-piece band called **Hart Wheeler's Showband** that often plays wild tunes from those precious days of yore. There are three shows nightly, and the weekends tend to have line-ups, so it is recommended that you get there early. Gold nuggets are accepted, but so are charge cards – you can be sure of that, pardner.

Edelweiss (598-1977), on the west island of **Ontario Place** on the waterfront across from the CNE grounds. This place is frequented by your standard, young beer-swilling set, 19-25. They're college kids and working-class types, mainly dressed in blue jeans and T-shirts, attracted by the lack of cover charge and the loud entertainment.

The food is no gourmet delight, but it's tolerable and moderately priced. As the name suggests, there is Bavarian weiner schnitzel, bratwurst, and sauerkraut. The music is the joy, of course; rowdy, oom-pah-pah band encourages sing-alongs.

His Majesty's Feast (769-1165), at the Seaway Motor Hotel, 1926 Lakeshore Boulevard W. at the South Kingsway. There is no cover, but you have to order the meal, which runs $16.95 on weekdays and $21.95 on weekends. No jeans are allowed and the drink prices are moderate.

The decor is pseudo-sixteenth-century English tavern, in a giant room filled with wooden tables and benches, lots of red velvet drapes, and a stage for the King and for the staff, who do singing and dancing routines. The clientele runs 19-60, wearing everything from three-piece suits to those illegal jeans.

There are numerous birthday celebrations, and audience participation includes choosing people from the tables to assist in the routines. Treats include choosing a woman – and a man – to be locked up in stocks, and having men and women in the audience come up and kiss the "victims."

Dick Turpin's Pub (368-2511), in the Royal York Hotel, 100 Front Street W., across from Union Station. No dress code, and no dancing, but a very casual atmosphere. Drinks are expensive. The decor? English Tudor again, which means that the sing-along music includes country, calypso, as well as English, Irish, and Scottish. There is a stand-up area at the bar for singles, and the clientele runs from 20-70.

Brunswick House (924-3884; 924-3833), 481 Bloor Street W. between Spadina and Bathurst. Where you'll find the university crowd, since the place is right on the edge of the U. of T. It's loud, raucous, beer-guzzling: everyone is in jeans and swilling draft – with quarts available.

Upstairs, university types pour in to hear eclectic music from across the country, including bluegrass, swing, country, and rhythm and blues. It's not audience participation, but it's good, solid entertainment, and less good, less solid fast food is available.

Back downstairs are some of the Brunswick Tavern's regular events: there's a talent night weekly, and every September (like clockwork) their annual wet T-shirt night, which has us as worried about the future of Canadian youth as you are. There are annual pie throwings, annual watermelon eating, and sing-alongs throughout the year.

Give Me a "P"! Give Me a "U"! Give Me a "B"!

Considering how strong the British influence is in Canadian history, it's rather odd that the first English pub, the **Duke of York** (now a chain of seven), did not open in Toronto until 1975. But now they are everywhere – foot rails, dart boards, draft by the half-pint (but not paid for by the half-pence, alas). Here are some of the most popular:

Ben Wicks Dining Room and Neighbourhood Pub (961-9425), 422 Parliament Street, between Carlton and Gerrard. An English-style pub where you can get continental cuisine as well as quaff Tartan or Murphy beer. There's no cover, and a jazz band performs Wednesday through Saturday 9:00 p.m.-1:00 a.m.

Wicks is the cartoonist from the Old Country who does the

little boxes on the front page of *The Toronto Star* each day, often on Canadian political issues, and a strip on the comic page. He's verrrrry cockney, as is his pub.

Duke of Kent (485-9507), 2315 Yonge Street, just above Eglinton. A marvellous selection of imported beers and ales – nearly a dozen Irish, Scottish, and English beers by the bottle and on tap. They even have the world's strongest beer – Hardy's Hymalt, which is 10.8 per cent alcohol, compared with Canada's average of less than 5 per cent.

You can get pickled eggs (95¢) or pickled onions (75¢) and can enjoy the grandfather clock, bar mistress, and deer's-head trophies staring down at you, inviting you to stay until someone cries out, "Time, gentlemen! Please!"

The Unicorn (487-0020), 175 Eglinton Avenue East, a few blocks east of Yonge. Many find the atmosphere here even more British than the Duke chain. There's a six-foot screen and a nice, homey atmosphere that lacks the pressure of all those single bars.

It's fun to see the "North American side," which is more reserved, and has a seating area for quiet conversation on the left; on the right, "the English side" is more rowdy – there is a piano and everyone sings along. You can get snacky food, such as chicken wings.

Duke of Richmond (598-4454), in the Toronto Eaton Centre. There's a Scottish quality about it, and the University of Toronto student handbook raves about it. It's part of the explosively popular Duke chain, with lots of small rooms and a dart-board lane (natch) in the rear. Meat patties and pies are available, as well as a charming view of quiet Old Trinity Church, just to the west of the Eaton Centre. Closed Sundays.

Duke of Gloucester (961-9704), 649 Yonge Street, second floor, a few blocks below Bloor. Another member of the Duke chain praised by the U. of T. handbook. Go to the bar and stand, if you wish to mingle. Radio provides the entertainment, but that seems enough, as people down the Beamish and Tennents lager and dream of the Old Country. A shepherd's pie, with vegie of the day, will run you less than $5, and a Scotch egg is even cheaper, including salad. Closed Sundays.

Rose & Crown (488-5557), 2335 Yonge Street, above Eglinton. As authentic as its name, and its bar is considered the most comfortable stand-up spot in town. A long and delicious bar menu (with things like chicken fingers for less than $4) is backed up by a large restaurant in the rear. A

Sunday menu offers many choices of eggs and sausages and steak.

Queen's Head Pub (929-9525), 249 Gerrard Street E., west of Parliament. As homey and warm as you would expect in Cabbagetown. Flowers on the wallpaper, pâté sandwiches on the plate, chandeliers on the ceiling, and beer in the belly. And tiny Union Jacks all over the dart boards, of course.

Balmy Arms (699-8467), 2136 Queen Street E., is way out in the east end, in the Beaches. Wonderful food, both hearty and pubby, and the strange, charming local crowd make this place one of the grand places in the city.

Duke of York (964-2441), 39 Prince Arthur Avenue, just north of Bloor and west of Avenue Road. As beautiful as the neighbourhood is classy. Solid, British lunches, and lots of good conversation and beer.

Duke of Westminster (368-1555), First Canadian Place, via Adelaide Street W. Right there in the biggest, tallest bank building of them all. Here is where you'll find the men who may well foreclose your house, tossing back beers imported from Germany, Holland, Denmark, Belgium, and – dare we say it – England. Beautifully served snacks in a beautiful atmosphere, for all you thirsty capitalists.

Nightlife: Très Gay

Numerous gay bars have popped up in Toronto over the past few years, which is not surprising. For Toronto's gay community claims to be the largest in North America after San Francisco. The following selection should appeal to a variety of different people, interests, and lifestyles. More information about gay bars and gay life in Toronto can be found in literature available at most of the spots listed below.

Dudes (923-6136), 10 Breadalbane Street, one block south of Yonge and Wellesley. This is a male western-style bar with lots of denim. It is best known as an after-hours spot, serving beer and wine at a "collegiate-type" bar. There is dancing, Wednesday through Sunday, a large pool table, and home-cooking at extremely reasonable cost (the house claims that it loses money on every meal served).

Buddy's Backroom (977-9955), 370 Church Street, below Carlton. The clientele are blue-collar workers; the "social bar" is mostly men; the music is loud disco. Nostalgia freaks may enjoy the music from the 50s and 60s, which is blasted on weekends. There is no dance floor. Inexpensive food and a full menu for both lunch and dinner.

Maygay's (Charlie's) (no phone), upstairs at the St. Charles Tavern, 488 Yonge Street, above College. There is a cover charge, and it gets crowded around midnight. There is no food upstairs but there is food downstairs, in the tavern. The music is heavy-duty disco. There is a DJ, and the clientele likes to dance. Maygay's is not for men only, but women tend not to go.

The Outpost (925-6215), in the Hotel California (downstairs), 321 Jarvis Street, below Carlton. Brick-and-mortar with farm implements here and there. There is also a dining room, closed Mondays, but no dancing. The music is mainly current; the clientele is strictly male, from age 19 to retirement. There are theme nights once a month, and this is known as a cruising spot.

Albany Tavern (861-1155), 158 King Street East, near Jarvis. Has a "sports" clientele. It's a baseball bar, and the hangout of the gay softball league. It has a disco dance floor, a small dining room, patio, and pool tables. Since the fall of 1982, a "guest house," alias a hotel, has been in existence.

Boots (921-3142), in the Selby Hotel, 592 Sherbourne Street, just below Bloor. Two bars with disco dancing: the emphasis is on the bars. The dining room has burgers and daily specials. There's a lounge with a dance floor, and a tavern on the other side. Less than ten per cent are female; the clientele is a mix of all types and ages.

Together Dining Lounge (923-3469), 457 Church Street above Carlton. This is *the* female gay bar, although there are usually some men in attendance. The food served here is moderate in price, and it is reportedly excellent. Two can eat for between $20 and $30. There is a lounge, a long bar, and a dining room. The decor is dark and intimate, and it tends to be busy from 9:00 p.m. until closing time (at 3:00 a.m. weekends).

Katrina's (961-4740), 5 St. Joseph Street, west of Yonge and north of Wellesley. On Fridays and Saturdays, this club is open to 4:00 a.m. (However, it cannot and does not offer drinks at that hour thanks to our liquor laws.) It has a dance floor with decor in the New York disco-style. On Friday to Sunday nights, there is a drag show. The evening crowd tends to be 19-30 years old; an older crowd comes in during the day. Two can eat, with wine, for under $30. It's not elegant but leans towards it.

Real Live Honest-to-Goodness Entertainment

There are many, many spots with live entertainment in Toronto; many are listed under other categories, such as rock, singles, punk, etc. Here is an assorted gathering, by *no* means exhaustive, ranging from high class to down-and-dirty.

Favourite Nightspots

Imperial Room (368-2511), in the Royal York Hotel, 100 Front Street West, opposite Union Station. The grande dame of Toronto. This is where Tina Turner, Ella Fitzgerald, Lena Horne, Burton Cummings, Ronnie Hawkins, Peggy Lee, and Lord-knows-who-else has played over the past few years. Suiting its entertainers and their audience, the decor is elegant, ritzy, with orange, high-back chairs, and white tablecloths. Chandeliers above, large marble pillars around, and a stage at the front of a large room with two levels.

Close to half the clientele are regulars, who are given priority, so tough luck. They tend to be from age 30 on. Many business people come here for lunch, as well.

Continental food is served noon-2:30 p.m. and from 6:30 p.m. on. Dinner with show will set you back over $25 in mid-week, and close to $30 a person from Thursdays to Saturdays. But you *can* take in the show only, if you wish, for prices varying between $15-22, depending on what Living Legend is there this week.

Show times are 9:00 p.m., Tues.-Thurs.; 9:00 and 11:00 p.m., Fri.-Sat. The later show usually less crowded. You'd be wise to reserve a week or more in advance.

Café on the Park Restaurant and Nightclub (483-3484), 174 Eglinton Avenue W., between Yonge and Avenue Road. A sit-down bar, stained-wood walls, natural-wood tables, lots of ferns, two levels, and no dance floor. The clientele is 20-35, middle-class, and happy to indulge in fried potato skins, burgers, peppercorn steak, and salads. But what they really come for are the popular bands which play here, from middle-of-the-road to jazz, reggae, 50s rock, and the occasional comic.

The cover varies with the act, but it's usually around $2, Mon.-Thurs. and Sun.; $3-5 on Fri.-Sat. It's a nice place, and when the entertainment is good, it's a great place. Open till 1:00 a.m. every night except Sunday, when it closes at 11:00 p.m.

The Black Knight (368-2511), in the Royal York Hotel, 100 Front Street West is for ballroom dancing, with a pianist playing middle-of-the-road stuff. The decor is captured (if not tortured) in the name: Mediaeval English, with a suit of armour at the entrance, and dark wood panelling, heraldry plaques, red curtains, and stained glass, just like great-great grandfather, the knight, used to love.

The clientele is mid-30s; affluent, upper crust, well-dressed, quite sophisticated. Fittingly (and if the jacket fits, wear it), men are required to don one. The cover is in the $2-3 range; food runs toward linguine, steak, crab, lamb, and around $40 for two. Open 11:30 a.m.-2:30 p.m. for lunch; 6:30 p.m.-1:00 a.m. for dinner.

Rivoli Cafe & Club (596-1908), 332 Queen Street W., west of University. A showcase for new, local artists not yet established enough to have their own gallery showings. And the back room functions as a club, featuring poetry readings, theatre happenings, "new music" (progressive rock and jazz), a Sunday-evening film society, and the already legendary Tuesday-night **Pan-Am Dance Discotheque** – a sophisticated, New Wave European-type dance hall, beginning at 9:00 p.m.

The menu is café food; cover varies with the show, usually $2-5. No dress code. The Rivoli is *it* for a growing number of people. Open Mon.-Sat., noon-1:00 a.m.; Sun., 5:30-11:00 p.m.

Yuk-Yuk's Komedy Kabaret (967-6425), 1280 Bay Street, just above Bloor. As its dreadful name suggests, comedians appear regularly, some much better than others. We caught the inspired Mort Sahl here some years ago, and it was a highlight of our nightclub lives. Monday evenings are amateur night, so be warned or be excited, depending upon your level of optimism. It has no dress code, "as long as the naughty bits are covered."

The clientele tends to be young – 16-30, although it's getting older with the years. The cover can run up to $4.50 weeknights and Sun.; up to $7.50, Fri.-Sat. A dinner-show package runs $16.50 on Thurs.; $19.50 on weekends. Show times are 9:00 p.m., Mon.-Thurs.; 8:30 and 11:00 p.m., Fri.-Sat.; 8:30 p.m., Sun. We who are about to laugh, salute you.

B.B. Magoon's (928-0768), 96 Bloor Street W. near Avenue Road. A real comer. In 1983 it had the city in an uproar by bringing in Jim Carey, the hottest new impressionist in the world, it seems. (Carey used to perform at **Café on the Park**.) It's an exciting new place in a superb location, and is rapidly becoming a favourite of Torontonians and visitors.

Don't Knock the Rock

There are piles of rock places and palaces in Toronto, often quite similar in crowd, decor, and style. What follows is the must list of popular rock places for diehards. And, as everyone over twenty knows, rock 'n roll will never die.

El Mocambo Tavern (961-2558), 464 Spadina Avenue,

just south of College Street, took on the establishment when the **Rolling Stones** performed here, and were heard, and joined, by a certain Canadian Prime Minister's wife, who will remain nameless, probably for the first time in her life. There is no question: the Elmo is *the* place for rock 'n roll in the city. **Levon Helm**, **Rick Danko**, the **Ozark Mountain Daredevils** – this is where to hear them.

The age range here tends to be 19-30, dressed mainly in jeans and T-shirts. (There is no dress code, naturally; this is rock remember?) The ventilation is smoky, the music loud, the natural-wood walls covered with posters of groups who have played within these hallowed, hollowed walls.

The downstairs never has a cover charge, and gets various rock bands performing 60s rock and roll. The upstairs has a cover ranging from $1 to $11.50, depending on the act. Many good Canadian rock groups play here, including **Billie Idol**, **Goddo**, **Oliver Heavyside**, **Rough Trade**, and **Downchild Blues Band**. It's no pick-up bar; it's rock, rock, rock. Sandwiches, pizza, drinks, and music from around 6:00 p.m.-1:00 a.m.

Stagger Lee's (596-1956), 368 Queen Street West, corner of Spadina. A former blacksmith's shop that became the Grand Old Opry of the North for nearly three decades under the name **The Horseshoe**. (**Charlie Pride**, **Tex Ritter**, **Hank Williams**, **Loretta Lynn** all played here.) It's now a very swinging rock palace, with free dance lessons at 8:00 p.m. on Tues.-Wed., buck-a-beer Wed., no cover Thurs. and $2 on weekends. There are pajama parties, and lots of rock and roll. Any place that has its taped phone message conclude with "Rock and roll *is* here to stay at **Stagger Lee's**- – see you later, alligator" can't be all bad. Closed Mondays.

D.J.'s (595-0700), 700 University Avenue at College Street. Live bands – three sets from around 9:30 p.m. to closing – play middle-of-the-road rock. Because of its expensive location (in the handsome Hydro Building, just southwest of the Parliament Buildings), the draw has to be very good. And most of the groups are both good and popular. There is dancing, with a disco system and DJ between sets, and the decor is turn-of-the-century New York saloon. The crowd runs to 20-25 year olds in the evening, and there's a small singles' bar as well.

The hip of beef buffet costs under $5 and is offered from 5:00-8:30 every night. Young singles predominate. No cut-off jeans or tank tops. Open Mon.-Fri., 11:00 a.m.-1:00 a.m.; Sat., 7:00 p.m.-1:00 a.m. Thurs.-Sat., usually a $4 cover.

Queensbury Arms (243-0660), 1212 Weston Road, above Eglinton in the west end. In a tudor-style building is a large, warehouse-style rock/new wave bar, crowded on weekends with young people in their 20s and 30s. Working-class locals love the very loud and very smoky atmosphere. The decor is early Marxist and late Engels; your basic tables and chairs packed very close together; like many rock places, it looks seedy, and has a first-rate collection of graffiti-covered washroom walls.

The large dance floor facing the band and the stand-up bar make this a fairly easy place to meet people, with the male/female ratio running a healthy 50-50. Almost everyone is wearing jeans and T-shirts, so leave the three-piece at home. Wednesday is "Ladies' Night," when it is, to quote the locals, "packed with chicks." Where are you, Gloria Steinem?

Live rock bands play 70s music; a snack bar provides burgers and roast beef sandwiches; moderate drinks; busiest on weekends. Mon.-Sat., 11:00 a.m.-1:00 a.m. There's a $3-4 cover Thurs.-Sat. We flatly refuse to mention the Wet T-Shirt contests on Monday evenings and the male strippers on Wednesdays.

Nickelodeon (unlisted phone number!), 279 Yonge Street, across from the Eaton Centre. Upstairs from the **Hard Rock Cafe**. This medium-sized rock bar caters to people in their 20s-30s, all uniformed in jeans and T-shirts. It's a popular Yonge Street spot, the crowd mainly rock lovers, with the occasional motorcycle gang to add some class. It tends to be loud and rowdy, with the poor ventilation that befits a rock bar. There's a dance floor, and live bands play 60s rock and new wave. It's slightly seedy and grimy, serves snacks and drinks, and is busy weekends.

Larry's Hideaway (Headspace Bar) (924-5791), 121 Carlton, east of Jarvis. Not far from Maple Leaf Gardens, and popular amongst the younger set, 19-25. It's dimly lit, the ventilation is cough-cough, and the cover varies, depending on the rock band playing the 60s and 70s rock 'n roll. The tables are packed close together, more males than females, and video shows are often screened. Bands start at 9:30, even later, and are known to be much better than the seedy bar and the less than desirable washrooms. There is a dance floor, plus snacks, burgers, and moderately priced drinks. Open noon-1:00 a.m.; closed Sundays.

Jarvis House (368-2034), 101 Jarvis Street, below Queen Street E. It's a great place to swill beer and mix with the working- and middle-class 20-30-year-olds, all dressed in you-know-what. The decor is somewhat better than most; natural-wood walls, brass railings, plants, black tables and chairs surrounding the smallish dance floor. There is a large stand-up bar, and a variety of snacks, including pizza with sausages. There is never a cover, and weekends are busy. Music runs from rhythm and blues to middle-of-the-road rock to hard rock. Open all week, 11:30 a.m.-1:00 a.m.; closed Sunday.

Ve Haf Vays Ov Letting You Tawk

Many bars, lounges, and watering holes in Toronto are so noisy, one might think they were created by hungry ear/nose/throat doctors to drum up – and we do mean drum up – business. But not *all* places in this city are loud and near-impossible TO HOLD CONVERSATIONS IN. HERE ARE BUT A FEW OF OUR FAVOURITES! (Sorry, but we just *had* to yell there.)

Note: There are numerous little places in Yorkville, running up and down Cumberland and Yorkville Avenues, between Avenue Road and Yonge Street. And since they are so numerous, we urge you to take a stroll and cafe-hop; this is the best way to dig them up, according to our archaeologist friend.

Le Select Bistro (596-6405), 328 Queen Street West, west of University. The perfect place for a romantic conversation and a fine meal. The clientele tends to be 25-35, with regulars often receiving special treatment (e.g., wine on the house, etc.). With seating for only forty-three, the tables are rather close together; but this only makes it more intimate, with hanging baskets of fresh bread and light, taped music of jazz of the 30s and 40s adding to the delight. We've mentioned this place before, with its underpriced $11.95 prix fixe meals; but we can't stop. Mon.-Thurs., noon-midnight; Fri.-Sat., noon-1:00 a.m.; Sun., 5:30-11:00 p.m.

Madcaps (593-1110), 335 Queen Street West. A charming restaurant with a long stand-up bar at the entrance. The age range here is 25-40, with lots of locals from the area, and none of your Yorkville Trendies. It's a good place for conversation, although it *can* get loud at times, with taped music of 50s and 60s rock, R & B, reggae. The food is very good, the drinks low priced. A winner. Open Mon.-Sat., noon-1:00 a.m.; noon-11:00 p.m., Sun. No Sunday brunch in the summer, alas.

Garbo's (593-9870), 429 Queen Street West, west of Spadina. Surprise! Pictures of Greta Garbo, as well as 1880s-style furniture (is she *that* old?) and lots of art nouveau. The place has a $2 cover on Friday and Saturdays, and will allow no cut-off jeans from its clientele of "real as opposed to plastic people." About half of the 20-55 year olds who go here are regulars, enjoying the small dance floor and romantic dining area. At lunchtime, businessmen come to nibble. And talk.

The music is live, seven days a week; the food is French, continental, and very good, served to 11:00 p.m. From then until 1:00 a.m., snacks are available. **Garbo's** is crowded throughout the year, especially after 7:30 p.m. The lunches are fine; drinks are reasonable. Open 11:00 a.m.-1:00 a.m., seven days a week; lunch, noon-3:00 p.m.

The Twenty-Two (979-2341), 22 St. Thomas Street, just south and east of Bloor and University. A quiet meeting spot for over two decades. There's no dress code or cover, yet one can count on lovely, live piano from 5:00-8:00 each evening, and piano with singing, 9:00-1:00 p.m. Until the summer of 1983 this place was not licenced for food, but there are free hors d'oeuvres at 5:45. So if you are hungry for fine food, drift over to the excellent **Courtyard Cafe**, in the same building.

The clientele at **The Twenty-Two** is the Bay Street business person. It's frequented by many big names in the city, but the management won't talk about them. Big deals and hot affairs go on here, but it's very discreet (dim lighting helps). Probably ninety per cent are regulars, who have good rapport with the staff. The decor is mostly tables for two, beige-and-dark-green chairs and walls, with lots of wood and different lighting. A sidewalk cafe has expanded its seating capacity. If you've got something to say to someone, this is one of the most pleasant places in Toronto to say it. Lunches are served from noon-4:00 p.m.; it's open until 1:00 a.m.

Dominic's (483-1444), 173 Eglinton Avenue East, west of Mt. Pleasant is an Italian restaurant (dinners run about $50 for two, including a half-litre of wine) that has a totally relaxed atmosphere that is great for talking. Its lounge, is set beside huge windows facing the street. Plants and comfortable chairs abound.

There are more females than males, but it's really not a meeting place for singles; it's a home away from home for its regulars. Visitors enjoy the superb pianist and singer who does requests. A small dance floor completes the picture; good service and unpretentiousness abound. It's a place to *talk*. Open noon-2:30 p.m. for lunch; dinner is served from 5:00-11:00 p.m., and closing time is 1:00 a.m. Closed Sunday.

Jingles (960-1500), 1378 Yonge Street, just below St. Clair.

A pub-like atmosphere and a good place for a nice talk, in spite of its jangley name. The small dining room serves continental food but stressing the Italian – the management claims that its lasagna is the best in the city. The clientele is a broad cross-section of people, heavy on literary types, with up to fifty per cent regulars. lunches and Saturday nights are busiest; Lunches of soups, salads, pastas, and desserts, are in the $5 range. Dinners run toward seafood, poultry, and steak ($10-12). Reservations are advised for the Saturday-night special, which is a prix fixe dinner, not a gun.

Much of the pleasure comes from the good pianist on Saturdays who plays ragtime and requests. But the lack of cover and the moderately priced drinks help. It's a nice break from the hustle of other places around town. There's another **Jingles** (964-7722), at 467 Church Street, but there's no pianist there. Both locations are open Mon-Fri., noon to 2:00 a.m.; Sat., 5:00 p.m.-2:00 a.m.; Closed Sundays.

La Serre (964-0411), in the Four Seasons Hotel, at Avenue Road and Yorkville. Once the **SRO**, it is now AOK with its large crowds. It has luxurious, old-European decor, with a stand-up piano bar and a pianist worth standing for. The crowd runs from 25-70, and classy; perhaps forty per cent are hotel guests. This place serves a cross-section of society, and no longer stresses singles.

Lunches are the most interesting, running from $5-8 for quiche, roast rib eye, shrimps, pasta, salads, etc. In the evening, a sushi bar; for cocktail hour (5:30-8:30), pâté maison, shrimps, cheese plate, etc. Drinks are expensive, but coffees, teas, and wines are not. Besides, the price is worth it for a place to talk. Open 11:30 a.m.-1:00 a.m., Mon.-Sat.; 3:00 p.m.-11:00 p.m. Sun.

Bloor Street Diner (928-3105), 50 Bloor Street West, near Yonge. Light taped background music, which is already something to recommend it for. The decor is what you might expect in a "diner" that rides on the second floor of the Holt Renfrew building at the most expensive intersection in Toronto: black formica, silver, black and white tiling, pink neon signs, fluorescent lighting. The clientele is everything and anything, from punkers to cabbies to high class to you and me. The food and service have been known to be uneven, but it is a gorgeous place. And open late. And fairly quiet. And to be open from 11:00 a.m.-3:00 a.m., seven days a week is, for *this* city, a very special find, indeed.

Cafe Goodyo's (489-3633), 2360 Yonge Street, just above Eglinton. That California feeling: ferns, natural wood, unnatural brass. There's no dress code and no cover, but there *is* a $5 minimum on Thurs.-Sat., so don't go then unless you plan to eat or drink something. The music is by two regular bands, which play Simon and Garfunkel, the Beatles, and other such Mon.-Sat. The menu is cafe food, the clientele rather young (20-35), and middle-class, fairly trendy, cafe-types. Let's just say it's sophisticated. And they can hear themselves think and their partners talk, which is more than you can say or scream about most cafes. Open Mon.-Sat., 11:30 a.m.-1:00 a.m., with food until 11:30 p.m.; Sun. 5:00 p.m.-10:30 p.m.

The Courtyard Cafe (979-2212), in the Windsor Arms Hotel, 22 St. Thomas St. Known as "Cafe Yoo-Hoo," with good reason. It's a place to see and to be seen. It is also physically beautiful, with tasteful modern decor and wonderful food. And those desserts! You don't have to die to go to heaven. The entertainment is piano music, trios, duets, or light classical music that goes well with the fine food and that wonderful person you came with. Service has a reputation for being, shall we say, poor, as in rude. But it's the perfect place for conversation, in between waving to friends and acquaintances – and famous strangers – across the room. And the pâté maison, galantine of duck, marinated seafood salad, Dover sole, fresh trout, veal paillard, bouchée of chicken with baby shrimps with green olives and almonds- -well, even without the most extraordinary desserts and ices in the city, this is a place to eat in and talk in and even *not* be seen by everyone in.

Breakfast, 7:00 a.m.-11:00 a.m., Mon.-Sun.; Lunch, noon-5:00 p.m., Mon.-Sat.; Dinner, 5:00 p.m.-12:30 a.m., but open until 1:00 a.m. Sunday brunch, 11:00 a.m.-4:30 p.m.; Sunday dinner, 5:00-10:30 p.m.

Dessert Dessert (485-1725), 2352 Yonge, just above Eglinton. It is mentioned in our **North Yonge Street** walk, but it should be noted again here, because of its lovely atmosphere and those five hundred different desserts, baked on the premises. The lovely patio is open April to October; from November to March, they are closed Mondays; otherwise, 11:00 a.m.-3:00 a.m., daily.

Zaidy's Restaurant (977-7222), 225 Queen Street W., noted on our **Queen Street** stroll, but it's also very good for very quiet conversation, helped along by excellent desserts. Open Mon.-Thurs., 11:30 a.m.-3:00 p.m. for lunch; 5:00-10:00 p.m. for dinner. Fridays and Saturdays 5:00 p.m.-midnight. Closed Sundays.

Montréal Restaurant-Bistro (363-0179), 65 Sherbourne, east of Jarvis and north of King Street E. Extremely popular, yet good for a good talk. Dinners tend toward steak, salmon, and pork, at $8-13. After decades of brutal competition between Toronto and Montreal, it's nice to have a restaurant by that name on our side. Open Mon.-Sat., noon to 2:30 p.m. for lunch; 6:00-10:00 p.m. for dinner. The Bistro is open Mon.-Fri., 11:00 a.m.-1:00 a.m.; Sat., 5:00 p.m.-1:00 a.m., Closed Sunday – this is Toronto, not Montreal.

The Jack Benny Memorial Award for Cheap Drinks This award, which, surprisingly, goes along with an award for decent food and attractive decor, goes to **The Keg Restaurants**. There are four, as of this writing: 12 Church St., just below Front (367-0685); 515 Jarvis Street, just above Wellesley (964-6609); 2300 Yonge Street, just above Eglinton (482-0304); and 1977 Leslie Street, south of the 401 (446-1045). Okay, okay, there's one west of Toronto, in Cooksville, at 2539 Dixie Road (279-9127). And note that The Keg at 515 Jarvis is in an old mansion that used to be the home of Governor-General Vincent Massey and his actor brother, Raymond, and is worth a visit for the architecture alone.

The pricing strategy at these restaurants aims for quality at a reasonable price. How reasonable? Well, they have raised their liquor prices only four times since 1971; during the same period most restaurants and bars went through half a dozen or more. So you can buy domestic beer for $1.75; imported suds at $2.50; a shot of liquor for $1.75; a "keg-sized shot," which includes an extra ounce, at $2.75; selected imported liquors at $2.75; a glass of white wine for $2.50; Spanish coffee for $1.95, and so on.

The Keg on Church has a bar and a dance floor, with a DJ providing the music Thurs.-Sat. At all the Kegs, the age is 18-45, the clientele, white collar, professional, middle-management. Tens of thousands of Torontonians swear by their steaks, and their onion soup is said to be the best in the city. And then, those cheap, cheap drinks.

Punk and New Wave
As of early 1983, Punk and New Wave clubs and bars are the most popular places in Toronto. The decor at these places is usually nothing to talk about, but that is not why the kids go. These places are trendy as all-get-out, and might be on their way out soon; but then that's what they said about Frank Sinatra and The Beatles.

Domino Klub (968-1010), 1 Isabella, at Yonge, just south of Bloor. A tough crowd between 18 and 30. You'll see lots of

FRED and GINGER
SLAM-DANCING
CHEEK-TO-CHEEK

leather, chains, and wild hair. Some of the patrons make E.T. look human. The decor is dark and dirty, and is suitably painted basic black. There is a dining lounge to the right, a disco to the left, and a bar at the back. The DJ doesn't play punk anymore, even though a good half of the clientele are punkers and many are regulars. Most of the music is new wave and disco. On Tuesdays and Wednesdays, a 75¢ cover pays for musical-video, such as a tape of a David Bowie concert, for which there is good visibility and sound.

The dress, to use the term loosely, is up from jeans and T-shirts to New Wave hairdos, such as the memorable Mohawk and Black Leather. Food runs from junk to sirloin; line-ups on Friday and Saturday nights suggest that mothers are still being hurt, even in the 1980s. Open weekdays, noon to 1:30 a.m.; weekends, 7:30 p.m.-4:00 a.m., which is late, man.

Nuts 'N' Bolts (977-1356), 277 Victoria, above Dundas, east of Yonge is a basement dive with the same nasty decor as the Domino. It's grimy, dark, with different coloured walls to keep you awake into the wee hours. Regulars call the music "fantastic for dancing," and who is to argue? It's hot and smoky, with 18-25 year olds everywhere in wild and weird clothes. It's trendy for a punk place, with lots of middle-to-upper-class rebels, James Deans, and students from Ryerson Polytechnic, nearby. It's most crowded on Thursday and Friday nights, listening and dancing to punk and new wave music on records. The food includes hamburgers, fries, and onion rings, beer, shots, cocktails, etc. Open Mon.-Wed., 11:00 a.m.-1:00 a.m.; Thurs.-Sat., 11:00 a.m.-4:00 a.m. Video also available for those who prefer staring to thrashing about. And with a capacity of close to three hundred, there is a lot of thrashing about.

Turning Point (967-4794), 192 Bloor Street West, west of Avenue Road. Live bands, mainly punk and new wave. The food is generally sandwiches for both lunch and dinner; the cover charge depends on the band. The crowd here has "society" – lots of multi-coloured hair and Mohawks. Chains and leather are often worn, to parents' horror. The capacity of the dance floor is about one hundred. It's a bit of a dive, but being so close to a major university probably helps. The crowd is extremely young. Open noon-1:00 a.m. nightly; a band plays from 9:00 p.m.-1:00 a.m.

Glitz, Glitter, and Gaudiness: The Atmosphere's the Thing

One common element in the following listings is an unmistakable emphasis on the decor and setting. Indeed, the service/food can be downright shabby.

And yet, for your money, you buy an "experience," as the trendies who package these things might say. It is no coincidence that some of the places below have achieved fame as discos, where fantasy atmosphere is achieved by sensory overload – LOUD music, fantastic light shows, and overwhelming decor.

It's also no coincidence that these spots have underplayed their disco theme; after all, rumour has it that disco is passé in the 1980s. But these *are* good places to go and dance, probably with a John Travolta lookalike you've never met before.

Heaven (968-2711), 2 Bloor Street East at Yonge. The management suggests reservations, which also suggests its popularity. In keeping with their modest name, they modestly describe themselves as "The Last of the Great Discos." It certainly ain't small-time: up to 676 people can squish in on Thursdays, Fridays, or Saturday evenings (The whole club can be rented for private parties on the other days.) and enjoy the floral-patterned couches, backgammon tables, and the superb sound system. A DJ plays funk, new wave, reggae, everything – and they have been experimenting with live rock bands.

The cover charge changes with the night: $3-5. And no jeans during Saturday night fever. Designer clothes are the way to Heaven. Lots of theme nights ("jungle night," "naughty nightie night," etc). Expensive drinks, no food. But with the monster light show and two huge dance floors, who could eat? After all, what's a Heaven for? Open Thurs., 8:00 p.m.-1:00 a.m.; Fri. 8:00 p.m.-2:00 a.m.; Sat., 8:00 p.m.-3:00 a.m.

Zodiac I (493-5511), in the Ramada Inn, 185 Yorkland, in the east end of the city, just south of Sheppard, near Victoria Park. Live entertainment plays reggae, funk, and disco, top forties, etc. No jeans, please. There's a fair-sized dance floor and a large singles bar, dimly lit for the working-class clientele and guests from the hotel. The age range is 20-45, and the good sound system may be too good for some. Lots of tables and seats – this is one big place. There's a $3.50 cover Fridays and $4.50 Saturdays. Cocktails run over $4, and service can be rude. But did you come here to dance or study etiquette?

Jacqui's (869-1600), in the lower lobby of the Toronto Hilton Harbour Castle, at the foot of Bay Street. There's no cover Mon.-Thurs., but you'll shell out $4-5 on weekends, when only designer jeans are allowed. It gets busy here from 11:30 p.m. to 1:00 a.m. on most days, and from as early as 8:30 p.m. on Saturday nights. A DJ plays disco tunes for the very mixed clientele, which runs from 25-45, depending on the night. They have theme nights, such as 50s rock.

Strange ratios here: more women on Fridays, but more couples on Saturdays. Regulars make up about half the crowd; the other half are from the hotel. Single men tend to hang out by the bar and railing that surround the dance floor, waiting like so many spiders for their victims to appear. It has a medium-sized dance floor, with disco-style decor; lots of brass and teak, strobe lights, tables for twos and fours, sofa lounges, and the ubiquitous stand-up bar. It's pointless to try and hold a conversation here. Open Mondays through Saturdays, 8:00 p.m.-1:00 a.m.; closed Sundays.

Le Club (444-2561) in the Inn on the Park, Eglinton Avenue E. at Leslie, just west of the Don Valley Parkway. They take reservations from their members (about 50 per cent of their clientele), but from others only on the day of the visit. People range from 25-50, most under 35; but a younger crowd comes out on Fridays and Saturdays. Members, of course, suffer no cover or line-ups, whereas *hoi polloi* can expect to pay $5 on weekends.

The room was designed for singles and couples, with mirrored pillars, rust carpet, and a cozy atmosphere for a place with a large dance floor and revolving coloured lights. Snacks and dinners are available. Music is disco all week. A warning to all you under-nineteens: they are *very* strict here about ID. Open Tues.-Thurs., 8:00 p.m.-1:00 a.m.; Fri. and Sat., 8:00 p.m.-3:00 a.m.; closed Sun. and Mon.

Sparkles (362-5411), in the CN Tower, 301 Front Street W. The world's highest free-standing dress code: jeans and sneakers are allowed only during the week. The clientele here is middle-to-upper class, with older folk on weeknights, and more women, tourists, and regulars Thursdays to Saturdays. There are lots of theme nights, disco, big band, 50s and 60s music, etc.

This is a tourist attraction, gang: imagine finding your beloved 1,150 feet above the ground – and revolving, no less! You can always plead insanity in the morning. The atmosphere, as you can imagine, is party party party. The lighting and the decor (and that View!) creates an environment that overwhelms the senses. The curved-space furniture, space-age fixtures and laser, smoke machine, and neon lights make this the best light show in the city. Drinks are expensive;

salads and snacks are available; the cover always changes
($2-5) so does the view as the world turns. And sexism lives:
Thursday nights are, believe it or not, "Ladies' Night," when
women (girls?) get in free and even are presented with a rose.
There is a reduced cover charge after midnight. And it seats
440! Open Mon.-Fri., 11:00 a.m.-2:00 a.m.; Sat., 11:00 a.m.-
3:00 a.m.

All That Jazz
The arguments are endless: New York City is Jazz City; New
York City is no longer the centre. Edmonton, Alberta is *the*
place for jazz in Canada; don't go to Edmonton if you want to
hear great jazz. All we do know for sure is that Toronto has a
number of extremely popular and trustworthy jazz places:
   Meyer's Deli (960-4780), 69 Yorkville. Live jazz is performed from 1:00 a.m.-3:30 a.m. each night except Sunday.
There is a full deli menu and its cheesecake is worth killing
for.
   Errol's (862-8431), 284 Richmond Street E., just west of
Sherbourne. It's considered the classiest, most comfortable,
and most successful jazz night spot in town. The off-beat
location adds to Errol Fisher's concept of a place where people walk in "and feel that it is their own private discovery."
The decor is muted browns, soft lights, mirrors, and brass,
with marble in the washrooms. The clientele is refined, professional, middle-to-upper class, with lots of beautiful
women, if that is your thing. The Italian cuisine is reportedly
very good, and a dinner for two plus wine runs close to $60.
The jazz starts at 9:00 p.m., and is played by a superb jazz trio
led by pianist Joe Sealy, with occasional blues vocals from the
room's proprietor. There is no cover and no minimum, but
proper attire is requested. Open Mon.-Sat., 9:00 p.m.-1:00
a.m. Closed Sundays.
   Lytes (368-2511), in the Royal York Hotel, 100 Front Street
W. A high-tech jazz club, with stark and glittery decor. It
competes with **Bourbon Street** for top of the line soloists,
mostly American, but it has a "house" rhythm section. With
its hotel location and relatively steep cover charges, **Lytes**
has been slow to get established, but it is now very much
appreciated by jazz aficionados. The music is usually main-
stream jazz – a mixture of mellow, warm, melodic, and swinging. The food is snacky. Cover is $3 on weeknights; $5 on
weekends. Open noon-1:00 a.m. daily. Music starts around
9:15 p.m.

George's Spaghetti House (923-9887), 290 Dundas Street E., corner of Sherbourne. The oldest continuous jazz club in the city. The atmosphere is gala, music starting at 9:00 p.m. The staff is friendly, the owner is maitre d', and the Italian food is served efficiently, and is better than over at Bourbon Street. This is not the place to look for a new lover; it tends to be frequented by couples and small groups.

Pictures of jazz artists line the restaurant walls, and fine performers line up to play here. The music covers a good range of the Toronto modern jazz community, with different local groups appearing each week. **Moe Koffman** and his Quintet (famous even in China for his *Swinging Shepherd Blues*) play the first week of every month, and reservations are urged up to one week in advance. Drinks are moderate; no dancing; casual dress and very good jazz. But use the washroom elsewhere. Open Mon.-Thurs., noon-1:00 a.m.; Sat. 5:00 p.m.-1:00 a.m.; Sun., 5:00-10:00 p.m., but no entertainment.

Bourbon Street (598-3020), 180 Queen Street W. Considered Toronto's most important jazz club, and has been for more than a decade. Major American soloists come in on a regular basis, to play with local rhythm sections. It's noisy and crowded, with so-so food. This place gets the cream of modern jazz, from vibraphonist Milt Jackson to guitarist Jim Hall to flugelhornist Art Farmer. The cover ranges from $1-4 and up, depending on the group. But be warned: the musicians are more likely to be asked to quiet down than the customers. Open 11:00 a.m.-1:00 a.m.; lunch from 11:00 a.m.-2:00 p.m. Entertainment runs about 9:00 p.m. to closing.

Chick 'N Deli (489-4161), 744 Mt. Pleasant Avenue, south of Eglinton. A popular uptown jazz spot. All ages, from 20-60, come up here to hear good jazz, mainly contemporary and swinging. Serious jazz listeners sit in the dining area, where they can purchase excellent honey and garlic chicken wings and a variety of chicken and rib dishes, from $4-9. Snacks are also available. An outdoor patio, in season, can be enjoyed with drinks and food. No dress code, but the cover runs $2-4, depending on the group. There is no cover for either the bar or the patio. There is dancing, and the entertainment starts at 8:30 p.m., with matinees on weekend afternoons. Open seven days a week.

In Deepest, Darkest Suburbia

Is there life after death? Is there life after forty? Is there life north of Bloor, west of Bathurst, or east of the Don Valley? For the first time, here are the answers to questions that have confounded philosophers and poets for milennia.

Tramps (231-8946), 2 Dunbloor, at Kipling and Bloor in the west end. A young clientele, no cover, and a not-too-restrictive dress code: no cut-offs or sweat pants. There's varied music, a restaurant, some theme nights. Open Mon.-Sat., 11:00 a.m.-1:00 a.m.; Sun. 11:00 a.m.-11:00 p.m.

Hannibals (223-1787), 5075 Yonge Street, about a kilometre north of Sheppard. The pick-up place of Greater Downtown North York. It has a lounge, a stand-up bar, a restaurant, and a patio. The clientele is mainly locals 20-30, nicely dressed, slightly trendy, lots of tiny alligators, listening to a DJ and dancing. Thursday and Friday nights are busiest, and they *do* check your age. Open Mon.-Sat., 11:00 a.m.-1:00 a.m.; Sun., noon-11:00 p.m.

Flanagan's (449-4111), in the Holiday Inn at Eglinton Avenue East and the Don Valley Parkway. A rowdy, sing-along Irish pub with dark wood panelling, green wallpaper, green carpets, green uniforms, etc. But it's so dimly lit, you'd hardly notice. There's a stand-up bar at the back of the room, but most of the action occurs on stage where Michael Shanahan leads the audience in songs, and elicits participation in singing contests and other delights. Since he's been playing here for over fourteen years now (and for previous fourteen at the *El Mocambo*), it's a known commodity. The age range is vast: 19 to 60. But it's mainly a younger crowd, with many regulars who come here for a good time. It is *not* a singles' bar, as the tables for twos, fours, and groups attests to. And it's quite busy on weekends. With its even male/female ratio, one understands why. No cover or dress code, and drinks are reasonable. Open Mon.-Sat., noon-1:00 a.m. Closed Sunday.

Faces East (439-6200), in Howard Johnson's, at Markham Road and Highway 401 in the east end. Plants, mirrors, and pictures of faces explain its name. The age range is 25-35, including lots of professionals. A DJ plays disco, funk, rock, and 60s music, and coloured lights help give out that Saturday Night fever, if it's still going around. (Get plenty of rest, drink fluids ...) There is a small cover charge on Fridays and Saturdays, and Wednesdays have themes: Greaser night, Western night, Beach party, etc. Patrons here often ask the hostess to seat them beside members of the opposite sex (whether the hostess gets invited to the weddings we have no idea), so this is a fairly easy place to meet people. It's a *very* singles-oriented place, with lots of suburbanites hanging around. Open Mon.-Sat., noon-1:00 a.m. Lunch available, noon-2:30 p.m. Closed Sunday, but **Bluffer's**, another bar in the same hotel, *is* open on the Lord's Day.

Tony's East (291-8736), 4900 Sheppard Avenue East at Bellamy. Once a rowdy bar, it is now more subdued like OPEC. There's lots of socializing here, some pick-ups, and a clientele of 19-30-year-olds. The music is rock 'n roll –usually MOR, with some R & B. Dig? The food is basic burgers/fish/chicken, with a $3-5 cover on Fridays and Saturdays. Open noon-1:00 a.m., six days a week. Closed Sundays.

Across town, there is **Tony's West** (665-1456), at 4749 Keele Street, just below the city limit of Steeles. A rowdy atmosphere and rock 'n roll for diehards.

Special Mentions in Suburbialand:
The Airport Strip is terrifically convenient for tourists staying at the hotels there. And these places are very busy, a popular alternative to downtown nightlife. We've mentioned some airport spots in other sections, so we won't repeat them. But other notables include:

Dr. Livingstone's (675-9444), in the Bristol Place Hotel, 950 Dixon Road. It is decorated in African motif. It's quiet, intimate, and has easy listening and dancing music nightly. Open Mon.-Sat., 11:00 a.m.-1:00 a.m. Closed Sunday.

5444 (624-1144), in the Ramada Inn, 5444 Dixie Road at 401. A two-level club with a dance floor, a fancy sound and light system, and lots of people. Open Mon.-Fri., 5:00 p.m.-1:00 a.m.; Sat., 7:00 p.m.-1:00 a.m. Closed Sunday.

Faces International Club (675-6100), in Howard Johnson's, 801 Dixon Road. A popular singles' bar, providing lunch as well as your future mate. The stained-glass window over the bar goes well with the green corduroy banquettes, and the medium-sized dance floor is crowded. Regulars and visitors enjoy dancing their feet off or watching others do it, as they lean on the brass rail around the dancing area. Open Mon.-Sat., 11:30 a.m.-1:00 a.m.; Sun. 4:00 p.m.-11:00 p.m.

Tally Ho (675-6100), also in Howard Johnson's, is a quieter lounge, but still a popular place for singles to try and become doubles.There is a fireplace and live entertainment. Open Mon.-Sat., 5:00 p.m.-1:00 a.m. Closed Sunday.

Rendezvous (244-1711), in the Skyline Hotel, 655 Dixon Road. A dimly lit piano bar on the ground floor, with easy listening and quiet conversation. And if things don't work out, you can just hop a plane somewhere else. Open Mon.-Sat., noon to 1:30 a.m.; Sun., 4:00 p.m.-11:30 p.m.

Is there life after death? Is there life after forty?
The Luck of the Irish
Any lover of the theatre must eventually come to the conclu-

sion that without the Irish, there is hardly any great drama in English. Well, aside from the Great God Shakespeare, who was probably Irish if he traced his family back far enough. From Sheridan to Wilde to Shaw to Synge to O'Casey to Friel, the Irish have blessed the stage with the most wonderful writing in our language.

Well, the Irish may not have built Canada or Toronto, the way the Scots did (back in the nineteenth century, if you yelled, "Hey, Mac!" on a Toronto street, five hundred people would wave), there are a number of Irish nightclubs in the city that are much loved. They tend to attract an older crowd, and often have an atmosphere that is far more interesting than most.

Dooley's (922-2626), 23 Bloor Street E., near Yonge. A place "where there are no strangers; only friends ye haven't met." The decor is – surprise – green, but it's also comfortable, with lovely memorabilia on the walls. It's busiest at lunch, with a steady two-thirds of their clientele of American tourists with Irish backgrounds. It has a lively ambiance, the service is excellent, and the staff has a fine rapport with the customers. Everyone really gets into the spirit of things here, with dancing, sing-along, etc. People tend to come in couples or groups, so don't expect to find your single wild Irish Rose in this place. The food is good Irish fare, served from 11:30 a.m.-5:00 p.m. for lunch. Main courses, such as chicken pot pie and steak 'n kidney run from $7-18. Moderately priced drinks go well with the comedy, live bands, and the champion Irish fiddler on weekends. No cover or dress code, but guess which colour is always welcome? Open 11:30 a.m.-1:00 a.m.

Kelly's Keg 'N Jester (596-7630), in Ontario Place, 955 Lakeshore Blvd. W. Runs from May to September only, so check your calendar before coming. Many visitors are over 35 or 40 here, so we middle-aged folk feel more at home than among the younger leprechauns elsewhere. There's a nice view of the yachts in the harbour, and you tend to meet new people here, because you sit at big tables. There's loud, Irish or popular music bands here, and enjoyable sing-along. The food is fast-deli-style, and is slightly overpriced; but the decor is true Irish, and the small dance floor, stand-up bar, tolerated jeans, and lack of a cover make it a homey place. No, Kelly's is *not* for a quiet rendezvous; but it's fun, and one feels that this place is *not* as impression-conscious as most in this city. Mon.-Sat., 11:00 a.m.-1:45 a.m.; Sun., 11:00 a.m.-midnight.

Nags Head (979-9250), in the Eaton Centre, Yonge south

of Dundas. An English tudor-style interior, decorated with plants and bric-a-brac, as well as wine-coloured drapes. The age range is 20-50, and seems predominantly middle-class, many dancing to the music of Irish and middle-of-the-road bands. Food is served – fish and chips, burgers, steaks, and snacks – but one senses that's not why people flock here. There's a large bar where singles tend to congregate, and the male/female ratio appears to be fairly even (which helps explain why there are so many Irish people around). And it's easy to meet people at the stand-up bar, where a lot of men "hover." There's live entertainment each Monday to Saturday, when you can quaff moderately-priced beers and cocktails. Two other downtown locations, 7 King Street W. (366-1194) and 74 York Street (368-6874), suggest that there are enough Irish and Irish-lovers to go around.

HOTELS, MOTELS, DORMS AND DELIGHTS: SOME GOOD AND BED PLACES TO STAY

Toronto does have lots of un-hostile hostels and hotels. Here is a selected list with some of the plusses that make these places into places to stay.

Very Cheap, Even in These Uncheap Times:

The Whitehouse (362-7491), 76 Church Street near King. Only thirty-five rooms, but they come in three different varieties, from a double bed with bath to a huge studio suite. At a price as low as $35-40 for a single/double, sitting only a few feet from Trinity Church, St. Lawrence Market, and most of the downtown theatres, you can't lose.

Neill-Wycik College-Hotel (977-2320), 96 Gerrard Street East near Church. Open only May through August. It is close to the Eaton Centre, and has a breakfast eatery that will fill you for under $5. Twin rooms are as cheap as $27-29; singles as low as $21-23; family rooms around $35. There's a great view of the city from its cedar roof-deck.

York University (667-3098), 4700 Keele Street north of Finch. One thousand barren, futuristic rooms available every summer for prices as low as $18 for a single, $26 for a double. Pity the students who have to live there. But it *is* a reasonable place to visit.

Karabanow Guest House & Tourist Home (923-4004), 9 Spadina Road at Bloor. Within walking distance of Casa Loma, Chinatown, U. of T., and Yorkville and costs about $25-35 for singles or doubles. Only twenty rooms, but it's in a lovely old Annex home only millimetres away from the Spadina/University subway line.

Hotels, Inns and Outs

The Guild Inn (261-3331) is truly extraordinary, out there at 201 Guildwood Parkway, south of Kingston Road. Built on fifty acres overlooking Lake Ontario and a ravine, it is more a resort than a hotel. Singles and doubles are in the $40-$65 range, so the trip out to Scarborough is worth it. And even if you don't stay there, just drive there and let your kids run wild in their labyrinthine gardens.

Sutton Place (924-9221), 955 Bay Street at Wellesley. Recently renovated, there is a new ballroom, restaurant, and bar, an indoor pool, and the rooftop restaurant has been redecorated. A single will run you close to $100, and suites cost anywhere from $195-$395 (the Prime Minister's Suite is only $700). This is a very posh place indeed, and a rather good location.

The Sheraton Centre (361-1000), 123 Queen Street West. Across from the New City Hall, it has two towers with 1,448 luxury rooms, cabanas, and suites. It's not cheap – singles run $94-$117; doubles, $116-$139, but with seven restaurants and lounges, forty shops and boutiques, and even two movie houses, this is a place to see, if not stay at. The two-acre indoor garden will delight all, and there are holiday packages that run as cheap as $39.50 per person per night. Their indoor-outdoor pool is glorious, the largest hotel pool in Canada.

The Westin Hotel (869-3456), 145 Richmond Street West at University. Beautiful glass-enclosed elevators and a marvellous location. While rates are up to $121 a night for one and $141 for two, they have weekend specials ($79 per night for two) and children can stay free. It just completed extensive renovations, making it an even better place to stay.

The Ramada Renaissance Hotel (299-1500), 2035 Kennedy Road at the 401, the road that goes to the airport, the zoo, and the science centre. Architectural critics are raving about its solar panels and bold lines. Opened in the summer of 1982, it offers special deals – as little as $50 per room per night, single or double, and use of their indoor pool, saunas, and whirlpool.

The Windsor Arms (979-2341), at 22 St. Thomas Street. Just a block east and south of University and Bloor, is important for its extraordinary restaurants alone: **Three Small Rooms** and the **Courtyard Cafe**. But its 82 charming rooms (as cheap as $65-$75 for singles and doubles) and its astoundingly good location make it an old favourite of many.

The Chelsea Inn (595-1975), 33 Gerrard Street West near

Bay. More than one thousand rooms, a convenient location, and cheaper prices than almost any other similar-quality hotel in the downtown area. But what impress us is their inspired children's centre, where kids can paint, make mucky in a sand-box, and gently squeeze live pets. The chance to leave the darlings for a couple of hours is a bonus, and we congratulate them on it. Senior citizens get ten per cent or more off the usual rates. Now that is creative and decent hotel thinking. Both deals (for kids and their grandparents) are offered at the **Delta Meadowvale Inn** (821-1981), 6750 Mississauga Rd. at the 401, near the airport.

Inn on the Park (444-2561), 1100 Eglinton Avenue East at Leslie. Right around the corner from the science centre and smack on some of the loveliest parkland in Toronto. Singles are in the $70-$100 range, doubles around $90-$115, and weekend rates are available. With good retaurants, and complimentary bikes, skis, toboggans, and skates, it is one of Toronto's finest hotels.

The Prince Hotel (444-2511), at 900 York Mills Road near the Don Valley Parkway and 401. Japanese-owned and luxurious. With fifteen acres of magnificent grounds and excellent Japanese dining, we have fallen in love with this place and have taken advantage of their reasonable weekend rates. Our greatest thrill is the year-round outdoor, heated pool; swimming while snow falls gently on our confused little heads is an amazing experience. And their Sunday brunch, while expensive, is perhaps the best in town. How many other hotels provide you with a putting green, a children's playground, and nature trails, for under $95 a night, kids included?

The Four Seasons Hotel (964-0411), Avenue Road at Yorkville, just above Bloor. Recently rated as one of the world's top forty hotels – number twenty-four, to be exact, and number three in North America. Recently renovated, this handy hotel has 463 guest rooms with standard Four Seasons flair: complimentary shoe shines, twice daily maid service, a bathrobe to use, oversized towels, and a fresh rose waiting in every room. It's not surprising that it's around $120 a day for a single and about $140 for a double. And if you want more of the best...

Toronto Hilton Harbour Castle (869-1600), One Harbour Square on Lake Ontario near Bay. A stunner. Newly renovated, it stands majestically by the lake, overlooking the Toronto Islands, just steps from Harbourfront and minutes from downtown. Rooms run around $100 for a single and up to $130 for a double; but their holiday packages include three days and two nights for around $150 per person, a gift breakfast in one of their fine restaurants, and a complimentary tour of either the CN Tower, Casa Loma or a boat tour of the the Islands and harbour. And don't forget the view - that glorious view.

The King Edward (863-9700), 37 King Street E. near Yonge. On the edge of the wonderful St. Lawrence area, and one of Toronto's landmark hotels. Newly refurbished and elegant in the best tradition of European hotels, it is expensive. But it does have honeymoon/anniversary/special-occasion packages that run $125 a couple per night, including a deluxe room (and they *are* deluxe), a bottle of champagne, and a "lovers' breakfast for two served in your room." There are also weekends for two for $90 a night. Ah, but Toronto has come a long way, hasn't it? And since the Beatles and Burton/Taylor stayed here, when they were still the Beatles and Burton/Taylor, you will be in good company.

OUT WITH THE INN CROWD: GREAT COUNTRY INNS WITHIN A DAY'S DRIVE

There's something satisfying in knowing that there are some spectacular hideaways within an hour or two of Toronto, where you can toast your feet near a roaring fire, cross-country ski, and enjoy some fine meals for a few days for only a few hundred dollars. These places are not cheap. But neither is a get-away to Morocco or the Bahamas or the Côte d'Azur.

Here is a personal, short list of some of the better country inns within driving range of Toronto.

The Millcroft Inn in Alton, Ontario. It calls itself the "definitive" country inn, but don't say that is presumptuous until you experience it. **George Minden** of the **Windsor Arms**, **Three Small Rooms**, and **Noodles** converted this 1881 knitting mill into forty-two elegant guest rooms, many furnished with old-fashioned beds and antiques.

All of the crofts (split-level units) are built on a hill near the banks of the Credit River. They are slightly more expensive, but each has its own fireplace, private patio, and enough room for a family of four. The inn has tennis courts, a heated outdoor pool, sauna, whirlpool, and, as if you need it, TV. Good cross-country and downhill skiing is nearby.

What cannot be overestimated is the superb food, which is understandably not included in the price of the rooms. From rabbit, trout, and pheasant to pâtés and terrines, this is city-level dining in the country.

Rooms run about $100 a night, with a deposit of one night's tariff to confirm your reservation. There are two-night specials – you get a room plus breakfasts for around $200 for two.

How to Get There:

It takes a little over an hour by car from Toronto. Go north up Highway 10 (west of the airport) to Caledon, left for five kilometres (three miles) on Highway 24 to Highway 136, then north to the village of Alton. The food is so remarkable that many drive up there just for a lunch or dinner. In Toronto, call 791-4422.

Benmiller Inn, outside Goderich. Little did the people who slaved away for pennies an hour in those grist and woollen mills know that a century later these mills would serve as expensive getaways for well-to-do Torontonians.

The 130-year-old woolen mill with its weather vane and gothic windows is a beauty, nestled beside the Maitland River and Sharpe's Creek in the charming village of Benmiller. You'll also like the indoor heated pool, jogging track, tennis, whirlpool, sauna – not to mention fishing, nature trails, and cross-country skiing. Ecologists will enjoy visiting and perhaps staying in the **Gledhill House**, heated by solar energy. (The panels on the roof gather sunlight to heat a 25,000-gallon water tank in the basement.) Some make this lovely place their base for a Stratford Festival weekend, since the theatre is less than an hour from Benmiller.

A double room will run about $100, a suite around $125, a double suite closer to $200. All rates include a continental breakfast.

How to Get There:

The **Benmiller Inn** is about three hours from Toronto, near Lake Huron. Take the 401 west to Kitchener, then west and north on Highway 8 to Stratford and on up to the Inn. It is about three kilometres (two miles) off Highway 8, eight kilometres (5 miles) from Goderich. Phone 1-519-524-2191.

Elora Mill at Elora, is more grist for the mill. This five-storey, renovated gristmill is one of the most original resorts around. And it isn't hurt by being near the scenic Elora Gorge and artists' studios or romantic St. John's Anglican Church (you didn't think Anglican churches were romantic?), whose pastor was the first lover of Florence Nightingale. The church forbade their marriage; he went to Elora, she went off to the Crimean War, and that was that.

The guest rooms at the mill are charming: pioneer reproductions, hand-sewn quilts, and matching curtains give new meaning to the word "quaint." The dining room gives a thrilling view of the Elora Gorge, and the roast duck Grand Marnier is renowned.

Bus tours of the lovely towns nearby are available, and you may wish to use the nearby racquet and squash club. And cross-country ski trails, hayrides, and sleigh rides will keep most visitors blissfully happy.

Double occupancy runs in the $60-80 range; suites between $100 to $125. Winter season packages are available between the beginning of November and the end of April and include breakfast and dinner.

How to Get There:

The Elora Mill is about 90 minutes northwest of Toronto (and about the same time and distance from Buffalo). Take Highway 401 west to Highway 6. Go north through Guelph, up to Fergus, then a brief jog southwest to Elora. Phone 1-519-846-5356.

Grandview Farm in Huntsville is a warm, sweet lodge whose main claim to fame was that it was, for many years, unlicenced for serving liquor or beer.

Located in the heart of Muskoka cottage country, your accommodation here could be an early 1800s four-poster bed or more modern facilities, and all the rooms in the main house face the lake. In the summer, there is tennis, golf, and water sports on the beautiful Fairy Lake – swimming, sailing, waterskiing, canoeing. Wintertime pursuits include alpine and cross-country skiing, sleigh rides, tobogganing, and ice skating. There is platform tennis year-round. Far more a family place than most, **Grandview Farm** is a marvellous escape any time of year.

All rates include meals, which is important to figure in your calculations: In the inn proper prices are around $55-$75 per person in a double room, and around $100 per person in a single. Various cottages and "tree tops" cost about $65-$75 per person. Children under twelve sharing a room with an adult pay one-half the adult rate.

How to Get There:

Approximately 225 kilometres (140 miles) due north of Toronto, **Grandview Farm** is about 2½ hours away. Go north on Highway 400 and then take Highway 11 to Highway 60. Go east six kilometres (3½ miles) and you are there. Phone 1-705-789-7642.

Deerhurst Inn, a Victorian stone-and-stucco estate in Huntsville, is a classic Toronto hideaway. The indoor pool, sauna, disco, and Las Vegas-type shows in the summer (including the Second City Cabaret), make this a very swinging spot, and less amenable for families who just can't leave the future prime minister at home.

Fifteen of the seventeen private cottages have their own fireplaces. One cottage even has its own whirlpool, sauna, fireplace, and stereo system. Suffer.

There are tennis courts, golf, waterskiing and a private beach. In that other, colder season, there is cross-country skiing, tobogganing, sleigh rides, and snow-mobiling, with all the equipment provided. And the food here is renowned throughout the Muskoka area. This is one classy place.

For around $80 per person per night, you can get a sports package including breakfast, dinner, access to ski trails, free ski lessons, and free use of snowshoes and ice skates.

How to Get There:
Deerhurst is less than three hours from Toronto. Go north on Highway 400, continue north on Highway 11 to Highway 60. Go east on 60 towards Algonquin Park, turning right on Muskoka Road 23 to Deerhurst Road. Phone 964-3925 for more information.

Prince of Wales Hotel, in Niagara-on-the-Lake, offers you a superb combination: a historic hotel, the oldest community in Ontario, and a very fine theatre – not bad at all. Built as a sixteen-room inn in 1864, it was handsomely restored in the mid-1970s and now has a grand total of ninety-four rooms. Where else can you request a brass or four-poster bed? Where else can you sit among plants and trees in a greenhouse for dining? Where else can you play tennis on the roof, swim in an indoor pool, and take a sauna afterward? What is extra special is that the Prince of Wales has top quality food – some of the best, in fact, outside of Toronto. From rack of lamb to sweetbreads in madeira sauce to saddle of hare, this place is as satisfying as an eatery as an innery.

And it's smack in the middle of one of the loveliest towns in Canada. Niagara-on-the-Lake (the first capital of Upper Canada back in 1792) is a living, breathing museum, with a rebuilt fort, pretty shoreline, charming inns, and beautiful nineteenth-century homes.

From May 1 to October 31, the Prince of Wales will run about $65-$75 for single, double or twin rooms, $75 for sitting rooms, and $85-$135 for suites. The neighbouring **Prince of Wales Court** costs about the same.

How to Get There:
It's about ninety minutes from Toronto. Drive west, south and east on the Queen Elizabeth Way (QEW) from Toronto,

circling around Lake Ontario. Go east on Highway 55 to the town of Niagara-on-the-Lake. The Niagara Parkway flows into Picton Street, where the hotel stands majestically. Phone 1-468-3246 for more information. And don't forget to book tickets for the Shaw Festival, short blocks away, between May and October.

The Briars, on Jackson's Point, is on the south shore of Lake Simcoe, barely 70 kilometres (45 miles) north of Toronto. Driving up Highway 404 (alias Woodbine Ave. or the northern extension of the Don Valley Parkway) takes only about an hour, in summer or winter. It's a lovely 200-acre estate, with guest houses and cottages snuggled amongst pine tree equivalents of the CN Tower. Attractions include tennis courts, an eighteen-hole championship golf course, that great lake, and two heated outdoor pools. Snowmobiling and cross-country skiing, as well as snow-shoeing, tobogganing, and ice fishing make winter more pleasant, as well.

A 1982 addition has an indoor pool with a whirlpool and sauna, plus a game room and lounge. Prices range from around $200 per person, double, meals included, for three-day long weekends, up to around $400 for one-week packages. You can come and go for just a day for around $70 per person, double, with meals.

How to Get There:

North on the Don Valley for about an hour into Sutton, Ontario. The Briars, Sibbald House, and Country Club are located on Hedge Road. Their mailing address is P.O. Box 100, Jackson's Point, Ontario. Phone, by direct line, 364-5937.

Toronto After Midnight:
The Joys (And Dreads) of Insomnia

A quarter-century ago, harsh critics used to moan, "The sidewalks of Toronto are rolled up at 10:00 p.m." Not so. It was more like 7:15 p.m. Sharp. In fact, the rolling up of the sidewalks occurred every night, back in the 1950s. It was the highlight of the day. Torontonians would stuff themselves with Yorkshire pudding and tea and walk slowly to their windows to watch workmen crank the sidewalks under the roadways, only to crank them out again early the following morning.

No one minded, particularly, because there was no reason to go out. It was not by chance that such Hollywood films as *Night of the Living Dead*, *One Million BC*, and *The Day the Earth Stood Still* were filmed in this town: design costs were nil.

No longer. Indeed, Toronto swings after dark. Well, let's say it moves. There are dozens, even hundreds, of eateries, movie theatres, vets, food markets, gas stations, drugstores, etc. that are open most of the night and even twenty-four hours a day.

Below is only a partial listing of the many establishments that might be of assistance to you, should you need services after the usual nine-to-five:

Birth Control Information: Which people often need after dark, let's face it. Call 947-7442 for a recorded message, twenty-four hours a day, about birth control clinics and over-the-counter contraceptives, compliments of **Family Planning Services.**

Bakeries: Commisso Brothers and Racco Italian Bakery has two twenty-four-hour locations in Toronto where you can obtain fresh baked goods and hot Italian foods: 8 Kincort Street, north of Eglinton and west of Dufferin, and 33 Eddystone Avenue, north of Sheppard near Jane.

Dental Work: Teeth are renowned for acting up at ungodly hours. The **Dental Emergency Service** at 1650 Yonge Street, north of St. Clair, is open until 2:00 a.m., seven days a week. Call 485-7121 for an appointment. And the **Academy of Dentistry** (924-8041) will provide names of dentists who treat emergencies as late as 1:00 a.m.

Bowling: Suddenly seized with a desire to knock down pins? There are **Bowleramas** at 45 Overlea Boulevard in the Don Mills/Eglinton area; 5427 Dundas Street W. in Etobicoke; and 1250 South Service Road in Mississauga. All three are open twenty-four hours a day.

Drugstores: The one twenty-four-hour store where you can obtain emergency prescriptions at any time is the **Boots Drug Store** (597-0001) at Bay and Gerrard streets in downtown Toronto. They are also willing to have them delivered to you by cab for an extra few bucks.

The **Caledonia Pharmacy** (783-5131) at 600 Caledonia Road, just above Eglinton and west of Dufferin, will fill prescriptions until 2:30 a.m. **Ford Drugs**, at 357A Yonge Street above Dundas, will sell you food and over the counter drugs twenty-four hours a day, but not prescriptions.

Eateries: We use that term because not all of the following will qualify as restaurants, by any means. But all of these places are open twenty-four hours a day, seven days a week, and they might satisfy that strange urge when it hits. Here are a few:

Fran's, 21 St. Clair Avenue W. near Yonge Street; 2275

Yonge Street just above Eglinton; and 20 College Street just west of Yonge are twenty-four-hours-a-day-seven-days-a-week places for reliable, if uninspired, food.

People's Foods, 176 Dupont Street, east of Spadina and north of Bloor, will give you what the name says.

Vesta Lunch, 474 Dupont Street at Bathurst, is where you'll find competent food and all the characters you've needed to use for gothic novel that you've been trying to write.

Howard Johnson's, near the airport at Dixon Road and Highway 27; and at Highway 401 and Markham Road out in the east end of the city. Well, Howard Johnson's food.

Fuller's, at 5238 Dundas Street W. in Etobicoke, and at 2829 Eglinton Avenue E., near McCowan in the east end, might make you full.

And there are nearly five hundred (count them) donut places across the city where you can fill your tummy with empty calories and caffeine, and wonder what went wrong.

Groceries have recently moved to twenty-four-hour-a-day service all over the city – except on Sundays, alas, alas.

Miracle Mart, a large Canadian chain with as moderate prices as you are liable to find in the city, now has thirty-six of its seventy-six locations open twenty-four hours. These include 2760 Bathurst Street below Lawrence in the north central part of the city; 2684 Eglinton Avenue E. at Brimley in the east end; and 853 Jane Street below Eglinton in the west end. Phone their head office at 744-3000.

A & P has quite a few twenty-four-hour stores around the city: in the north-central part of the city, 3142 Yonge Street above Lawrence; in the far north-west, 1735 Kipling Avenue near Steeles; and in the east end, 682 Kennedy Road near Eglinton, and 3485 Kingston Road near Markham.

Bloor Super-Save, at 384 Bloor Street West, west of Spadina Road, is open twenty-four hours. And **Variety Food Fair** at 37 Charles Street W. near Yonge is open until 2:00 a.m. A second store of the same name is just east of Yonge and south of Front, way downtown, at 49-53 Lower Jarvis.

The Kitchen Table (487-1527), at 2287 Yonge Street, just a few steps above Eglinton, is handy to most hotels in north-central Toronto. Its fruit and vegetables are as fresh as the lovely atmosphere. The branch at 1110 Bay Street, just south of Bloor, is open until 2:00 a.m. every day, including Sundays and holidays.

And don't forget those marvellous fruit stores along the Danforth east of the Don Valley Parkway; most are open twenty-four hours a day, and all are top quality. See the **Greek Toronto** section (pp. 118-120) for further information.

Full-service Stations, and Twenty-Four-Hour Gas Stations: And when else would the car break down but in the middle of the night with the kids crying in the back. Well, **Cross Town Service Centre** in the very heart of Toronto at 1467 Bathurst Street at the corner of St. Clair Avenue West, has all-night gas, towing, and emergency service. It will do minor repairs after midnight.

All-night gas stations have been appearing across our city. Here are some well-placed ones:

Agincourt, in the northeast end: **Imperial**, 2901 Sheppard and Victoria Park.

Scarborough, east end: **Imperial**, 800 Lawrence E. and Leslie.

Don Mills Esso, Don Mills-Wynford Drive.

Downsview, northwest: **Esso**, Jane and Finch.

Thornhill, north of the city: **Esso**, Yonge and Steeles.

Willowdale, northeast: **Esso**, Don Mills and Sheppard.

Rexdale, northwest: **Imperial**, 1104 Albion and Islington.

Mississauga, west end: **Imperial**, 5725 Airport Road.

Etobicoke, west end: **Imperial**, 1000 The Queensway and Islington.

Toronto: north central: **Esso**, Lawrence W. and Bathurst; **Shell**, Yonge Street and York Mills; east central: **Gulf**, 2544 Bayview and York Mills; east: **Gulf**, 2250 Victoria Park and York Mills; west: **Gulf**, 2747 Keele and Wilson; downtown: **Gulf**, Bay just above Dundas.

Pet Emergency: What's wrong with Fido now? Well, if "now" is between 6:00 p.m. and 10:00 a.m. there is a **Veterinary Emergency Clinic** (226-3663) at 201 Sheppard Avenue E., about a km (half a mile) east of Yonge Street and just above the 401. In the east end, the **Emergency Animal Hospital** (698-0888) at 2646 Danforth Avenue, east of Main, might be able to help, 8:00 a.m.-midnight, seven days a week.

Laundromat: Lipstick on your collar told a tale on you. **Ted's Launderama** at 1610 Bayview Avenue about a km (half a mile) south of Eglinton is open twenty-four hours a day.

Limousine Service: Want to impress someone at 4:00 a.m.? **Rosedale Livery** (677-9444), will provide a Lincoln Mark VI (black exterior, grey interior, four doors) for $20 per hour, twenty-four hours a day. We *are* impressed!

Big Dipper Blues: Can't find your star? Want to be sure which sign you were born under? There is a twenty-four-hour-a-day **Astronomical Hot line**, compliments of the

McLaughlin Planetarium. Call 978-5399 to discover the position of the planets, what to look for, and what frequency to tune in for the music of the spheres.

Weather Information: American visitors are used to a simple number such as Greenwich 21212, which gives them the latest weather, twenty-four hours a day. In typical Canadian fashion, our weather number is not easy to memorize, nor is it well known. But it does exist: Call 676-3066, twenty-four hours a day, for the latest weather conditions and predictions. If you must hear a human voice, try 676-4567 for more weather information.

Emergency Road Service: If – and only if – you are a member of the Ontario Motor League or its equivalent provincial affiliate of the Canadian Automobile Association (south of the border, the Automobile Association of America), phone 966-3000 for twenty-four-hour help with batteries, tows, and pushes. We *told* you to join!

The Major Number: Thanks to the foresight of Miss Suzette, founder of **The AHA Corp. (After Hours Assistance)**, information on the hundreds of other stores, services, restaurants, etc., now open late into or throughout the night is readily available. Their twenty-four-hour telephone directory and answering service is 964-1575. The **AHA Corp.** also sells cards that will give you further access to these businesses, for only $5.00.

Quit Playing With Your Food
What to Do, See, and Eat With Kids
Child's Play: Kiddies See, Kiddies Do

Toronto is wonderfully sensitive to the needs and interests of its younger citizens and visitors. Indeed, a large number of previous listings are ideal for children, as well as mature adults like you.

For this reason, we are *not* about to list, at length, everything that has gone before. What we *will* do is recommend some easy fun things to do and remind you of other ones already mentioned. This listing will be based on where they can be found, and whether they are free or costly. In the case of previously discussed highlights, we shall merely mention what kids like best about them. You can then read the appropriate section to find out more about them.

Free or Close To It:

Great Views of Toronto: There are a number of places where you can go for free views of this city, which are almost as exciting (and terrifying) as the CN Tower. The **Westin Hotel**, at University and Richmond, and the **Toronto Hilton Harbour Castle**, at the foot of Bay St., both have outdoor, glass-enclosed elevators, which provide hair-raising – and free – rides up and down, with spectacular views. The Hilton one is only open from noon-2:30 p.m., and 5:00 p.m.-1:00 a.m., since it goes up to their Lighthouse Restaurant. Another freebie *view*, but with the traditional, boring, inside elevator, is the **Toronto-Dominion Tower**, where you can get eerie overviews from their top floor.

The **Riverdale Farm** in Cabbagetown (pp. 84-86) can provide a lovely, free outing for children, near the centre of the city.

The **High Park Zoo** (page 78) is charming, and with swimming, skating, picnicking, and so much more to offer, is a perfect, free day for all ages.

Conservation Areas are sprinkled all around Metro Toronto, and usually cost no more than a few dollars to park the car that takes you there. These places have swimming, fishing, boating, cross-country skiing, and much more. Phone 661-6600 for information.

The **Toronto Islands** (pp. 75-77) provide swimming, skiing, and so many joys, for no more than the cost of the ferry boat ride over. And don't forget **Far Away Farm** in **Centreville**, on **Centre Island**, which is free. A trip to the Islands *can* cost next to nothing.

Skating, Skiing, Tobogganing, and so much more is available, for free, at most of the major Toronto parks and ravines (pp. 89-90). Don't forget the **skating rink** in front of **New City Hall**, and the often terrifying hills at **Winston Churchill Park** (pp. 82-83), **High Park** (pp. 77-79), **Earl Bales Park** (p. 89), and **Riverdale Park**, at Broadview and Danforth, just southeast of where the Don Valley Parkway intersects the Bloor-Danforth bridge.

The **Children's BookStore** in Mirvish Village (pp. 152-153) can provide hours of free fun for children. And do not forget to buy at least some of the record albums made by the inspired performers and composers who have made this city a Mecca of kids' recordings: **Sharon, Lois, and Bram; Raffi; Bob Schneider; Jerry Brodey; Ken and Chris Whiteley**. Visitors to France used to smuggle home dirty postcards; the wise visitor to Toronto freely trots home with albums by these brilliant artists.

Apple Picking can provide hours of excellent exercise and pleasure for kids and adults, and at no more than the cost of what you pick. (We also recommend strawberry and rasp-berry picking – in season, of course.) Our favourite place is **Al Ferri's**, which is only about fifteen minutes west of the airport: take 401 west to Mississauga Road; go north to Steeles Ave., then a left and the first right. Their apples come in from early September to mid-October, and they are Incredi-ble! Call 965-7701 for a free list of all the places where you can go to pick various vegetables and fruits in the vicinity of Toronto.

The **Haida**, at Ontario Place (p. 35) can provide hours of joy for slightly older children, who thrill to climbing in and out and around and through all the portholes and levels of this giant destroyer, at the cost of just pennies per person.

The Art Gallery of Ontario (pp. 160-161) has a Hands On room (open Sundays, holidays, and school vacations), which is wonderfully creative and entertaining for younger kids. And then there's the fascinating historic **Grange** house behind, and the **Henry Moore** in front to play on.

The David Dunlap Observatory in Richmond Hill, just north of Metro (pp. 168-169) and the **McLaughlin Planetar-ium**, next to the **Royal Ontario Museum** (pp. 167-168) both provide reasonably priced entertainment and tours for older children.

The Royal Ontario Museum (pp. 157-159) is heavenly for children of all ages. The dinosaurs send kids into ecstasy, and the **Discovery Room** can provide hours of joy for kids, especially junior high and older. A full morning or afternoon at the ROM need not set a family back very much, financially.

Casa Loma, that magical castle in the heart of Metro (pp. 29-31) is much loved by older kids – but even children under eight will love the views from the towers, and the long, eerie tunnel that leads to the stables. It's an inexpensive morning or afternoon.

Fort York (pp. 54-56) down near the Exhibition grounds, is fascinating for older children.

Harbourfront (pp. 37-39) almost always has free or nearly free entertainment, whether painting, sculpting, building with giant wooden blocks, concerts, or plays. Check their monthly newspaper, which tells you all about it, as well as their ads in the daily papers.

The **Puppet Centre** (p. 170), **Hockey Hall of Fame** (p. 95), **Sugar Museum** (pp. 170-171), **Water Filtration Plant** (p. 62), **New City Hall** (pp. 48-50), and even the **Metro Toronto Library** (pp. 173-174) all provide free or cheap tours and visits. And don't forget the **Marine Museum** (pp. 169-170) and the **Railway Museum** at Harbourfront (364-5665), which is open on weekend afternoons, from 1:00-5:00 p.m.

The major Toronto newspapers – *The Toronto Star, Sun,* and *Globe and Mail* often provide free tours for schoolkids of their plants, offices, and printing presses, which can be greatly engrossing. Call each, and see if you can join one.

More Expensive, Both in and Out of Town:

Ontario Place (pp. 34-37) need *not* be fiercely expensive; the **waterplay area** and the astonishingly inventive **Children's Village** are both free, and the **Cinesphere** and **Haida** are both reasonable. And the **Forum** concerts are free, with entry, as are the frequently excellent shows in various pods.

The Ontario Science Centre (pp. 31-32) is a *must*; don't miss the free movies, and the thrilling space, communications, laser, and electricity exhibits.

The CN Tower (pp. 27-29) is not cheap, but remember, there are many things to do in the area of the tower, beyond the elevator ride to the top.

The Metro Toronto Zoo, once you pay to get in, can provide a full day of pleasure, from cross-country skiing to just enjoying the animals and the gorgeous scenery. It's one of the world's great zoos (pp. 39-43).

Black Creek Pioneer Village (pp. 53-54) can also provide close to a full day of entertainment, from watching a blacksmith ply his trade to petting sheep and seeing an old mill do its stuff.

In season, such events as **The Canadian National Exhibition** (pp. 67-69), **The Royal Winter Agricultural Fair** (p. 74), **The Binder Twine Festival** (p. 73), **Caravan** (pp. 70-71), **Caribana** (pp. 72-73), **International Picnic** (page 70), **Mariposa Folk Festival** (page 71) can provide whole days of fun and frolic.

Even More Expensive and Often Worth It

The Young People's Theatre Centre (pp. 180-181). Very good work in live performance.

The Childrens' Concerts at the **Roy Thomson Hall** (pp. 182-183). Top-quality, enjoyable ways to lead a kid to culture, and even get him or her to drink.

Canada's Wonderland (pp. 43-45). Toronto's frozen version of Disneyland.

African Lion Safari, west of Toronto (pp. 46-47), is fabulous; take a car, if possible, to get that giraffe to put his head in your child's lap.

Marineland, in Niagara Falls (pp. 45-46), is top quality entertainment for the underwater zoo crew.

Family Kartways, east along 401 to Whitby and then north about 8 km (5 miles), can run you a lot of money; but for kids over ten, it is glorious to ride his/her own little go-kart for a thrilling few minutes around the twisty-turvy track. Have they been *really* good?

Many Toronto Hotels offer **Brunch-and-Swim** deals, where you can stuff yourself sick, and then learn first hand why you should never swim when your stomach is full. Costly, and great fun.

Youth Yummies:
Restaurants that Both Welcome and Entertain Kids
One of the most powerful arguments ever made for Zero Population Growth is to try and enjoy a meal in a restaurant and be bombarded by the grumbling, whining, and crying of children. And if your kids are doing the complaining it's all the worse.

Children, certainly under age ten or so, were not made for fine dining. They get justifiably bored and fidgety. Weaned on *M*A*S*H* or *Sesame Street*, they find all the ordering and sitting and waiting much ado about nothing. And unless the parents have been wise enough – and most of us are not – to bring along favourite books or quiet games, the restaurant experience can be torture for the parents, tedium for the children, and maddening rage for everyone else in the place.

Toronto *does* have, however, a number of charming, and even good-quality-food restaurants that *do* cater to children and not always at the expense – epicureally or financially – of the parents.

Toronto has as many fast-food outlets as any other major North American city, and you don't need our book to remind you of them. But our city *does* have some real winners, where kids (and adults) can be entertained and competently fed. Try some of these, the next time junior has been really good.

The Old Spaghetti Factory (864-9761), 54 The Esplanade, one block south of Front and one block east of Yonge Street. This place is beautiful to look at and nearly always overflowing with families. With good reason. First, what kid does not love to eat spaghetti with five sauces to choose from, and with or without meatballs? Even if they eat with their hands, no one will mind much. And parents will be much relieved to hear that there is chicken and steak available for more mature palates.

Second, the atmosphere is a delight: the building was once a blacksmith's shop, and they've filled the cavernous room with thousands of Tiffany lamps, huge posters, antiques, and a 1902 streetcar. Food for a family of four is under $25, including bread, butter, coffee or tea, spumoni ice cream, and salad.

The Organ Grinder (364-6517), 58 The Esplanade. As its noisy name implies, there is a massive Wurlitzer organ on the premises. Kids will thrill to the look and the sound (*you* will thrill only to the look) of the walls covered with xylophones, marimbas, glockenspiels, and dozens of other absurd-looking and absurd-sounding instruments, all played by remote control by **Craig Stevens**, who performs Tuesday through Saturday evenings.

There are ten different kinds of pizza served, as well as burgers, lasagna, and chicken, between the horses' clopping, the bells ringing, the sirens blaring, and the birds whistling. It's great, great fun. About $35 for a family of four.

The Market Grill (366-7743), 15 Market Street just a few blocks east of Yonge and just south of Front. Children's portions of chopped steak, roast chicken, and prime rib, with a free salad bar if you order the dinner.

The handsome place also has a lovely Saturday breakfast and Sunday brunch where kids can dig into the hefty buffet, filled with things that most kids love: home fries, ham, sausages, bacon and eggs, hot roast beef, fresh pineapple slices, honeydew and watermelon balls, muffins, and cake. Fresh fish is also available for most lunches and dinners. You can get away with lunch for 4 for under $25; dinner, $35.

Lord Stanley's Feast (363-8561), 26 Lombard Street at Victoria, two blocks north of King St. E. It is exactly what it calls itself. It's all shove-it-in-your-mouth-without-any-utensils. Kids will love the onion rings, mushrooms, spareribs, chicken, shish kabob, corn, fruit, and even soup. And no cutlery. Clowns, magicians, and minstrels drift about throughout the evening, making this entertaining for the eye as well as the palate. Adults pay around $15-$17. Kids under 12 pay less than half of that.

The Carrousel (865-0033), is in the **Merchants Mall** of the Royal Bank Plaza at Front and Bay, that gorgeous golden tower in the heart of downtown. This place is open for breakfast lunch and dinner for big people, but it's Saturday when The Carrousel really swings for kids – there's a children's menu at that time, with hamburgers and hot dogs in the $2.50-$3.00 range, and a magic show at 1:30 p.m. and 6:00 p.m. A stunning carrousel is available for free rides, and there are free hats and balloons. A family of four can ride on the horses, eat well, and get out for under $30.

Mother Tucker's Food Experience has two locations: one at the airport, 15 Carlson Court (Dixon Road at Highway 27, 675-8818); another in the east end, at 1920 Eglinton Avenue East, at Warden (759-5688). There are children's portions, and kiddie prices. Their world famous log cabin salad bar has more than four dozen choices, and is a meal in itself for little salad freaks. Most important, kids are invited to visit the bakeshop on the premises where the bread and apple pies are created. They find this extremely enjoyable, bless their expensive little hearts. A family of four should spend in the $40 range.

Ginsberg & Wong (979-3458), is as silly, crazy, and comic as its wonderful name. It's in the **Village by the Grange**, 71 McCaul Street, three short blocks west of University and about a block north of Queen Street West. The idea of bringing together Jewish deli and Chinese food sounds coy. But the owners have wisely jazzed it up, with massive, oversized hamburgers and giant hot dogs. Some of the food is surprisingly good. And with the magicians, clowns, and mimes who regularly drift through the **Village by the Grange**, this place is great fun. Between $25 and $30 for a family of four.

INDEX